THE HOLY SPIRIT

Studies in the Person and Work of the Holy Spirit

Herb Hodges

HOLY SPIRIT

Studies in the Person and Work of the Holy Spirit

©2013 Herb Hodges

ALL RIGHTS RESERVED

No part of this publication may be reproduced, stored in a retrieval system, or transmitted in any form without prior written permission.

Spiritual Life Ministries
2916 Old Elm Lane
Germantown, TN 38138
Herb Hodges -- Executive Director

Web site: herbhodges.com
E-mail – herbslm@mindspring.com

Table of Contents

THE HOLY SPIRIT—WHO, WHERE AND WHY?
John 14:16-18 9

THE DAY OF PENTECOST
Acts 2:1-4 21

THE BAPTISM OF THE HOLY SPIRIT
1 Corinthians 12:12-13 29

THE HOLY SPIRIT AND GOD'S TRUTH
Part One—How the Holy Spirit Publicizes God
I Corinthians 2:9-13 41

THE FOUR KINDS OF PEOPLE GOD SEES ON EARTH
Part Two: What Kind Of Person Will Receive God's Truth?
I Corinthians 2:14-3:3 51

THE IMPORTANCE OF ILLUMINATION
Ephesians 1:15-23 73

THE CONVICTING WORK OF THE HOLY SPIRIT, THE NECESSARY PREPARATION FOR SALVATION
John 16:7-11 93

AVAILABLE POWER FOR AVAILABLE PEOPLE
Ephesians 1:15-23 117

THE IMPERATIVE OF THE SPIRIT-FILLED LIFE
Ephesians 5:18 127

A FORMULA FOR SPIRITUAL FULLNESS
I Corinthians 6:19-20 155

A RIVER RUNS THROUGH IT
John 7:37-39 167

SHALL WE GATHER AT THE RIVER?
Ezekiel 47:1-12 185

FAITH'S FINEST FORMULA OR BEHOLDING BY BECOMING
2 Corinthians 3:18 . ……………………………...…..……….. 201

THE SADDEST OF ALL SINS
Ephesians 4:30 …………………………..……................……... 233

THE HOLY SPIRIT — GRIEVED OR GRATIFIED?
Ephesians 4:30 ….........…......................……………………….. 243

INTRODUCTION

Recently, I found a note I had written, apparently taken down as I was listening to a lesson or testimony or sermon somewhere, probably in a Bible Conference or a Spiritual Life Conference. The note contained this quotation: "The Church was supernatural in her *entrance* into the world; the Church will be supernatural in her *exit* from the world. Doesn't it make sense that the Church would be supernatural in her *existence* in the world?" What makes the Church's existence supernatural? It is the Presence and Power of the Holy Spirit dwelling in each member and compounded in the Church.

Jesus could not minister while in human flesh without the Power of the Holy Spirit, and neither can we. We cannot do without what the Lord Jesus Himself was in need of. All true spiritual leadership is Spirit-leadership. The supreme concern among Christians should be the deficit in Divine unction. A Christian without Power is like a sailing vessel fully rigged but without wind, or like a light bulb without electricity.

When the Holy Spirit is invited to control individual Christians, He takes the things of Christ (His Person, His history, and His benefits) and applies them to their lives. His work is to take the objective events accomplished for us by

Christ and make them into subjective experiences in our lives. The permanent historical events of the life of Christ become lasting personal experiences in our lives. For example, His Death (a single historical event) becomes our death (an enduring spiritual reality in us—see Galatians 2:20, 6:14; Romans 6:6, 11, etc.). So our lives should reflect His personal history, and provide echoes of His glorious Gospel. All of this is the work of the Holy Spirit. Thus, it is absolutely vital and indispensable that each Christian understand the ministry of the Holy Spirit. Bill Bright, the late founder of Campus Crusade for Christ, said, "If I had a lost person on my left hand and a Christian who doesn't understand the work of the Holy Spirit on my right, and I only had ten minutes, I would talk to the Christian about the work of the Holy Spirit."

One of the greatest Christian witnesses and soul-winners in the modern church was a medical doctor in Kansas City named Walter Wilson. Wilson's great fruitfulness for Christ began when he heard Dr. James M. Gray preach as a guest in the church Wilson attended. That Sunday morning, Dr. Gray preached on Romans 12:1, 2, perhaps the greatest call for Christian consecration in all of the Bible. Paul wrote, " I beseech you therefore, brethren, to present your bodies a living sacrifice." Holding his glasses in his hand, Dr. Gray leaned forward with his elbow on the pulpit and gently asked, "Have you noticed that this verse does not tell us to Whom we should give our bodies? It is not the Lord Jesus. He has His own body. It is not the Father. He remains on His throne, and doesn't need a body. But Another has come to earth without a body, and God gives to you and me as followers of Christ the indescribable honor of presenting our bodies to the Holy Spirit, to be His dwelling place on earth." Wilson returned home from that service and fell on his knees beside a chair in his living room. There in the quiet of the hour, he said, "My Lord, I have treated You like a servant. When I wanted You, I called for You. You have been My vassal. Now I give this body from my head to my feet to You. I give you my hands, my limbs, my eyes and lips, and my brain. You may send this body to Africa, or lay it on a bed with cancer. From this moment on, this body is YOURS." The remainder of Wilson's life was a remarkable history of the Spirit's accomplishments through a dependent man. May God awaken each of us to the same possibility.

Chapter One

THE HOLY SPIRIT — WHO, WHERE AND WHY?

John 14:16-18:

"I will pray the Father, and he shall give you another Comforter, that he may abide with you for ever; Even the Spirit of truth; whom the world cannot receive, because it seeth him not, neither knoweth him: but ye know him; for he dwelleth with you, and shall be in you. I will not leave you comfortless: I will come to you."

Late in the last century, Nelson Bell, father-in-law of Billy Graham, former missionary to China, and a regular contributor to *Christianity Today* periodical magazine, said, "Ignoring the place of the Holy Spirit in individual salvation and in the life of the church might well be called the great omission of the twentieth century." Carl F. H. Henry, himself the editor of *Christianity Today* just before Dr. Bell spoke those words, echoed this truth in similar words when he said, "The most misplaced person of the twentieth century is the Holy Spirit." Although much has been done to correct this sad assessment, it still must be admitted that the typical Christian is woefully ignorant of the Person and ministry of the Holy Spirit.

A Christian's practice will result from his perception, so this ignorance is costing us dearly in the at-large Christian community. One great pastor said, "The church has majored on mechanics and minored on the Divine dynamic of the Holy Spirit." A veritable army of Christians who will depend on the Holy Spirit is needed in the church today like never before.

As we consider the Holy Spirit we will look at His Personality and His Presence, with some attention given also to His power and His purpose.

I. The Individual Personality of the Holy Spirit

First, Jesus spoke in these verses of the *individual personality* of the Holy Spirit of God. I must confess at the outset that any discussion of the Holy Spirit as a Person is perfectly unnatural to me, not because I have any questions about His personhood, but rather because I am so certain of it that a discussion seems almost artificial and unnecessary. After all, I never try to prove or substantiate the personhood or existence of a very dear personal friend, and that is the way I regard the Holy Spirit. It is so obvious, so sure, so evident to me that the Holy Spirit is a Person that it seems unnecessary for me to have to prove something that I presume upon and now take completely for granted.

Note the clear *revelation* of the Personhood of the Holy Spirit in the Bible. In just the fourteenth, fifteenth and sixteenth chapters of John, Jesus firmly and fully established the identity and individual personality of the Holy Spirit. Of the Holy Spirit, Jesus said, "*He* will abide with you forever." "The world seeth *Him* not, neither knoweth *Him*." "*He* dwells with you." "*He* shall teach you all things." "*He* shall testify of Me." "I will send *Him* unto you." "When *He* has come, *He* will reprove the world." "When *He* has come, *He* will guide you into all truth." "*He* shall not speak of *Himself*." "Whatsoever *He* shall hear, that shall *He* speak." "*He* will show you things to come." "*He* shall glorify Me: for *He* shall receive of mine, and shall show it unto you." "*He* shall take of Mine, and shall show it unto you." Were you watching thoughtfully as you read those words? No less than nineteen times in a span of nine

The Holy Spirit-- Who, Where, and Why?

verses, Jesus Christ spoke of the Holy Spirit as "He" or "Him," thus establishing beyond doubt or debate the individual personality of the Holy Spirit. His Personhood is clearly revealed in Scripture.

It is necessary that we simply *recognize* and acknowledge the Personhood of the Holy Spirit. If you saw the *Star Wars* movies, you will remember the phrase, "May the Force be with you." That's how many people think of the Holy Spirit—as a mysterious force from heaven that somehow helps us on earth. Well, *the Holy Spirit is very forceful, but He is not a mere force.*

I am aware as I write these words that there are multitudes of church people, and many sincere, conscientious Christians, who refer to the Holy Spirit as an "it." Admittedly, the expression may simply reflect an unfortunate choice of words, and in that case, the Christian should be much more careful in his choice of words. But some Christians are so careless that they glibly think of the Holy Spirit as a mighty influence, as an ecstatic vision, as vague essence, or as a nebulous power, but *not* as the Person that He is. Perhaps one reason for this sad circumstance is the unfortunate use of the word "Ghost" in speaking of the Holy Spirit since the translation of the King James Version of the Bible. To most people today, the word "Ghost" conveys the idea of a haunting disembodied spirit floating across the earth on an arbitrary errand of harm and fear. In fact, I have had several fine Christian people confess to me that they had at one time been very frightened of the Holy Spirit. This is partially true because the Holy Spirit has been regarded as an "it."

Reuben A. Torrey, the great evangelist of a past generation, once said, "If we think of the Holy Spirit as an 'it,' then our chief concern is 'How can I get hold of *it* and use it for my purposes?" You see, it makes a great deal of difference whether the Holy Spirit is a force or a Person to you. And it makes a great deal of difference to Him, also!

Nobody likes to be called an "it"! How would you like it if a dear friend walked up to you and said, "How is *it* getting along? It surely is looking well." You have probably seen something like this: a young mother is standing in a group of people with a young baby in her arms. Speaking from a mixture of politeness and ignorance, someone says, "How old is *it*?" "How much does it weigh?" "What is its name?" And you saw the young mother step back in mock rebuke (although it was probably more than *mock* rebuke), and say, "I'll have you know that this baby is not an 'it.' My little boy is a 'he,' thank you!" You see, it is an insult to personality to call a person by the impersonal pronoun "it." And how true this is of the highly sensitive Spirit of the living God! How can He possibly do His desired work when we maintain an attitude that violates His great Personality?

Furthermore, there are certain "proofs of personality" which can be seen in the Holy Spirit as He is revealed in the Bible.

For example, the Holy Spirit has the *traits* of personality. He has intelligence. "The Spirit of God knows" (I Corinthians 2:11). We are told that He has a "mind" (Romans 8:27). Every work of the Holy Spirit is marked in Scripture by infinite wisdom. The stamp of His intelligent mind is upon all that He does. Then, the Holy Spirit has emotion. He can be grieved (Ephesians 4:30). No impersonal object can experience grief; only a person can be grieved. The Holy Spirit loves, too (Romans 15:30), and He provides love for the children of God (II Timothy 1:7). The Holy Spirit also has will, or volition. He distributes spiritual gifts in the church "as He wills" (I Corinthians 12:11). He has the traits of personality.

Then, the Holy Spirit performs the *tasks* of a person. Jesus said that He does these things: He teaches, He reminds, He testifies, He reproves, He guides, He speaks ("He who has ears, let him hear what the Spirit says unto the church"), He hears, He shows, He glorifies, He receives, He takes. Elsewhere in the Bible, we are also told that He comforts, He strives, He searches, He sanctifies. Without a single exception, these tasks are performed generally (if not only) by persons. The Holy Spirit is a Person!

Then, the Holy Spirit receives such *treatment* as only a person can receive. The Holy Spirit can be grieved. Now, you cannot grieve a pulpit, or a desk, or a book, or a microphone, or carpet on the floor. Only a person can be grieved. And the Holy Spirit can be lied to (Acts 5). Now, you cannot lie to an impersonal object. You can lie *at* it, perhaps, but not *to* it! But you can lie to a person, and you can lie to the Holy Spirit. So the Holy Spirit is a Person!

The final proof of the personality of the Holy Spirit I would mention is that He *talks* like a person. He is often represented in the New Testament as speaking. Let me cite an example. In the tenth chapter of Acts, Peter was in a quandary about accepting the invitation to the home of the Gentile, Cornelius. In Acts 10:20, we read, "While Peter thought on the vision, the Spirit said unto him, Behold, three men seek thee. Arise therefore, and get thee down, and go with them, doubting nothing: for I (Greek, *ego*) have sent them." All psychologists declare that the very center and essence of personality is summed up in the word "ego." "Ego" is a person's basic selfhood. It is a transliteration of the Greek first personal pronoun "I." And the Holy Spirit claims this selfhood—the basic mark of personality—for Himself! The Holy Spirit is a Person, the blessed Third Person of the Holy Trinity. And He is as much a Person as God the Father is a Person, or as God the Son is a Person.

One final truth concerning His personality: if you have the Holy Spirit in your heart, you have all of the Holy Spirit any human being can have. Because He is a Person, He does not parcel Himself out piece-meal. When you received Jesus Christ into your life by faith, you did not receive half of a Person, or part of a Person, you received all of Jesus. Possession of Him is personal and total. Furthermore, it is the Holy Spirit, His "Other Self," Who mediates the Presence of Jesus in your inner person. Like you, the Holy Spirit is an individual Person.

II. The Immediate Presence of the Holy Spirit

Then, Jesus spoke in these verses of the *immediate presence* of the Holy Spirit. For over three years, the disciples had been with Jesus day and night. In every emergency—doubt, temptation, persecution, discouragement, defeat—Jesus had been present to strengthen them. But now He is about to leave them. What will they do when He is gone? In this last discourse before His arrest, trial, and crucifixion, Jesus made this great promise to His disciples:

"I will not leave you comfortless: I (myself) will come to you." This is why Marcus Dods called the Holy Spirit "Christ's alter ego," or "Christ's other self."

The word translated "comfortless" in the text has been translated in various ways—"I will not leave you leaderless, forsaken, desolate, friendless, unrepresented." But none of these words adequately conveys the full idea. The Greek word is *orphanous*, from which we derive our English word, "orphan." "I will not leave you orphans," Jesus said. An orphan is a person whose parents are dead, a person who is left alone, a person who is without guidance or instruction. The disciples must have felt that these things would be true of them if Jesus should go away. But He said, "I will not leave you orphans in the storm; I myself will come to you in the Person of the Holy Spirit." So the Holy Spirit is perpetually, permanently present with every Christian. He is present in two senses:

First, He is *with* us. "He will abide *with you* forever." "He dwells *with* you." The fourth chapter of the Gospel of Mark records the story of the storm on the Sea of Galilee which threatened a boat containing Jesus and His disciples, several of whom were professional fisherman and thus not unaccustomed to such severe storms on the sea. Jesus was asleep on a pillow in the back of the ship. The storm became so severe that even those professional fishermen became afraid for their lives. They awoke Jesus from His sleep, crying, "Master, don't you care that we perish?" From our modern vantage-point, we can look back upon that incident and know that however rough the elements were, there was, in fact, nothing for them to fear as long as Jesus was with them in the boat. The same thing is true of us. *The Holy Spirit is "in the same boat" with us!* The Holy Spirit is *here* (actually *here, at this moment, wherever you may be reading these words*), in our midst, in the very thick of our trials and our circumstances. He has cast His lot with us and stands ready to abide by the position He has taken.

Someone has told a story of a father whose little son was to have an operation. The boy asked the father to promise him that he would stay in the operating room through the operation. The

The Holy Spirit-- Who, Where, and Why?

father obtained permission from the doctors and made the promise. He entered the operating room with the doctors, and although it was hard to have to watch the little son take the anesthetic and slip into unconsciousness and then watch the doctors as they cut into his little body, the father kept his promise and stayed in the operating room. As soon as the little boy opened his eyes in the recovery room, he looked up and saw his father, and the first thing he said was, "Dad, did you stay all the way through?" The father said it was worth more than anything to him to be able to say, "Yes, son, I stayed all the way through." One day soon each of us will stand face to face with God. Jesus the Son will be as the right hand of the Father securing our case as our Advocate. And the Holy Spirit will be at our side. If we should turn to Him and say, "Did you stay through?" He would reply, "Yes; I stayed through; I stayed all the way through with you. There were some things that hurt Me deeply, and some things I didn't like, but I stayed all the way through. I often didn't like the way the world treated You, and I certainly didn't like it when the world anesthetized you—and you often didn't even know it—and I often didn't like the way you treated Me, and I sometimes didn't like the way I had to treat you, but *I stayed through, I stayed all the way through with you."* Jesus said, "He will abide *with you* forever."

But there is a second even more intimate and wonderful way that He is present. He is not only *with* us, He is *in* us. Jesus said, "He dwells with you, and *shall be in you."* It is as if Jesus had said, "There is a better form of possession opening before you, which will begin at Pentecost, and will last forever after." The Holy Spirit dwells at this moment within every true believer in Jesus Christ, that is, in every born-again person.

Very early in Christian history, there lived a great Christian named Ignatius. Ignatius was finally martyred because of his faith in Jesus Christ. Ignatius refused to bear the name given him at his birth by his parents. He rather introduced himself as "Theophorus," or "the God-bearer." When he was questioned at his trial, the examiner asked him why he had refused his birth-name. He respectfully answered, "Because since I have been born again, I always bear about with me and in me God the Holy Spirit." In this sense, every born-again person is a *Theophorus*, a "God-carrier." Every Christian has the Holy Spirit tabernacling in his breast. He carries the Holy Spirit, Who is God of very God, literally living as Another Person in his heart.

Christian, *are you courteous to the indwelling Holy Spirit? Or are you impolite or discourteous to this Divine Tenant who lives in you? Would you treat any guest in your home like you treat this honored Guest in your heart?* Do you wonder that He is often pained and grieved? But He is courteous, and has never forced Himself upon you. Instead, He has waited, working through spiritual pressures and impressions, maximizing truth within you and minimizing errors of concept and behavior. He is patiently waiting for you to give Him your courteous full attention, as well as access to all the compartments of our hearts and our habits. He urges you to commune with Him, to cooperate with Him, and to convey His Presence and power into your surroundings. He will act through you if you will only maximize His Presence within you. Will you give Him the right-of-way at every intersection of your life?

III. The Indispensable Power of The Holy Spirit

I do not want to leave this study without isolating at least briefly two other related matters about the Holy Spirit. One is an examination of *the indispensable power* of the Holy Spirit. I have written about this power in other studies, but it seems remiss to omit a consideration of it in any study about the Holy Spirit. I am personally convinced that maximum attention is often given to the minimal aspects of His power. His interests are from eternity and for eternity, and though He is here and now harnessed with us in the fast-moving streams of time and history, He still has eternity as His primary agenda. His power is best maximized when we recognize that He is deeply interested in our time-bound concerns, but He is monopolized by the eternal issues He is working out in and through us. I do not personally believe that the "big" issues have to do with my physical welfare or with some local outward "manifestation of His Presence."

The Holy Spirit-- Who, Where, and Why?

I would not be misunderstood at this point. I repeat: He is here and now harnessed with us in the fast-moving streams of time and history. He *is decisively interested in the things that concern us here and now*. But against the foil of the circumstances of our lives, He is working toward character transformation, Gospel communication, conviction of sin, conversion of total individual life, full implementation of *His purposes and His strategy* (the strategy clearly stated by Jesus Christ)—in short, the Holy Spirit is dominated by the desire to see each believer come to genuine likeness to Jesus Christ—goals that are often very elusive because they are hidden in outward manifestations of "spiritual things". These outward manifestations include such things as going to church, teaching, preaching, witnessing, etc. In no way am I reducing or minimizing the importance of these and the many other activities that constitute the "outward manifestations of spiritual things." But the subtle danger is this: our quest is often one of "spiritual search for carnal things." All of the above-mentioned priority activities of the Spirit-character transformation, heart-penetrating and life-transforming Gospel communication, conviction of sin (both in lost people and saved people), full and radical conversion of *total individual life*, full implementation of *His purposes and His strategy* (the strategy clearly mandated and modeled by Jesus Christ), may easily occur in very quiet and unobtrusive ways (study all of the personal, "private" encounters that are recorded between Jesus and *individuals)*.

I am convinced that "boom" power is not the primary exercise of the Holy Spirit, but rather "blessing" power (as seen in Ephesians 1:3 and II Peter 1:3-4 and *multitudes of other similar and supportive passages*). This power is quiet, rich, deep, penetrating and active within the Spirit-walking believer. This may be further seen as I mention the other related matter about the Holy Spirit.

IV. The Imminent Peril(s) We Always Face With Regard to the Holy Spirit

The other related matter which I want to briefly discuss is the *imminent peril* we constantly face with regard to the Person and Presence of the Holy Spirit with and in each believer. There are several sins against the Holy Spirit which are mentioned and exposed in the Bible. I have written about these elsewhere, but again I feel that this treatment of the Holy Spirit would be very inadequate if I did not mention them here and warn myself and you against their occurrence in our lives.

Four sins in particular are mentioned in the New Testament with regard to possible offences we may commit against the Person and Presence of the Holy Spirit. Let me give an outline of them.

> "Resisting the Holy Spirit", Acts 7:51 – a sin against *salvation*.
> "Blaspheming the Holy Spirit, Matthew 12:31-32 – the so-called "unpardonable sin," a sin again *spiritual sensitivity*.
> "Grieving the Holy Spirit," Ephesians 4:30 – a sin against *sanctification*.
> "Quenching the Holy Spirit," I Thessalonians 5:19 – a sin against *service*.

Let me note that the first two of these sins can only be committed by lost people, people who have never been born again. The last two can only be committed by saved people, people who *have* been born again. Any person who has committed the first sin mentioned, the resisting of the Holy Spirit as He works generally to convict and convert sinners, is flirting at all such times with the committing of the hopeless second sin against the Holy Spirit, the unpardonable sin of blaspheming Him. That is, as a sinner resists the Holy Spirit, he is establishing direction and momentum toward the unpardonable sin. So the only offered time to be saved is "NOW" (see II Corinthians 6:1-2) and the person who is awakened to consider Christ, eternity, heaven and hell, sin and salvation, should respond to Christ at today's opportunity. A lost person's "casual" procrastination with regard to his own eternal salvation (the opposite of his own eternal *damnation*) is Satan's chloroform that slowly causes character immunity to the convicting, converting work of the Holy Spirit, and each such postponement brings him closer to the committing of the unpardonable sin. There is a full-length study of the unpardonable sin available, and this sin needs to be studied carefully—and every possible action should be

The Holy Spirit-- Who, Where, and Why?

taken to help that "casual" procrastinator to correct the direction and momentum he establishes through his postponement of his own salvation.

The last two above-mentioned sins are sad indeed. Having God within, the Christian may grieve Him into silence and inactivity. Note that this sin is committed *against the Holy Spirit who dwells within the Christian.* The "engines" of the Christian life are shut down and the believer reverts tragically to carnal control for his motivation, momentum and mentality. He invites misery with every moment he pursues this course, but selfishness is a powerful driving force, and he may court misery almost deliberately because of his stubbornness and sin. This is the Christian's sin against his own sanctification, the "grieving" of the Holy Spirit.

The other sin the Christian may (and does) commit against the Holy Spirit is a sin against *Christian service.* The "grieving" of the Holy Spirit takes place *within* the believer, where He seeks to do His sanctifying work. The "quenching" of the Holy Spirit takes place *around* the indwelt Christian, where the Spirit is seeking to release His Presence and Power and accomplish massive Divine purposes in the service of the individual Christian. Dear Christian, please re-read the previous sentence and remember that you are the "individual Christian" referred to. Yes, God the Holy Spirit fully intends and purposes to release His Presence and Power through you in all situations and accomplish His own massive Divine purposes through your moment-by-moment individual service. Now you can see why this service you perform must be defined and standardized by the Mandate, Model and Method of Jesus. Otherwise, mere tradition and much guesswork will determine the insipid "service" of the individual Christian.

One paraphrase of I Thessalonians 5:19 says, "Do not smother the Holy Spirit," and a footnote suggests that the action is like that of throwing a wet blanket over a fire to put it out. What would happen if each Christian lived with an ungrieved, unquenched Holy Spirit all day long every day? The knowledge, power, and activity of the Holy Spirit would "cover the earth as the waters cover the sea." May God give to us, one by one, this lifestyle of living with an ungrieved, unquenched Holy Spirit until an army of Spirit-walking, Spirit-monopolized, Spirit-manipulated, Spirit-empowered, Spirit-manifesting, love-dominated, others-centered Christians are found in every community on earth—and Jesus is "happening" to people in deep and profound ways. May God hasten that day, and may He graciously use us to do it.

Chapter Two

THE DAY OF PENTECOST

Acts 2:1-4:

"And when the day of Pentecost was fully come, they were all with one accord in one place. And suddenly there came a sound from heaven as of a rushing mighty wind, and it filled all the house where they were sitting. And there appeared unto them cloven tongues like as of fire, and it sat upon each of them. And they were all filled with the Holy Ghost, and began to speak with other tongues, as the Spirit gave them utterance."

The Book of Acts has been appropriately called "the most exciting book in the New Testament." The leading contribution to the excitement of the book is made by an event which is recorded in the second chapter. The story of one of the most exciting and spine-tingling days of world history is told in this chapter. The occasion was the Day of Pentecost, the day on which, as someone has said, "God opened the shutters of His nature and let men feel the size of His power." It has been said that "power is the forceful expression of personality," and that is certainly true of God's power. The Day of Pentecost exemplifies that power. That day marked the coming of the Holy Spirit in the full release of God's redemptive power, and it was the Holy Spirit's power that endowed the church with the spiritual strength that has been the source of its true life and of its highest (indeed, its *only*) success. I invite you to examine with me today the Biblical record of that all-important day. I want to use three guide-words that will help us investigate and interpret the Day of Pentecost.

I. PROPHECY

The first guideword is the word *"prophecy."* The day of Pentecost was a day of prophetic significance. The very wording of the first verse of the second chapter of Acts suggests that the day of Pentecost was a well-known day *before* this great event occurred. There were three great Jewish festivals—religious celebrations—to which every male Jew who lived within twenty miles of Jerusalem was legally bound to come—the Passover, Pentecost, and the Feast of Tabernacles. The word "Pentecost" is the Greek word for "fiftieth," and it was so called because it fell on the fiftieth day after the Passover. The Passover celebrated Israel's deliverance from Egyptian bondage. It was during the Passover that the lamb was slain that secured Israel's freedom. During the Passover, on the day after the Sabbath, the Jews were to offer before the Lord "a sheaf of the firstfruits." Then, fifty days later, on the day of Pentecost, a loaf, known as the "bread of the firstfruits," was presented unto the Lord. The twenty-third chapter of Leviticus should be carefully studied by any student wanting to understand this feast and the other feasts of Israel.

This was another of God's ways of preparing His people for the coming of Christ and the development of the Gospel of Divine salvation. The lamb that was slain represented Jesus, the Lamb of God, who was slain during the Passover week. Then, the day after the Sabbath, Christ was raised from the dead, the first ripe sheaf of the vast harvest of humanity which is maturing for its Lord. He was taken out of the grave, where the rest of the harvest still lies, and presented in the very Presence of God as the firstfruits of the harvest of humanity. In I Corinthians 15:20, we read that "Christ has risen from the dead and become the firstfruits of them that sleep." At the Passover, a single sheaf was presented to God; at Pentecost, the sheaf has become a loaf, signifying the completion of the work that was begun at the Passover. On the day of Pentecost, the potential bread became the actual bread, the sheaf became a loaf.

Thus, in the two feasts, the entire plan of world redemption was symbolized. The Cross of Christ was symbolized by the Lamb that was slain at the Feast of Passover. The resurrection of Christ was symbolized by the sheaf of firstfruits. And the application of "the power of the resurrection" was symbolized on the annual day of Pentecost.

It was on the day of Pentecost recorded in the second chapter of Acts that the redemptive power of Christ in the Holy Spirit was released among men. Now the Holy Spirit applies and appropriates the redemption of Jesus to each human heart when Christ is received by faith, and brings to completion in each life the work of redemption. The day of Pentecost was a day of prophetic significance.

II. PRAYER

The second guideword toward understanding this red-letter day of Pentecost is the word *"prayer."* Prayer was a never-to-be-forgotten feature of preparation for and participation in that transforming Pentecost. Now, we must be careful to note that the praying of the Apostles and disciples did not *produce* or *cause* the visitation of the Holy Spirit on the day of Pentecost. That date was already set on God's calendar of world redemption before anyone present that day had been born. In fact, all of the red-letter days on God's calendar of redemption had been "fore-ordained" of God before they occurred in history. In fact, Pentecost was an *annual* day and feast on the Jewish calendar. So the praying of the disciples did not produce or cause Pentecost. The release of the Holy Spirit in full redemptive power on the day of Pentecost would have happened whether they prayed or not. Their praying served one indispensable purpose. Their praying made the human vessels ready to receive the Divine infilling. Their praying "took the lid off their souls" so they could become receptacles for the outpouring of the Holy Spirit. As it was then, so it is now; waiting on God in humble, believing prayer will bring the Holy Spirit in fresh power on the church. What kind of prayer was it that prepared those disciples to receive the benefits of the outpouring of the Spirit on the day of Pentecost?

First, it was *united* prayer. Verse one says, "They were all with one accord in one place." What a victorious note that is! They were "all" there! It is a simple fact, but history cries aloud in its testimony that God has never been able to do much with absenteeism. God would give many more Pentecostal experiences to His people if they did not forsake the assembling of themselves together. And they were not only there, they were there "with one accord." And they prayed! Praying together emptied those disciples of all discord. There had been strife and competition among them before, but all that was now gone. They were ready to throw their total weight in a united way into the task of prayer.

Then, it was *expectant, specific* prayer. They were pleading a clear promise of Jesus. He had promised to send His Spirit upon them, and this promise gave their prayer concentration and anticipation. It was this promise, also, that gave expectancy to their prayers. There was something majestic and mysterious about Christ's promise of the coming Spirit, but they expected His promise to be fulfilled, though they didn't know how. Only God knows how much His work depends upon our faith and expectancy.

A young man in Charles Spurgeon's class for young preachers one day sadly reported that he had not had any conversions in a long while. Spurgeon remarked, "But surely, you don't expect conversions every Sunday." "Oh, no," the young preacher replied. "Then that is one reason you don't have them," Spurgeon said gently. How much easier it is for God to work when His people expect it.

The phone rang in the office of a famous church in Washington, D.C., early one Sunday morning. The pastor answered the phone. A voice said, "Will the President be in your church this Sunday?" The pastor replied, "I don't know, but God Almighty will be here. May I invite you to come and join us in worshipping Him?" When we expect to meet God in prayer, and at church, as

The Day of Pentecost

eagerly as we expect to meet our friends, God will move upon us in Pentecostal power. Their prayer was expectant prayer.

Again, their prayer was *bold* prayer. For the first time in history, the disciples were actually praying "in Christ's name." They had seen Jesus ascend to heaven. They now felt a new and holy familiarity with heaven. God was no longer just a vast, baffling infinity. As they now looked up to heaven they saw God looking down on them through a human face, the face of Jesus. They were on covenant ground with God through the blood of Calvary and the ascended Lord. They came "boldly before the throne of grace" (Hebrews 4:16).

And their prayer was *continual* prayer. They met for self-examination and prayer for ten full days before Pentecost. I wonder if Peter's impatient, impetuous nature found the eighth and ninth days rather taxing to his faith? But there is nowhere in the story a suggestion of anything but quiet determination to wait upon God until the windows of heaven opened, and the promised Spirit came in great power. How many times have we missed God's best blessing because we failed to prayerfully, patiently "wait on the Lord." The day of Pentecost was a day of united, eager, bold, continual prayer.

As it was in the days of the Apostles, so it is and shall be in the twentieth century! "Call unto me, and I will answer thee, and show thee great and mighty things, which thou knowest not," saith the Lord. *A prayerless Christian is a sterile Christian. A prayerless church is a sterile church.* But a church full of praying Christians will be powerful for God. Things begin to happen for the glory of God only when God's people gather regularly and systematically to pray.

III. POWER

The final guideword in interpreting Pentecost is the word *"power."* Just a few days before the day of Pentecost, Jesus had said to His disciples, "Ye shall receive power, after the Holy Spirit has come upon you." Throughout the Book of Acts after Pentecost the record is one of persistent, overcoming power. *The Holy Spirit was*

Himself the power for the "blast-off" of the early Church! This power of the Spirit manifested through the Book of Acts is symbolized by the signs that marked His coming on the day of Pentecost. There were three of these miraculous signs. *They* were *temporary*, but the *reality behind each symbol was permanent.* You see, the day of Pentecost, like Bethlehem, like Calvary, like the resurrection, were unique events and will never be reproduced. However, they were each "specimen days" which released something and represent something that is eternally permanent. Since God gave the signs of the day of Pentecost, we can expect them to be symbolic of the age-long mission of the Christian and the Church.

The first sign of the day of Pentecost was *audible.* "Suddenly there came a sound from heaven as of a rushing, mighty wind." This was a miracle of *sound.* A heavenly wind was the first symbol of the Holy Spirit's power. What could be a better symbol of the boundless, irresistible, sweeping, overwhelming might of the Holy Spirit to *envelop* ("clothe," the Bible says) believers in power, and to overthrow the citadels of evil? Wind is independent and powerful. And it was a "rushing, mighty" wind, more like a tornado than a gentle June zephyr or soft summer breeze.

In the Bible, wind is the symbol of *regeneration* and *new life.* Remember, dear Christian, that it was the wind that breathed into Ezekiel's valley of dry bones and stirred them into life so that they "stood up as a mighty army" (Ezekiel 37). And it was to the wind that Jesus appealed to point out the mystery and reality of the new birth and of spiritual realities (John 3:8).

Wind is also the symbol of cleansing and separating. It was the wind blowing over the threshing floor that was used to blow away the light chaff and leave only the heavier golden grain. And that is what the Holy Spirit does in our lives if we are willing. The old dead chaff of the world covers up the golden grain of our lives. No Christian can be useful to God until the holy wind of the Spirit has been permitted to breathe into him and blow over his life. "A rushing, mighty wind filled all the house where they were sitting" on the day of Pentecost, and the same heavenly atmosphere is needed in our lives, our fellowship, and our churches today, free

The Day of Pentecost

from the dust and dirt of the world. When this atmosphere prevails within and without, the Christian may be described as Spirit-filled and Spirit-anointed, and the same is true of a church.

The second sign of the day of Pentecost was *visible*. "There appeared unto them tongues like as of fire, and it sat upon each of them." This was a miracle of *sight*. The second symbol of the Spirit was *fire*. Fire suggests the searching, purifying, refining work of the Holy Spirit. It is a known fact that fire *purges* and *purifies*. It burns out the dross and leaves the durable.

Many years ago, the city of London, England, was hit by a terrible plague which sacked the city and left its pollution everywhere. It was believed that its progress could not be stopped. But then a great fire swept over the city and burned away all the lurking disease, and its progress was arrested. The Holy Spirit acts the same way on every life into which He comes; all dross is burned away. But fire also *hurts!* Yes, and until we are willing to permit God to come into our lives and burn us until it hurts, we shall remain far too worldly and far too unfulfilled and dissatisfied as Christians. And fire also *warms!* Many orthodox Christians and churches are so chilling that they resemble ice chests more than warm, glowing furnaces that warm those that have the chill of sin and death upon their lives. Dwight L. Moody once prayed, "**Lord, make me not only warm, but red hot!**" May this be my prayer, your prayer, *our* prayer.

But verse three says that "there appeared unto them cloven tongues (distributed tongues) like as of fire." The fire was not a shapeless flame; it came in distributed *tongues*. *The symbol of the new age was to be the tongue of fire—human speech aflame with the Divine Presence.* The tongue of fire was to be the Church's great weapon from that time on. Note that the fire "sat on *each* of them." No exceptions were made, even as no exceptions are made today. *The resource—and the **responsibility**—of the tongue of fire were to belong to each Christian.* And "it *sat* upon each of them"—an indication that it came to stay! In I Thessalonians 5:19 the Bible tells us that we are to "quench not the Spirit." We are not to "smother" (The Living

Bible) or put out the consuming and purifying fire that the Holy Spirit brings into our lives.

The final sign of the day of Pentecost was lingual. "They were all filled with the Holy Spirit and began to speak with other tongues (languages), as the Spirit gave them utterance." This was a miracle of speech. Remember, these were the same men who, only weeks earlier, had retreated furtively behind closed doors "for fear of the Jews." Their timidity has now become radiant audacity to make Jesus known. "They began to speak"! They spoke with other dialects, or other languages. Each man present, no matter what his nationality or native language (and there were at least fifteen ethnic and national lingual groups present, Acts 2:9-11), heard the Gospel in his own mother tongue. This is a perfect token of the age-long work of the Holy Spirit. Under the leadership and empowerment of the Holy Spirit, there shall not be a man of any tongue on the face of the earth who shall not hear the Gospel in his own tongue. There is no problem of communication that the Holy Spirit cannot solve.

This, then, was the day of Pentecost. Remember that it was a special, unique, red-letter day on God's calendar. It will never be reproduced. We should not seek "another day of Pentecost." However, it was a kind of "specimen day," and the realities that were released on that day are permanent. Our individual experience of the fullness of the Holy Spirit usually begins with a kind of "day of Pentecost" in our inner lives, when, in utter yieldedness to Jesus Christ as absolute Lord, we honor the Spirit's Presence in our lives and receive by faith the power of the Holy Spirit in our lives. Christian, are you filled with the Holy Spirit? Have you appropriated by faith the power that is available through His Presence in you?

Chapter Three

THE BAPTISM OF THE HOLY SPIRIT

I Corinthians 12:12-13:

"For as the body is one, and hath many members and all the members of that one body, being many, are one body: so also is Christ. For by one Spirit are we all baptized into one body, whether we be Jews or Gentiles, whether we be bond or free; and have been all made to drink into one Spirit."

In Bible study and in Christian experience, it is wise for a Christian to begin with his *position* (*where* he is — "in Christ"), and *then* to think of his *condition* (*what* he is in his present experience). Once an individual has truly received Christ as personal Savior, he is *positionized* "in Christ", and all the benefits, privileges, and security of that position belong to him. On the other hand, his *condition* may fluctuate and change with changing feelings and circumstances. In this study, we are dealing with a truth concerning our *position* in Christ. Our theme is "The Baptism of the Holy Spirit."

I. PLAINLY PREDICTED

First, we note that the baptism of the Holy Spirit was *plainly predicted* before it occurred. No less than five times, "baptism with the Holy Spirit" was predicted and promised before it took place. *On four of the occasions, the predictions were made by John the Baptist.* In Matthew 3:11, Mark 1:8, Luke 3:15, and John 1:33, John said, "There will come one after me who shall baptize you with the Holy Spirit." Then, in Acts 1:5, during the forty days between His resurrection and ascension, Jesus said, "Ye shall be baptized with the Holy Spirit not many days hence."

In each of these instances, there is a contrast made between water baptism administered by John the Baptist and the baptism of (with, in) the Holy Spirit. It is only in reference to the prophecy of John the Baptist concerning the ministry of Christ that the baptism of the Holy Spirit is mentioned. The contrast between the two baptisms can be summed up this way: *Baptism in water by John the Baptist did not save (in fact, no baptism in water saves). Baptism by, and with, and in, the Holy Spirit, though it does not save per se, occurs precisely at the moment of the soul's salvation.* As a careful exegesis of the one text which explains this baptism will disclose, the baptism of the Holy Spirit occurs simultaneous with the moment of the new birth, or salvation. Immediately, some Christian will protest, "But that didn't happen to *me* when I was saved. Or if it *did*, I certainly didn't *know* it!" Dear Christian, there are *many* things which happened to you when you were saved, things which you certainly did not know at the time, just as there were many things which happened to you at the moment of your *physical* birth, *things which you did not know at the time.* However, at this point, I am only establishing that the baptism of the Holy Spirit was plainly predicted before it occurred.

II. HISTORICALLY FULFILLED

Then, the baptism of the Holy Spirit was *historically fulfilled* on a *specific calendar date*. In Acts 1:5, Jesus said , "Ye shall be baptized with the Holy Spirit *not many days hence.*" This suggests that this baptism was immediately coming. This is a plain and obvious reference to the day of Pentecost, the story of which is recorded in Acts 2. The day of Pentecost is the historical fulfilment of the predictions of the baptism of the Holy Spirit. So the baptism

The Baptism of the Holy Spirit

of the Holy Spirit occurred *after* the events recorded in the four Gospels, *after* the Ascension of Jesus into heaven and His enthronement at the Father's right hand. In Ephesians 4:8, we read, "When he (Jesus) ascended up on high, he led captivity captive, and gave gifts unto men." And the first of those "Ascension gifts" was the gift of the Holy Spirit Himself. We must always distinguish between the Gift of the Holy Spirit and the gifts of the Holy Spirit.

The Holy Spirit came in the full release of redemptive power on the day of Pentecost and baptized all true believers in Christ in, and with, and by His Presence. The explanation of this will be given later, but the baptism of the Holy Spirit occurred historically on the day of Pentecost. Dwight L. Moody often said, "The day of Pentecost was a specimen day. It does not need to be repeated any more than Bethlehem, Calvary, the Resurrection, or the Ascension need to be repeated." And he was right! Since the day of Pentecost, believers in Christ do not experience *another* Pentecost; they simply enter into participation of privileges and experiences given on that great day.

It must be noticed that on one instance *after* Pentecost, the baptism of the Holy Spirit is spoken of. This has to do with the conversion of Cornelius and his family in the tenth and eleventh chapters of Acts. *On the day of Pentecost, the baptism of the Spirit came to Jews and Jewish proselytes, but the baptism was not given to Gentiles. So the tenth and eleventh chapters of Acts record a great crisis in the history of the church.* The conversion of Cornelius marks the official opening of the door of faith to the Gentiles (including ultimately you and me). When the Gentile Cornelius and his family repented of sin and received Christ, they were saved and baptized with the Holy Spirit (Acts 11:16).

From the time of Acts 2, any Jew who truly receives Christ is *"baptized with the Holy Spirit"* at the moment of conversion. And since the eleventh chapter of Acts, any Gentile who truly receives Christ is *"baptized with the Holy Spirit"* at the moment of conversion. The moment any true believer receives Christ, he is simultaneously *"baptized with the Holy Spirit."* This is possible since the "specimen day" of Pentecost. That day fulfilled the predicted "baptism of the Holy Spirit."

III. BIBLICALLY INTERPRETED

Then, the baptism of the Holy Spirit is *biblically interpreted*. In I Corinthians 12:12-13, we find *the only doctrinal interpretation of the baptism of the Holy Spirit found in the Bible*. This is an example of the necessary "didactic passages," the teaching passages which, in the case of each key doctrine of the Bible, best explain that doctrine. The interpretation of that particular didactic passage which explains any doctrine is absolutely crucial to a proper understanding and presentation of that doctrine. Again, I Corinthians 12:12-13 is the passage which didactically explains the baptism of the Holy Spirit.

In this passage, we read, "As the body (the human body) is one, and hath many members, and all the members of that one body, being many, are one body: so also is Christ. For *by one Spirit are we all baptized into one body*, whether we be *Jews (since Pentecost)* or *Gentiles (since Acts 11*, the official reception of Gentiles into the body), whether we be bond or free; and have been all made to drink into one Spirit."

In investigating the meaning of these verses, there are several key words that need to be defined, interpreted, and explained. One such word is the little word, "one", which occurs some *six times* in those two verses. So *the baptism of the Holy Spirit is to accomplish a "oneness," a oneness between all members of the body which was newly formed by the baptism of the Spirit on the day of Pentecost*. From that time on, there would be a oneness, a *union* between each member and each *other* member, and between each member and the Head of the Body (Christ).

None of us has ever seen a nose moving alone along the street, or a foot walking by itself. All the members of a body must be joined and fitly knitted together. If an organ is independent, it is not a member of the body. And if it is a member of the body, it cannot be independent. Furthermore, each member of a body unites two other members. For example, the forearm unites the

The Baptism of the Holy Spirit

hand with the upper arm. Again, each member nurtures other members of the body. Each member receives nourishment for itself and passes it on the other members around it. Also, each member of the body relays orders it receives from the head to other adjacent members. The head does not send orders to the hand without going through the other members that connect the head to the hand. So it is evident that elasticity, utility, and health depend fully on a marvelous internetworking among all the members of a body. This oneness is initially produced by the baptism of the Holy Spirit, and then regular adjustments must be made within the body to retain it.

The second key word in the passage is the word "body." You see, the day of Pentecost marks a new departure for the Kingdom of God and for the Holy Spirit on earth. On the day of Pentecost, for the first time, the Holy Spirit created a body for Himself, and by the "baptism of the Holy Spirit," He incorporated all believers into that Body so that they became "members" of it. God the Father does not need a body (John 4:24); God the Son received a body at conception and birth (by the supernatural work of the Holy Spirit); and now, at Pentecost, the Holy Spirit takes a body. Jesus, in the Person of His "other Self," the Holy Spirit, takes a body for Himself. I say it reverently. At Pentecost, Jesus mystically became a Baby again, and the 120 believers were His infant Body. Immediately, the "members" of His Body were increased by 3,000, and His Body began its age-long growth toward full maturity.

The third key word in the passage is the word "into." Thus, the baptism of the Holy Spirit positionizes the believer into the Body of Christ. On the day of Pentecost, believers were incorporated into the Body of Christ. Since that day, every believer is joined to the Body of Christ by the baptism of the Holy Spirit at the moment of conversion. So the baptism of the Spirit is a gracious act of the Lord whereby He joins His people to the Body of Christ. It has been illustrated like this: It's like a mason taking a brick and placing it into the wall which he is building. The brick still retains its own identity as a brick, but it also become a part of a larger wall. Even so, at the moment of conversion, the Holy Spirit baptizes the believer into the Body of Christ, and thereafter he is a "member" of that Body. In this manner, dead and isolated stones become "living stones," incorporated into the Church, which is God's building.

A fourth key word in the passage is the word "all." "By one Spirit are we *all* baptized into one body." The baptism of the Spirit is universal among all believers. Remember, Paul wrote these words to a troubled, disturbed, disordered, carnal church. The Corinthian church was divided--over preachers, over doctrines, over religious practices, over legal matters, and over discipline. But Paul says that they had **all** been baptized by the Holy Spirit into the Body of Christ. Not merely one here and one there; not those who had met certain moral qualifications, but **all**. The moment any person was born of the Spirit, he was also baptized by the Spirit into the Body of Christ.

Now, these facts explain why we are never told, or invited, or urged, or commanded to seek the baptism of the Holy Spirit. **Never, ever, are we exhorted to seek the baptism of the Spirit in the New Testament**! The baptism of the Spirit is not something for which the believer must earnestly ask and beg, not something to be waited for or sought after. Many sincere, faithful, true Christian people mistakenly seek, pray, and wait for an "experience" of the baptism of the Holy Spirit. They expectantly, prayerfully, and sometimes agonizingly wait before the Lord for this baptism. Some even build whole systems of theology upon it. However, this is alien to the New Testament. Nowhere is it recorded in the New Testament that anyone ever prayed for or sought the baptism of the Holy Spirit. In Ephesians 5:18, we are commanded to "be filled with the Spirit," but **never** are we commanded to be *baptized* with the Spirit. Furthermore, the baptism of the Spirit occurs once-and-for-all; "by one Spirit are we all baptized (an aorist tense verb, describing action that occurred at the moment of conversion) into one body." A Christian can be *filled* with the Spirit many times, but he can be *baptized* with the Spirit only once. And it is really useless to pray for the baptism of the Spirit, because every Christian has *already been* baptized by the Spirit. The baptism of the Spirit is Biblically interpreted.

IV. BEAUTIFULLY SYMBOLIZED

Again, the baptism of the Holy Spirit is *beautifully symbolized* in the New Testament and in Christian experience. In I Corinthians 12:13, Paul said, "We have been all made to drink into one Spirit." This verse literally says, "We have all been *saturated with, drenched with, immersed in, thoroughly soaked in* one Spirit." Here, Paul uses the suggestive symbol of water baptism to illustrate or symbolize the baptism of the Holy Spirit.

Here is the baptismal pool in which the believer has just pictured his death to sin, burial with Christ, and resurrection to walk in newness of life. There he stands, drenched to the skin, thoroughly soaked. This is a picture of the believer becoming a part of the Body of Christ *"by being drenched in His Spirit,* by being thoroughly soaked in His Spirit." By the birth and baptism of the Spirit, every true believer becomes a participant in the death and resurrection of Christ (Romans 6:3-5). Water baptism is a beautiful and meaningful picture of this participation.

Water baptism is like a one dollar bill. A one dollar bill has two types of value. One is its *intrinsic* value, the value of the paper and the ink that constitute the bill. Intrinsically (the value of the paper and ink), a one dollar bill has very little value. But it also has *extrinsic*, or *assigned*, value. The value of a one dollar bill is not in the paper and the ink, but in the fact that it is assigned to be an official certificate of the federal reserves of the United States government. So it is with water baptism. The water and the ceremony by themselves have little value. But when water baptism is assigned value by the Word and Spirit of God, and backed by the death and resurrection of Jesus, it possesses great value as a testimony. It is a picture and a testimony of the Spirit's baptism of the individual believer into the Church as the Body of Christ.

Both of these baptisms — water baptism and the baptism of the Spirit — stand in the New Testament at the *beginning* of the Christian life. Water baptism was plainly an initial rite. Baptism in water marks the formal introduction of the believer into the church, but this is the *symbol*, not the *substance*. Observe the identity in form between the symbol and the substance. John said, "I indeed baptize you in water, but He that cometh after me... shall baptize you in the Holy Spirit and in fire." *As in the one instance the disciple was submerged in the element of water, so in the other he was to be submerged in the element of the Spirit* And thus it was in actual historic fact. If we may say it reverently, the upper room became the Spirit's baptistry. And since the day of Pentecost, every believer in Christ has been made a participant by the baptism of the Spirit in the benefits of the perpetually abiding Holy Spirit of God. Water baptism beautifully symbolizes the baptism of the Holy Spirit.

V. PRACTICALLY EXPLAINED

Finally, the baptism of the Holy Spirit should be *practically explained*. What does it mean for us in this place at this hour? It means that this local Body of Christ — made up of each true believer here and now — is indwelt by the Holy Spirit. When the Body was formed, *Christ* became the *Head* of it, and the *Holy Spirit* became the *Heart* of it. The Head provides the direction, the Heart provides life and vitality. If this Church is healthy, it is being governed by Jesus Christ and empowered by His Holy Spirit.

Furthermore, since we have been baptized by the Holy Spirit, we are now residents in the Divine element, the Holy Spirit. This explains much of the language of the New Testament. We are "not in the flesh, but *in the Spirit*" (Romans 8:9). We are called "to live according to God *in the Spirit*" (I Peter 4:6). We are commanded to "*walk in the Spirit*" (Galatians 5:25). And we are to "pray always with all prayer and supplication *in the Spirit*" (Ephesians 6:18). May God grant us the grace to live in the Spirit!

In a practical way, this means that the glorified Christ manifests Himself to the world through His Body. This is the same way *I* manifest *myself*, or *you* manifest yourself — through your body. How important it is that we see this and act accordingly! *Any individual Christian by inconsistency and unfaithfulness can weaken the life of the church, Christ's Body,* and the spiritual vitality and power of the entire Body can never exceed that which is possessed by its combined membership. Let's maintain constant correspondence between the members of the Body (us) and the Head of the Body (Christ), so that there will be a true, accurate, adequate manifestation of Jesus to the world — through His Body!

GENERAL NOTES AND QUOTES ON THE BAPTISM OF THE HOLY SPIRIT

If there was only a birth of the Spirit and no baptism of the Spirit, you would be an isolated Christian. But by the baptism of the Spirit, you become an incorporated Christian, and isolationism is no longer validly possible.

It is often the sad case that many true and ardent followers of the Lord Jesus Christ frequently use the wrong terminology to express their experience of the things of Christ. The use of the term, "the baptism of the Holy Spirit," is a good case in point.

There are only two references to the "baptism of the Holy Spirit" in the book of Acts (1:5 and 11:16). *This is absolutely amazing*. Due consideration must be given to this fact when considering the overuse of the term by many today.

The baptism of the Holy Spirit is the miraculous "placing-work" of the Divine Spirit. Every believer, no matter what his spiritual attainment (or lack of it), shares in this blessing. He may be completely ignorant of it at the time of its occurrence, for it is a work done *to* him and *for* him, and which he is not conscious of at the moment. Indeed, there are many things Divinely done for the believer at the moment of his salvation which he may not even be aware of, and he certainly is not intelligent about any of these until his study of Scripture allows him to "catch up" with his experience. This ignorance at spiritual birth is comparable to a baby's ignorance of human life and truth at physical birth. Babies simply do not understand embryology, but they are born, anyway! Then, they may spend their entire lives exploring biology and embryology, "catching up" in understanding with their birth-experience.

The truth of I Corinthians 12:13 is further amplified and the books of Colossians and Ephesians. In *Colossians*, Paul sets forth *Christ* as the *Head of the Church*, which is *His Body*, while in *Ephesians* he sets forth *the Church* as *His Body*, with *Christ as the Head.* *Colossians* spotlights *Christ*, *Ephesians* spotlights the *Church*.

According to Scripture, Paul's words were chosen for him by the Holy Spirit when he wrote his letters that form part of the New Testament, and I am sure that when we ignore the Spirit's use and meaning of these words, we are in danger of creating a false theology. When I have studied foreign languages in school, it has become very evident to me that the professor is *absolutely rigid and intolerant* about the correct use and understanding of words that make up the lingual vocabulary. Jesus showed this same spirit when He said, "Man lives ....by every word that proceeds out of the mouth of God." The practice (and regular habit, for some!) of idly stretching and glibly employing Biblical words in indiscriminate ways is an extremely dangerous procedure. See the similar paragraph later on this page.

The baptism of the Spirit gives us our *position in Christ*. The baptism of the Holy Spirit is never commanded in the New Testament. Instead, it is merely *stated* in an aorist tense verb form (I Corinthians 12:13). The aorist tense verb form points to point action and one-time occurrence. Our position is established in Christ and in His Body, the Church, once and for all at the moment of conversion. This is the only interpretation given of the baptism of the Holy Spirit in the New Testament.

The fullness of the Spirit, on the other hand, gives us our *power* in Christ. There is a command to be filled with the Spirit, and it is in the present tense verb form. The present tense verb form points to maintained action, and the necessity of renewal and restoration when the maintenance of the fullness breaks down. So the *baptism* of the Spirit is for *position,* while the fullness of the Spirit is for *character and power.*

When the Holy Spirit baptizes us into the Body of Christ, it is no longer possible for us to live in the singular. A "solitary Christian" is a contradiction in terms.

It has been my experience in dealing with Christians that many are too careless and not selective enough about their Christian vocabulary. All great Christian terms have their own distinct and decisive shades of meaning. It is "graveyard serious" that we "compare spiritual ideas with spiritual words" (I Corinthians 2:13), and that we use our words with great caution and care. The subtle differences between Gospel words give us added insight into what God has done for us through our Lord Jesus Christ.

I took ten hours of Spanish language study in college. Unfortunately, much of it has been lost through disuse! We had a time in each class session for "vocabulary." The professor was very intolerant if I confused one term with another! "Buenos noches" could not validly be translated "good morning", however much I might confuse the terms. If that was true in a college Spanish class, how much more careful should we be in dealing with the vocabulary of eternal revelation as recorded in the Bible. Remember that we live "by every word that proceeds out of the mouth of God," and it will become evident that we cannot assume the prerogative to change, misinterpret, abuse, misuse, or be careless about the words of the Word.

A good working formula for a Christian is "ONE BAPTISM, MANY FILLINGS, and CONSTANT ANOINTINGS." The ONE BAPTISM is for our *larger position;* the MANY FILLINGS are for the experience of *God's living power* for the formation of Christ's character in us and the forceful expression of His Personality through us; and the CONSTANT ANOINTINGS are His special equipment for each *local performance* in the Christian life.

Some baptisms in the Bible are *wet* baptisms, and some baptisms are *dry*. The baptism of the Holy Spirit is a dry baptism. Example: when Jesus said, "I have a baptism to be baptized with," He certainly did not have water in mind!

It is vital to note the great difference between the baptism of the Spirit and the fullness of the Spirit. No one would object to being baptized in a thousand gallons of water, but no one would want to be FILLED with a thousand gallons of water! In a *baptism, the subject goes into the element,* but in a *fullness, the element goes into the subject.* These are quite different in *direction* and in *determination.* Let me urge the reader to give prayerful and repeated attention to the two preceding sentences.

Studies in the Person and Work of the Holy Spirit

If Pentecostalism is correct, then there must be (at least) two baptisms of the Spirit--one at conversion (clearly taught in the New Testament), and another at a subsequent time (not taught in the New Testament); one for position (clearly taught in the New Testament), and another for power (not taught in the New Testament). Compare the "one baptism" statement of Ephesians 4, and note that the list in which that expression occurs is a list of spiritual things, not mechanical or material. So it is likely that the "one baptism" is a reference to the baptism of the Spirit, not baptism in water.

And note that there is *only one such baptism.*

When the church comprehends the glory and simplicity of the believer's position in Christ, there is the possibility of great peace and power, but when it does not, doctrinal and denominational errors prevail and confusion and division follow.

The baptism of the Spirit is not repeatable and cannot be lost, but the filling of the Spirit can be lost, can be repeated (and should be repeated), and should be maintained. The Holy Spirit is "grieved" (Eph. 4:30) by sin, and ceases to fill the saint, but the baptism of the Holy Spirit cannot be altered by the performance of the Christian. The Christian's position does not vary, but his power fluctuates with his walk and his faith.

Bibliography:

John R. W. Stott: The Baptism and Fullness of the Holy Spirit.

Merrill Unger: The Baptism and Gifts of the Holy Spirit.

Chapter Four

THE HOLY SPIRIT AND GOD'S TRUTH

Part One—How the Holy Spirit Publicizes God

(I Corinthians 2:9-13, the first of a two-part message)

"As it is written, Eye has not seen, nor ear heard, neither have entered into the heart of man, the things which God has prepared for them that love Him. But God has revealed them unto us by His Spirit: for the Spirit searches all things, yes, the deep things of God. For what man knows the things of a man, except the spirit of man which is in him? Even so the things of God knows no man, except the Spirit of God. Now we have received, not the spirit of the world, but the Spirit which is of God; that we might know the things that are freely given to us by God. Which things we also speak, not in the words which man's wisdom teaches, but which the Holy Spirit teaches; comparing spiritual things with spiritual."

This study could also be called, "The Holy Spirit and the Mind of God." The Scripture which provides the text is a vast gold-mine of exploration of the relationship between the Holy Spirit and God's Truth or God's Mind—and how He reaches our hearts with His Truth. It is my objective to "mine" some of these truths as deeply as possible.

Studies in the Person and Work of the Holy Spirit

The entire Bible points out the place of the Holy Spirit in implementing the Life and Truth of God in a believer's life. The New Testament is filled with information about the Holy Spirit and His relationship to God's truth. We will confine ourselves to one brief but full passage on this theme. What does it tell us? It reveals that the Holy Spirit is not optional but obligatory if we are to understand the things of God. Let me divide the text according to its various themes.

I. The Revelation of God's Truth, 2:10-11

First, it tells us that the Holy Spirit is essential in the *revelation* of God's truth. Verses nine through eleven record these words: "As it is written, Eye has not seen, nor ear heard, neither have entered into the heart of man, the things which *God* has prepared for them that love Him. But God has *revealed* them unto us by His Spirit: for the Spirit searches *all things*, yes, the deep things of God. For what man knows the things of a man, except the spirit of man which is in him? Even so, the things of God knows no man, except the Spirit of God." I have taken the liberty to italicize three terms in the text recorded above; these three terms bear major emphasis in the original Greek text. The best way to understand the major and minor emphases of the Greek text of the New Testament is that, in a minor emphasis, the Holy Spirit (in effect) raises His voice from the printed page, and in major emphasis, He *shouts!* Read the text recorded in this paragraph and shout the words in italics, and you will catch the meaning

The first verse of the text recorded in the previous paragraph is almost always misinterpreted in preaching and teaching. It is taught and preached as if it were a reference to *heaven* (read it with that idea in mind, and see how attractive that interpretation is), but the context reveals that it doesn't (*couldn't*) refer to heaven at all. The first sentence in the following verse (vs. 10) seals this by saying, "But God has (already) revealed these truths unto us by His Spirit," and that simply does not (*cannot*) apply to the truth about heaven. Verse nine refers to things that God has already revealed to living people on earth, to "them that love Him" (verse

The Holy Spirit and God's Truth

9)--and is continuing to do so today. That is, it refers to spiritual truths which God reveals in this present life to the ready heart of the spiritual believer.

In verse 9, the three primary means of natural knowledge are mentioned—the eye (knowledge received by physical vision), the ear (knowledge received by audible hearing) and the heart (knowledge received by intuition). One Greek lexicon says that the word "heart" in the New Testament includes the "thoughts, reasonings and understandings of a human being—that is, the word 'heart' is used as a metonym for the mind in general." To explain the obscure word in that sentence, a "metonym" uses the name of one thing for another thing to which it is related, like "scepter" for "sovereignty" or "the bottle" for "alcoholic beverage". However, the text firmly declares that *these three means of receiving natural knowledge (eye, ear and mind), if unaided, are useless in understanding the things of the Spirit of God*, the things which God wants to reveal *today* to *"them that love Him."* The understanding of the things of the Spirit of God must come from another source altogether.

Focus on verse ten. "God has revealed them unto us by His Spirit: for the Spirit searches all things, yes, the deep things of God." Remember that the terms "revealed" and "all things" are major emphasis in the Greek text. Read the verse aloud and strongly emphasize these two terms in the verse, and you will get the meaning. What does this verse actually say? It indicates that *only God can reveal God*. It also identifies the only Teacher who can reveal "the deep things of God" to men. "God has revealed these things unto us *by His Spirit: for the Spirit searches all things, yes, the deep things of God."* The second part of the verse reveals why/how the Holy Spirit is qualified to reveal the things of God to us. He can teach us "God from the inside" because He, being God, can search out and explain anything pertaining to God. "The Spirit searches . . . the deep things of God." The word "search" means " to explore," or "to examine," or "to probe." Only the Holy Spirit "reads God" from the inside, and He does this because He is God. Having perfect inside information from within God, He can perfectly reveal God.

Then Paul presents a classic ad hominem argument. An ad hominem argument is an argument that begins with what we know about man and then argues in another direction. In this case, Paul begins with man and then shows what we can deduce from man about God. Verse 11 says, "For what man knows the things of a man, except the spirit of man which is in him? Even so, the things of God knows no man, but the Spirit of God." That is, he argues from what we know about a man to what we then can deduce about God. For example, if man is made in the image of God, and man is intelligent, then surely God is intelligent as well. Since an individual man knows himself better than others do because he lives "inside" of himself, the same is true of the Holy Spirit of God. The Holy Spirit, because He is God, lives inside of God, and thus He fully knows God. In Paul's argument here, he establishes that the Spirit of God alone is competent to make any revelation of God, because He alone searches ("explores," "examines," "probes") the deep things of God. The Holy Spirit accurately and thoroughly knows the things of God; there is nothing in God unknown to the Holy Spirit. The Holy Spirit alone can fathom the plans, purposes, thoughts—"the deep things of God." And thus He alone can make them known to us. But there is a further Divine premise in these verses: not only is the Holy Spirit the only one who can make God known, but He must do so if we are to know God. We simply cannot discover God or His Truth by our unaided reason or by our unassisted investigation; we must have Divine revelation.

This passage proves at once the personality and the Deity of the Holy Spirit—that is, that He is *a person*, and that He is *God*. It shows His personality by ascribing intelligent activity to Him—He "searches" God from the inside, and it shows His Deity by attributing omniscience to Him—He knows all that God knows. Knowing God perfectly, He reveals God to men. The Spirit's work of revelation is primarily done through the Bible, which presents a perfect revelation of God and His Purposes. So the Holy Spirit it essential in revealing God and His Truth.

II. The Illumination of God's Truth, 2:12

Second, the text tells us that the Holy Spirit is essential in the *illumination* of God's truth. *Revelation* is the *objective* side of the Spirit's work with regard to God's truth, and *illumination* is the *subjective* side. Revelation presents recorded truth; illumination presents relational truth. Revelation is basically prepositional (the recorded truth of Scripture), while illumination is personal.

Verse twelve of our text says, "Now we have received, not the spirit of the world, but the Spirit which is of God; that we might know the things that are freely given us of God." Again, several words bear major emphasis: the first "we" in the verse (meaning "we alone," i.e., we Christians), the word "world," and the first use of the word "God" in the verse. Note immediately that this verse concerns something that we "received"; we simply cannot *achieve* this. We *obtain* this as a gift of God (it is "freely given to us by God," the text says); we simply cannot *attain* it by our own efforts. Both revelation and illumination are gracious gifts of God, but there is one condition: *the recipient's heart must be open, teachable and receptive.* These characteristics should mark every Christian, though we must sadly admit that they are often absent, in which case the believer is tragically carnal.

When a telescope is directed to some distant scene or landscape, it enables the viewer to see what he could not otherwise have seen; but it does not enable us to see anything that does not have a real existence in the distant scene. Even so, subjective illumination never goes beyond the objective revelation of Scripture. God does not illuminate our hearts to anything except what He has already recorded in His Word. *Revelation* gives the Word of God to the world; *illumination* gives Him and His Truth to the heart of the receptive and spiritual believer. Revelation puts the truth of God on the sacred page; illumination turns on the lights in the believer's heart so he can understand God's Mind when reading His Truth. Psalm 25:14 says that "The secret of the Lord is with them that fear Him"; all the rest of humanity must just keep guessing! Revelation may pierce an individual reader's *head* with truth, but illumination will penetrate his *heart* with Divine light. Your *reason* will give you *your own* understanding of truth, but *the Spirit's illumination* will give you *God's understanding of His Truth.* I can personally attest that this is not surmise or guess-work; I have known both kinds of knowledge--that which can be discerned by one's unaided mind, and that which can only be known by Divine *revelation*, the *objective* side, and Divine *illumination,* the *subjective* side).

Note too that the "world" also operates by a "spirit," an aura, a philosophy, a mindset, a world-view, and note that it is not on the same frequency as the Spirit of God. We are to operate, "not by the spirit of the world, but by the Spirit Who is from God." We will learn more of this later in the message. Note, too, that it is God's intention "that we might get to know the things that are freely given to us by God." "We have received . . . . that we might know." The tragedy of many Christians is that although they have "received", they still do not know. How can this be? Well, they have received salvation—they have been converted, they have been "born again," and thus they have received the indwelling Holy Spirit—but this reception of the Spirit for illumination must occur regularly **and miraculously** after conversion. All of the promises of verse 9, all the things which God has prepared for those who love Him, are ours now. Thus the Christian life becomes a treasure hunt, a possessing of possessions, a daily unfolding of the things freely given of God. But it is precisely this quality of Christian living which is unknown to so many of God's people today. Why? Because those Christians, while attending church often and regularly, take the stewardship of God's truth for granted and never seek the illumination of the Spirit for GOD'S understanding of these things. So they are sterilized of full fruitfulness and the churches are neutralized in their power and in the world-impacting individual service God wishes out of each Christian.

This text indicates that a Christian has no excuse for being ignorant of the things of God, even the deep things of God. After all, *the Christian has "the Author of the Book" and "the Illuminator of the heart" inside of him,* and He is always eager to reveal the truth to us

The Holy Spirit and God's Truth

and to enlighten our hearts so we can understand it. So what excuse can we offer for ignorance?

One of the greatest problems in the fellowship of faith is that Christians take for granted spiritual truths and the exposition of those truths in preaching and teaching. According to the Bible, this is the most dastardly of sins. Yet, in spite of all of God's warnings and threats to a person who so listens and so sins, the typical Christian drifts into casual ("lazy"or "slothful," the Bible calls it, Hebrews 6:12) listening which aborts the Spirit's purpose in him/her. This happens increasingly in most Christians, without their conscious awareness. The Bible warns every Christian against this kind of "drifting" (Hebrews 2:1). Every Sunday, the typical church building is crowded with unfruitful listeners who have assumed that hearing the truth and perhaps rendering small services in the church fellowship is the desired purpose of the Christian life and in going to church. This reduces the Christian life of the New Testament to next-to-nothing. The Bible says, "Be DOERS of the Word, and NOT HEARERS ONLY" (James 1:22). And no Christian can look at a Bible and suppose that this demand can be fulfilled only be activities confined inside a church building! A casual reading of the Book of Acts, or of the Ministry of Jesus, will reveal that on-the-job, on-the-move ministry by each Christian which impacts the world with the dynamic of the Gospel is the intent of Heaven. If each individual Christian would appeal to Heaven in every service for the giant Divine miracle of personal illumination, this problem could be corrected quickly.

It is my personal practice to pray Paul's prayer for illumination, recorded in Ephesians 1:17-19, as often as I remember to do so—and I pray it for every person who comes to mind at any time (saved or lost), as well as for myself. Personally, I believe it is by far the most important prayer any Christian can pray at any time for himself or for anyone else. The prayer needs to be studied to the bottom line, until we can be sure we understand (and obey) the substance of it. Please read the previous paragraph and this one several times, and even regularly for weeks or months, so you can begin to obey its truth. This is vital enough to post it on your refrigerator door and read it daily for the rest of your life.

So two things need to be understood before we dig into God's treasury of truth, the Bible. The first is that these things are already *freely (graciously, gratuitously) given to us by God.* Because they are already given, we don't have to spend days or weeks or years asking for them. We have only to take what God has already given, and say ,"Thank You." I had to learn in a very childlike way that you don't ask for a gift that is being offered to you, you just receive it and say thank you!

The second thing we must understand is that *we have received God's Spirit in order that "we might know."* This is not a matter of speculation or guesswork, or trial or error, but a definite positive reception of Divine illumination. In a world loaded with uncertainly, bewildered by doubt and darkened by cynicism, the true spiritual Christian is the only one who can validly take a full stand and say, "I know, because I have the open Textbook in front of me and the Teacher in me, and He is doing His work there." The Holy Spirit unveils (actually, literally and plainly) the most significant of all truth and reality to the believing, obeying, spiritual Christian.

The Holy Spirit of God is indispensable if we are to have the necessary illumination of God's truth.

III. The Communication of God's Truth, 2:13

Third, the Holy Spirit of God is essential for the Spirit-filled *communication* of God's truth. Verse 13 says, "Which things (i.e., 'the things that are freely given to us by God') also we speak, not in the words which man's wisdom teaches, but which the Holy Spirit teaches; comparing spirit things with spiritual." Again, two terms (opposite terms, in this case) bear major emphasis in the verse, the terms, "man's wisdom", and the term, "Holy Spirit." These are the only two possible sources for man's understanding—His own wisdom or the wisdom of God which comes to him by the illumination of the Spirit.

Note the main ideas of this verse: "We speak ....in words ....which the Holy Spirit teaches, comparing (literally, 'combining')

The Holy Spirit and God's Truth

spiritual ideas with spiritual words." This means that *you can't have Divinely-inspired ideas without Divinely-inspired words.* A Christian is to speak with "words which the Holy Spirit teaches"—words of the inspired Word, words of Divine wisdom, words of a Divine Gospel. These words are given by the Holy Spirit, and our speech should be filled with these words.

Very early in the history of the Christian movement, the first Christians said, "We are witnesses of these things, *and so is also the Holy Spirit" (Acts 5:32).* Our witness is a mutual witness: First, it is inspired by the Holy Spirit as its Source, and then it is endorsed by the Holy Spirit's power as we speak it. Often, conviction of sin, conversion to Christ and transformation of character follow the speaking of Christian witness. This should occur every time Truth is told, and would be more likely to do so if Christians were dependent, prayerful, obedient and faithful to witness concerning Christ and His Truth.

Throughout Christian history, spontaneous witnessing has come from the personal infilling of the Holy Spirit. Luke 1:41 says, "Elizabeth was filled with the Holy Spirit, and she spoke . . . ." Luke 1:67 says, "Zachariah was filled with the Holy Spirit, and he prophesied . . . ." This course is followed regularly throughout the New Testament. On the Day of Pentecost, "they (all believers in Christ) were all filled with the Holy Spirit, and began to speak . . . ." (Acts 2:4). The Holy Spirit fills and teaches, and the Christian bears witness and bears fruit.

A perfect illustration of this truth occurs just preceding and just following the Outpouring of the Holy Spirit on the Day of Pentecost (Acts 2). Previous to Pentecost, ten earnest disciples tried to convince Thomas, who was absent when the Risen Christ appeared among them, that Jesus was alive, and they could not do so. Thomas adamantly replied to their witness, "Unless I see the scars where the nails entered His hands and feet, and can put my hand into the spear-scar in His side, I will not believe." Ten sincere, honest, Godly men could not convince one man that Jesus was alive, although their verbal testimony to His resurrection and their eye-witness observation of it was unanimous, and though he had no real reason to doubt that *testimony!* But, when the Day of Pentecost came and the Holy Spirit was sent from Heaven in the full release of redemptive power, just a handful of disciples convinced three thousand people to abandon all self-trust, all trust in other things, and to fully and exclusively trust Jesus Christ alone for Eternal Life Now and Forever!

The Holy Spirit is indispensable for the powerful communication of God's Truth.

At this point, I am going to divide this message, because beginning with I Corinthians 2:14 and extending through 3:3, the great truths contained therein need to be treated in isolation in order to fully magnify their significance. So I will simply leave you with these truths (gleaned from I Corinthians 2:9-13) for now, and will take up the remainder of the text (I Cor. 2:14-3:3) in the next study. Please pray for the illumination of the Spirit for yourself and for me as we think upon these pages of God's Truth, and as we anticipate the next study about "The Four Kinds of People" God sees on earth. May God fix our hearts upon Himself and His Truth by the Miracle of Illumination.

Chapter Five

THE FOUR KINDS OF PEOPLE GOD SEES ON EARTH

Part Two: What Kind Of Person Will Receive God's Truth? (A Study of The Natural Person, The Spiritual Person, and The Carnal Persons)

I Corinthians 2:14-3:3:

"But the natural man receives not the things of the Spirit of God: for they are foolishness unto him: neither can he know them, because they are spiritually discerned. But he who is spiritual judges all things, yet he himself is judged by no man. For who has known the mind of the Lord, that he may instruct him? But we have the mind of Christ. And I, brethren, could not speak unto you as unto spiritual, but as unto carnal, even as unto babes in Christ. I have fed you with milk, and not with meat: for hitherto you were not able to bear it, neither yet now are you able. For ye are yet carnal: for whereas there is among you envying, and strife, and divisions, are you not carnal, and walk as men?"

We now come to a passage that I regard as one of the most important in the Bible for understanding Divine truth. If a believer in Christ will master this passage by much study, meditation, dependence upon the Spirit for illumination, and practical implementation of its truth into his life, he will learn essentially what he will need to know about His life in Christ. Of course, any passage of the New Testament is only partial, or the rest of the New Testament would be unnecessary. As important as this passage is, it is only foundational for the many, many other truths of the New Testament about spiritual truth. However, if a person tried to build a house without a foundation, the consequences are predictable. The same is true of the Christian who does not master this crucial passage of God's Word.

I have heard or read many messages on this passage that speak of "Three Kinds of People," and these messages always treat the "three" as if that were an exhaustive treatment of this text. A superficial reading of this passage may yield that kind of thinking, but, as we shall see, this is neither accurate nor adequate. There are actually *four kinds of people* pictured in this text, and every person on earth is one of them at this very moment.

In exploring the passage, we will begin with the theme we followed in a previous study in examining I Corinthians 2:9-13, the theme of "The Holy Spirit and God's Truth." However, at this point the thrust of the passage changes to become fully personal. The passage is no longer merely theological, theoretical, or hypothetical; it is intensely personal. Now, each human being may see himself as God sees him. The passage now concerns *my own present appropriation, and the present appropriation of every person, of God's truth.* What role does the Holy Spirit play in my personal *appropriation of God's truth?* Here, a division is made between four different kinds of people and their personal reception, appropriation and application of God's truth. Also, I will simply continue the enumeration of the points made in the earlier study. Let me repeat: the first three points are presented in the previous study. This is point four in that succession.

IV. The Reception and Appropriation of God's Truth, 2:14-3:3

The fourth topic in our study of "The Holy Spirit and God's Truth" is this: The Holy Spirit is absolutely indispensable for the proper *reception and appropriation of God's Truth*. Here, Paul presents three general categories of men, with the third category subdivided into two smaller categories, making four kinds in all. Though we will distinguish between the two kinds of "carnal" when we discuss the carnal person, at the beginning we will examine the three large and general categories—the "natural," the "spiritual" and the "carnal" persons.

A. The "Natural" Man (2:14) — Reception is Impossible

We will begin with *"the natural man"* of I Corinthians 2:14. This is crucial, because most people on earth are merely natural people. This is *extremely* crucial—just read what the text says about the natural man! The *reception of God's Truth* is totally *impossible* for the natural man. We must not ignore anything that the Holy Spirit says about this man in our text. The text says, "But the natural man receives not the things of the Spirit of God: for they are foolishness unto him: neither can he know them, because they are spiritually discerned."

Let's begin with the crucial words in the vocabulary of the text. The very first word of the verse is crucial if we are to fully understand the natural man. The first word is "but." Grammatically, this is an adversative conjunction, which means that now an opposite truth to the preceding ideas is going to be presented. "But" is a counter-stating word (giving an opposite or counter truth). In verses 9-13 (see the previous study), Paul has shown the place of the Holy Spirit in revealing the things of God to men. Now, he will introduce a man (a person) who has never experienced such a work of the Holy Spirit as is necessary to know spiritual *revelation* and spiritual *illumination*, and thus the reception of God's Truth is absolutely *impossible* for him.

The second crucial word of this verse is the definitive word for this person, the word "natural." So the first of the four people is simply called "the natural man." To simplify the word at the beginning, the "natural" man is a man who *just does what comes naturally*. He has never been born of God, so he has no Divine, supernatural possibilities in his inner life. His understanding is natural, his emotions are natural (for example, he cannot experience the "joy unspeakable and full of glory" of I Peter 1:8), and his choices are natural. And all of this seems so *natural* to him that he scoffs at any other possibility. He simply knows not his own ignorance, an ignorance enforced in him by the absence of relationship with God.

The Greek word for "natural" is *psukikos*, which means, "adapted to the soul" (the "ikos" part of the adjective means "adapted to" whatever is at the head of the word; the "psuche" part of the word is the Greek word for "soul"). The next paragraph will show us why the natural man *must* adapt his inner life to his own soul and draw his inner resources for living from himself instead of God. He simply *cannot* adapt to the Holy Spirit because the Holy Spirit does not dwell in his human spirit. Therefore he is dead toward God, spiritually dead, "dead in trespasses and sins" (Ephesians 2:1).

The natural man is described in Jude verse 19 in the Bible, where the same word is used, *psukikos,* or "natural," in describing a man, and there it is added that he "has not the Spirit." There it is! The natural man has not the Holy Spirit, thus he has no Divine Life and no true supernatural frame of reference in his life. Another translation calls him "the animal man," which is a good translation because he is devoid of the one thing that makes a human being *true* man, the presence of God in his inner spirit. When God made Adam, he endowed him with *a live and healthy body, a live and happy soul*, and *a live and holy spirit*, made so by God's own Presence in him. When God made Adam, His Holy Spirit occupied Adam's human spirit. However, when Adam sinned, God departed from Adam's spirit, and he died spiritually. His spirit, the organ of relationship with God, became an instantaneous death chamber. Since that time, every person merely born of Adam (any typical human being) has been born in sin and spiritual death. So God's problem is this: *How do you convince a dead man that he is dead?!* Now we will look at the descriptive characteristic of the natural man that is mentioned in the text.

The Four Kinds of People God Sees on Earth

The third key word is the word "receives." "The natural man receives not the things of the Spirit of God." There are two Greek words that translate into our word "receive". One is the word *lambano*, while the other is *dechomai*. One refers to aggressive reception, the other refers to a passive reception. Another difference between the two words is that the first one gives more attention to the *object* of the reception (for example, John 1:12, "receive *Him*"), while the other focuses on the *manner* and *spirit* of the act of receiving. The word here is the latter word, *dechomai*, "to passively receive." This word "receives" simply means to "welcome," and is the word used for welcoming a guest. The text says that "the natural man receives not the things of the Spirit of God." Thus, the natural man gives no welcome and no room to God and His Truth. The natural man puts out no Welcome Mat at the door of his heart to God or the Truth of God. If he *did* welcome Divine "things" without a miracle birth (a real, radical, revolutionary Birth From Above—I know, because it has happened to me), the entire Bible would be a lie!

What " things of the Spirit of God" does the natural man not receive? All of them! In the preceding verses, Paul had been defining the works of the Holy Spirit in human experience, particularly the work of *Divine illumination*, but this man has never known any of these works of the Spirit. The previous paragraph must not be misunderstood; not *all* natural men are *passive* in their rejection of God and His Truth. Many kick and scream and protest, but all to no avail. Neither God nor His Truth consult the vote, or need the support, of a human being. I read a clever sign which said, "Even if all the dogs in the world bark up the wrong tree, *that doesn't make it the right tree.*" Take heed, Mr. "Natural," your ageless eternity is at stake!

For a clearer, fuller understanding of the natural man, we would do well to go back to I Corinthians 1:20, where Paul mentions "the wise," and "the scribe," and "the disputer of this world." Also, in I Corinthians 2:6, 8, he mentions "the princes of this world." He seems to deliberately avoid the mention of low and vulgar forms of "the natural man" (and there are plenty of them), and chooses "up-and-outs" as his typical examples. To the natural man, the *intellectual* is the highest department. He may have great genius for the sciences, or for literature, poetry, painting, sculpture, etc., but he can never transcend the sphere of mind. The natural man is the man whose perceptions do not extend beyond the region of the intellect. The natural man is the man in whom pure intellectual reason and the merely natural affections predominate. As a general rule, the concepts and conduct of the natural man will be ruled and toned by considerations of self-centeredness and self-pleasing. This may be tempered by goodness of the natural disposition, or by culture and self-mastery, even by "good deeds" (which tend to make him even more satisfied in his subtle self-aggrandizing accomplishments), but the tendency of the natural man's existence always moves toward *self*, his final point of reference.

> "Only two philosophies occupy life's shelf,
> You will either live for God and others,
> Or you will live for self."

A careful and clear word of caution is due here: We need not undervalue the natural man's sphere or his accomplishments, so far as they go. The question is, How far can they go, or, How far can this perspective take the natural man?

The picture is not finished until the Holy Spirit says that these "up-and-outs" *crucified the Lord of glory* (2:8). Does this not suggest a serious misunderstanding and malfunction in the lives of natural men? It is not only the brutal mob, but the best specimens of mankind according to public opinion in every age, *whom the Holy Spirit defines as condemned natural men.* It is evident today that the natural man has made vast advances and shows astounding capability, but all this has brought him no nearer to "the mind of Christ" (2:16). Because the Center of God's Heart is Christ, and the Centerpiece of Heaven is Christ, the natural man is haplessly lost—even while being dreadfully deceived about himself, about his capabilities, and about God. The next crucial word of the text will enforce these truths.

The Four Kinds of People God Sees on Earth

The fourth key word of the text is the word "foolishness." "The natural man receives not the things of the Spirit of God, for they are *foolishness* unto him." The Greek word is "moria," which speaks rather loudly for itself. It is the word from which we derive our English word, "moron." Two simpletons were talking, and one said to the other, "My girl friend has been ignoring me, and if there's anything I can't stand, it's *ignore-ance.*" The "foolish" (color that, "moronic") natural man is exposed by his ignoring of God, of His Truth, and of all Issues that derive from His Truth. Remember, we are only talking about *GOD! And eternity!* What wise man, surrounded by so much testimony and evidence about God and especially about Christ, His Life, His Death and His Resurrection, not to mention the incredible content of the Bible, God's Word, would just foolishly go through his short life-span willfully ignoring all of these things and gambling with the possibility of living forever while bound to his Godless choices in this life? Remember, *God always bats last!* If even a fraction of these things are true, the man is abjectly foolish who stubbornly resists them.

In his commentary on I Corinthians, Dr. G.G. Findlay says, "The Gospel appears on trial before the *psuchikoi*, the 'natural' men of the world. Like the Athenian philosophers on Mars Hill in Athens (recorded in Acts 17), they may give the Gospel a patronizing hearing, but they have no equipment by which to test it. Indeed, the natural man cannot perceive that it is actually *he* who is being spiritually searched and exposed by the Gospel he is 'evaluating'. The incompetence of the jury invalidates their inquiry. The unspiritual (the natural men) are out of court as spiritual critics; they are deaf men judging music."

Next, the text says of the natural man that "he cannot know the things of the Spirit of God, because they are spiritually discerned." The word "know" is the same word that is used to describe marital intimacy. This means that God expects intimate interaction between himself and each human being. It is His design and intent that each person be lovingly related to Him in intimacy of person and Person. But the natural man cannot "know" Him or His Truth—because he is improperly equipped. "These things are *spiritually* discerned," and the natural man has no spiritual equipment. The word "discerned" may be translated "investigated," or "evaluated," or "understood." A human being must be *born of the Spirit*, thus, *indwelt by the Spirit*, and necessarily *taught by the Spirit*, before he can "discern" spiritual things. This is not theoretical; it is a constitutional impossibility for a natural man to "discern" the things of the Spirit of God. Puritan Thomas Boston rightly wrote, "Natural men may be eagle-eyed with regard to the trifles of time, but they are like owls and bats in the light of true spiritual life. The life of every natural man is but one continued self-centered dream and delusion, out of which he never awakes, until heaven opens his eyes, or in hell he lifts up his eyes." If a natural man should be reading these words, he likely will protest them in disgust—but he will prove their truth forever if he continues to live and die without the Omni-capable Christ.

Many were blessed by the excellent movie entitled "Amazing Grace," the remarkable story of the spiritual Christian, William Wilberforce, who was instrumental in abolishing the wide-spread slave trade of Great Britain. If you saw the movie, you will recall that two of the main characters were Wilberforce and William Pitt the Younger. Though this account was not shown in the movie, Wilberforce once hopefully took his lost friend to church to hear the Gospel. When the service was over, Wilberforce eagerly asked, "What did you think?" But Pitt forlornly answered, "I couldn't make any sense of it at all." Pitt was simply being an honest natural man!

One modern commentator said that the natural man is like an AM-FM radio. It is as if God is transmitting spiritual truth on an FM frequency, but the FM part of the natural man's "receiver" is totally broken and incapacitated ("dead," the Bible says). Only his AM intake works, and thus he has no capacity to receive the Divine transmission of truth, which comes on a different frequency altogether.

The natural man considering "the things of the Spirit of God" is like a man trying to study the stars through a microscope instead of a telescope. He is improperly equipped; he may focus the microscope endlessly, but no star will come into focus. He needs a telescope! You see, the New Birth is an actual spiritual *birth*, and *it installs spiritual equipment into the born-again person.* That is, *an actual spiritual DNA attends an actual spiritual birth*! A natural man cannot understand spiritual truth any more than an animal can comprehend computers. The natural man must abandon his own vaunted intellect as a means of knowing God, and must cast himself as a helpless sinner into the arms of grace which God opens to him, and instantly the New Birth will occur and the new life (Life) will begin that will allow him to know these things. Jesus prayed, "I thank You, O Father, Lord of heaven and earth, because *You have hidden these things from the wise and prudent*, and *have revealed them unto babes*" (Matthew 11:25). Though this is very humbling to the person who has undue pride in his intellect, this humbling is the way to Life. "Whoever exalts himself will be abased, but whoever humbles himself will be exalted." *The natural man only has worldly wisdom, UNTIL God gives the miracles of regeneration (the new birth, or "birth from above", John 3:3, 7) and illumination.* The word "until" supplies the natural man his one and only hope. We will turn now to explore the alternative, the "spiritual" man.

B. The "Spiritual" Man (2:15-16) — Reception is Inevitable

The second man described in the text is called *"the spiritual man"* (I Corinthians 2:15). With this man, *the reception of spiritual truth is inevitable.* When exposed to God's Truth, He will receive it and understand it. As long as he "walks in the Spirit" (Galatians 5:16), the reception of God's Truth is automatic in his mind and heart. He has a predisposition (the new birth and a spiritual walk with God) that guarantees this reception of spiritual truth. "He that is spiritual," the text says. The word "spiritual" occurs some thirty times in the New Testament, and almost always with the same meaning. Here it refers to the believer of highest standard in God's Purpose. The spiritual man is the Divine ideal, the man God has in mind when he saves any sinner. This should be the normal designation of every believer; each one should be accurately described as "spiritual".

The text is quite explicit in describing this man. "But he that is spiritual judges all things, yet he himself is rightly judged by no one. For 'who has known the mind of the LORD that he may instruct Him?' But we have the mind of Christ." Again, the first word of this description is the word, "but." The Holy Spirit has been describing "the natural man" (verse 14), and he now introduces his opposite (verses 15, 16). Note that this "spiritual man" discerns "all things," yet he himself will never be accurately or adequately understood by natural or carnal people. He discerns "all things" because he walks in the Spirit and the Holy Spirit thus can teach Him "the deep things of God." When Paul asked, "Who has known the mind of God that he may instruct Him?", he means that no mere human being is smart enough to teach God anything. Then, he adds a startling truth: "But *we* have the *mind of Christ*." Note again the beginning word "but." None of us is smart enough to teach God anything—*but* the spiritual man still has the mind of Christ. In the Greek text, the two italicized terms in that sentence ("we" and "mind of Christ") bear *major emphasis,* which is the equivalent of a *loud shout* from the page. The word "we" thus means "we and we alone", and refers to spiritual men. Only spiritual men have and can employ within themselves the mind of Christ. The term "mind of Christ" also bears major emphasis in the text, which shows the incredible character and capacities of the spiritual man. "We who are spiritual have the *very mind of Christ!*" Every normal man has a mind—but *does he think? Does he think in a way that uses the potential of his mind?* Most people would be forced to say "No" to these questions, and sadly, the same questions may be addressed to a Christian with regard to the mind of Christ which is in him, but still may be only poorly used. Christian, be very careful with these truths; the full use of your resources in Christ may be dependent upon *your thinking at this point. Will it reflect the Mind of Christ, or only revert back to your own carnal thinking?* More about this later.

Let me explore this concept in a practical way for just a moment. What happens to a sinner when he is saved? What happens when he is "born again"? Basically and simply, Jesus

The Four Kinds of People God Sees on Earth

Christ literally comes into his spirit by the mediating Person and Presence of the Holy Spirit. I repeat: through the Presence of the Holy Spirit, Jesus Christ literally comes into the sinner's previously dead spirit and enlivens it with the very Life of God. At one crisis moment of time, the Jesus Who said, "I am ... the Life" comes into the once-dead spirit of the repenting, trusting sinner. This is an absolute, top-drawer, "heavyweight championship", miracle of God! This does not occur by the mere making of a moral or religious decision. It occurs when a miraculous faith-reception is generated by the Holy Spirit in the sinner's needy heart. At that moment, the sinner "receives Christ" (John 1:12), is forgiven of his sins (Ephesians 1:7), and receives the Gift of Eternal Life (John 3:16). Christ also comes alive (!) in his consciousness; in short, he is born of God, or "born from above".

I repeat: this is a miracle performed in a person by the Holy Spirit of God. When the Holy Spirit comes in, mediating the Presence of Jesus Christ to the sinner's dead heart, the sinner is instantly saved. When we are saved, we receive the Holy Spirit, or conversely, when we receive the Holy Spirit, we are saved (see Romans 8:9). When we receive the Holy Spirit, suddenly Jesus takes on a new attractiveness to us. We see Him in an altogether new light; His Personal glories which were previously hidden to our carnal eyes instantly come bursting forth to our new spiritual sight--all because of the Holy Spirit Who is *seeing Jesus through us*. Thus, we see Jesus as the Holy Spirit sees Him, and this is only the beginning of the miraculous new illumination the Spirit gives.

Think very carefully at this point. Is Jesus a happy Person? Indeed, yes! Then, remember that He is now within you if you are saved, willing to share His Joy as the dominant disposition of your inner life. Is Jesus an intelligent Person? Really a quite stupid question! Well, at the moment of a sinner's new birth, this intelligent Person comes into him with His total mentality, presenting to that Christian the option of reproducing His thoughts in him. Thus, it is true that "we (that are spiritual) have the (very) Mind of Christ"!!! When we say that "we have the mind of Christ," this is not the same as having "the mind of Plato or Tennyson," which would be gained by reading their works and studying their lives. But we mean that Christ is actually in us, developing His own mind through our thoughts, that His mentality is in union with ours and can come to dominate ours. No wonder God wants all of His children to be "spiritual" and not "carnal" (we will talk about the "carnal" person later).

Remember the earlier analogy of the AM-FM radio, and let's go further with it. You see, the spiritual man is also like an AM-FM radio. At conversion he doesn't get rid of his old, worldly, self-centered AM frequency. No, he simply receives a new FM system. The Christian now will face a choice at each step. Will he choose to relocate himself on the old, carnal AM dial, or will he turn on the FM dial? The spiritual man is the man who daily turns on the FM dial, and thus he cultivates a taste for Heaven's best, "the milk and honey of God's Promised Land," and he replaces his earlier taste for "the leeks and garlic of Egypt."

In summary, the spiritual man's inner life has had a vast renovation. "If any man be in Christ, he is a new creation; old things have passed away, behold, all things have become new" (II Corinthians 5:17). Only a spiritual man knows the incredible dimensions of that statement. The spiritual man has been "born from above," to use the exact expression of Jesus in John 3:3 and 3:7. The spiritual man is Spirit-led (Romans 8:14). The spiritual man is spiritual-minded (Romans 8:5, 6). The spiritual man is Spirit-filled (Ephesians 5:18), which means that vast horizons "in Christ" are now open to him. Notice that in each of these texts, the spiritual man has made a God-designed, God-desired adjustment to the Holy Spirit. The spiritual man is a Christian in whom an unhindered, ungrieved Holy Spirit manifests Christ. The spiritual man has been instantly endowed (through his new birth) with a totally new perspective and totally new capacities. He instantly has new motives, new desires, new aspirations—an entirely new mentality, *the very "mind of Christ."*

Again, I must write a word of caution because of a tendency in the thinking of natural men today. The term "spiritual" is often used with a lower-case "s" today, but this must be sharply distinguished from "Spiritual" with a capital "S". With a capital letter, Spiritual refers to the Presence and activities of the Spirit of God within us, but with the lower case, spiritual may refer to anything that addresses or proceeds from man's inner life.   Author Denis Duncan wrote that "there are many approaches to wholeness today that make "spirit" with a lower-case 's' very important but do not give validity to 'Spirit' with a capital 'S'. These approaches do not recognize the essential factor, the crucial component of the activity of the Spirit of God in man. Such people may make statements that are 'true' in themselves, but not Divine Truth. For example, they may say that to be in a loving or caring relationship is to be involved in a 'spiritual' undertaking. That may be true in a very limited way, but it falls far short of the Christian 'Spiritual' (Spirit-generated) experience. In my view, the full integration of the human personality is impossible without the 'activity and control of the Holy Spirit' within that personality." Let me add a word of clarification which applies to this paragraph alone. It is not my intention to use the upper or lower case letters elsewhere in this study to distinguish between the two views. I only use them in this paragraph to distinguish between a *merely human* use of the word "spiritual" and the *Divine* use of the same word, which has *an entirely different meaning.*

C. The "Carnal" Man (3:1-3) — Reception is Inadequate

There is a third general category of people mentioned in the text. These people are called "carnal," and their *reception of God'sTruth is possible, but inadequate.* They may make an excited response to God's Truth when they hear it in a public gathering, but they have no consuming appetite for it which would cause them to cultivate the habit of "self-feeding" on that Truth. Their response to God's Truth is both the cause and the effect of their carnality. Their inadequate response causes their carnality, on the one hand, and is the result and symptom of their carnality on the other hand.

(1) "Good" Carnal

This truth must be carefully noted and studied from the text (I Corinthians 3:1-3): There is a clear distinction between *two kinds of "carnal"* in these verses. We might call them "Carnal # 1" and "Carnal #2", or (can you believe it?), ""*Good* carnal" (!!!) and "Bad carnal." Most of the teaching we have received leads us to think only of "bad" carnal, but a close examination of the text will allow us to see that this evaluation is a misinterpretation. As is often the case, tradition lodges an idea in the minds of church members and casual Bible students, and it is never challenged. This is a mistake! Every believer should be a "Berean believer," described in Acts 17:11 in these words: "These were more noble than those in Thessalonica, in that they received the word with all readiness of mind, and searched the Scriptures daily, whether those things were so." Every church should have an ever-enlarging "bunch of Bereans" in its fellowship!

Now, let's examine the two "carnals" in the order of their identification in the text. In I Corinthians 3:1-2, Paul wrote, "And I, brethren, could not speak unto you as unto spiritual, but as unto carnal, even as unto babes in Christ. I have fed you with milk, and not with meat: for hitherto you were not able to bear it." The chronology of this statement must be established carefully and clearly. Paul is speaking of the time *when he first came to Corinth, won people to Christ, and established a vital fellowship of believers there.* Note that he is writing only to Christians—he refers to them as "brothers" and "babes in Christ." We must make a vital distinction here. When a person is saved, or born-again, he is Spirit-filled immediately—but only to the degree of his baby capacity. Because his spirit is that of a new-born, and thus that of a baby, it has only a very small capacity for receiving the Holy Spirit. This new-born is necessarily a babe in Christ and not a spiritual person, since a spiritual individual, as defined in I Corinthians 2:15-16, is necessarily mature. This leads us to establish a very important principle: a Christian can be Spirit-filled and not be spiritual. This is always true of new-born Christians. Christ is in them. The Holy Spirit indwells them. However, their undeveloped spirit has only a small capacity for the Person of the Holy Spirit, and thus they are less than the full definition of "spiritual" used in our text.

The Four Kinds of People God Sees on Earth

The word for "carnal" in I Corinthians 3:1 is not the same as the word for "carnal" in I Corinthians 3:3, 4, but the variation is very slight (though very significant). In verse one, the word for "carnal" is *sarkinos*. The root form is *"sarx,"* which means "flesh." The *inos* ending implies nature and constitution. So, *sarkinos* means that the person described is still constitutionally more flesh than spirit though he is truly saved, truly born-again. What does this mean? The word "flesh" describes what a human being is by his first birth. "That which is born of the flesh is flesh" (John 3:6). Technically, the "flesh" is the combination of a person's body and soul, acting independently of the spirit (or the Holy Spirit in the human spirit), because the spirit of the individual is still dead in sin. So the "flesh" is all that a lost person has and is, and his soul must provide all of his inner resource for living (and bear all the *pressure* of living).

Note that Paul said about these new-born babes, "I could not speak unto you as unto spiritual, but as unto *sarkinois* (the plural form), even as unto babes in Christ." The "could not" suggests that Paul had attempted to carry these new converts further in the faith, but their small baby capacities would not permit it. "For not yet (while I was first with you) were you equal to it." We must be clear that these new converts were not to be blamed for their baby capacities—after all, they had *just been born*! *This is "good" carnal.* There is hardly anything more beautiful than to see a person when he has just been saved, truly born-again, but necessarily only a baby. He is so alive, but he only shows the life of a baby. He only shows the mind of a baby, the actions of a baby, the appetite of a baby, but *is alive in Christ.* When a person has just been saved, it is never blameworthy for him to be a baby—that is all that he *can* be. But we must remember that Paul's goal, God's goal, the Christian goal, is for all Christian babies to become full-grown, productive adults in Christ (Colossians 1:28). We must remember for now that the word "babies" in describing Christians has both a good and a bad sense. There is a "good" carnal (*sarkinos*, verse 1*)* and a bad carnal (*sarkikos*, verse 3). In its good sense, it implies *humility, teachableness* and *developing maturity.* Examples: I

Corinthians 14:20, "In malice be babes"; I Peter 2:2, "As *newborn babes*, desire the pure milk of the Word, that you may grow thereby"; and Matthew 11:25, where Jesus prayed, "I thank Thee, O Father, Lord of heaven and earth, because Thou hast hid these things from the wise and prudent, and hast revealed them unto babes." *These* babies are *child-like*, but now we must deal with "carnal # 2," the "bad" carnal baby. These babies are *childish*, even though they have had plenty of time and opportunity to grow to spiritual maturity and great usefulness.

(2) "Bad" Carnal

We will now examine the *other* carnal mentioned in these verses. This is the "bad" carnal, and that will become evident as we investigate the text. Paul had referred to the Corinthians as newborn "babes in Christ," a reference to the time when he first came to the city, led some people to Christ, and established the new fellowship of believers there.

In verse one, Paul had used the softer of the two words for "carnal" (sarkinos), and had simply described new Christians, or "babes in Christ." He uses the other word, the word for "bad" carnal, the much severer word (sarkikos), twice in verse 3. "You are yet carnal: for whereas there is among you envying, and strife, and divisions, are ye not carnal?" Remember that the Greek ending, inos (used in the "carnal" of 3:1), means to be constitutionally defined and described by the term that begins the word, as sarkinos in 3:1. The Greek word sarx means "flesh." In the New Testament, the word "flesh" does not usually refer merely to the meat that covers a skeleton of bones. Rather, it refers to the selfish tendency and disposition of each sinful human being. Someone said, "The flesh is not what you see when you look in the mirror, but it is likely the reason you look." So the new-born Christian is still more "fleshly" than "spiritual", though he has been born of the Spirit—because he has just been born and his spirit has not had time or opportunity to develop, so he is still largely controlled by his own resources. In that case, he is called "sarkinos."

In the Greek word *sarkikos* (the word that is used twice in 3:3 and translated "carnal"), the ending of the word, *ikos*, means that

The Four Kinds of People God Sees on Earth

the person is *adapted to* the "flesh." The word is *sarkikos* in 3:3, defining a believer who has been born again, but has persisted in adapting his life back to his self-will and to his own resources—though *he has the Holy Spirit and all of the potential of His indwelling Presence within him.* Paul is writing this letter *years after he had established the church in Corinth,* and through those intervening years the carnal people he is now addressing had become stubbornly set in self-will of mind and selfishness of lifestyle. Because of their independent and self-dominated decisions and choices, they were still dominated by the flesh and revealed only the characteristics of personality that had resulted from willful selfishness. During the passing years, the beautiful spiritual babies of verse one had become the badly spoiled brats of verse three. Were they Christians? To help us see the answer, let me ask the question in another form: Is a spoiled brat still a member of his parents' family? The answer to both questions is "yes". Yes, a carnal believer is a Christian, but he has become a *sub-standard* Christian, unlike what Jesus had in mind when He saved him. Christian, beware, because this is an ever-present danger for every born-again person. Why not at this moment conduct an inventory of your own spiritual life? Are you as a Christian more adapted to your own decisions, your own choices, your own inner resources, your own hopes, your own plans, etc., or are you "walking in the Spirit" (Galatians 5:16), deferring all decisions, choices, hopes and plans to His will, and drawing the resources for living on a daily basis from the indwelling Holy Spirit?

In a study of "The Holy Spirit and the Truth of God," we have examined the four types of men God sees, and have shown their responses to that Truth. It is *impossible* for the *natural man* to receive the Truth of God, because that Truth is spiritually discerned, and he is stone dead in his spirit, dead toward God. It is *inevitable* that the *spiritual man will* receive the Truth of God (as long as he is "walking in the Spirit"), because the Spirit who controls him has His own affinity for the Truth of God. Both *carnal men,* the "good" carnal and the "bad" carnal, may spasmodically receive the Truth of God, especially in moments of excitement in public preaching or teaching services, but their reception of that truth will always be inadequate because they are usually "walking in the flesh." The *natural* man has *no diet at all* of spiritual food. The *spiritual* man *daily feeds and feasts* on spiritual food. The *carnal* men only have *an occasional snack* of spiritual food.

In concluding this study, I will give a brief verbal summary of the three. Then I will give a popular illustration of the three types of men.

The summary of the three kinds of men.

I will begin by pointing out the essential need of each of these kinds of men. The **"Natural Man"** needs a new **ENDOWMENT**, a miracle endowment of Spiritual Life through a New Birth.

The **"Spiritual Man"** needs only **CONTINUING DEVELOPMENT**, the development of the Spiritual Life he *received* through the New Birth. That development will take him through spiritual growth that corresponds to early childhood, adolescence, young adulthood, and maturity (compare I John 2:12-14).

The **"Carnal Man"** needs **A RADICAL ADJUSTMENT**. If he is "sarkinos," a new-born baby, he needs *the Continual Adjustment of Regular Growth*. If he is "sarkikos," stubbornly adapted to his flesh and living selfishly, he needs *a Crisis Re-adjustment in which he brokenly confesses his sin and selfishness, repents of them, and re-establishes the practical Lordship of Jesus Christ over his life.*

In summary: The "Natural Man" (Psuchikos, "man of soul") is *constitutionally soulish*. Because he has no other interior resource except his own soul, he must adapt himself to his soul as his source of feeling, thinking and choosing. Since *his spirit is dead*, his soul is his only inner resource; so he lives in constant adaptation to his own soul (his own mind, his own emotions and his own will). The "Spiritual Man" (Pneumatikos, "man of Spirit") is *constitutionally spiritual* (through a spiritual birth and regular spiritual growth), and is consistently adapting himself to the indwelling Holy Spirit, who in turn implements the Lordship of Christ in his life. I will anticipate the sub-division of the third category, the "Carnal Man," by stating that the "Carnal Man" is of two types (Sarkinos, a

The Four Kinds of People God Sees on Earth

new-born baby, and Sarkikos, a nominal Christian who continues in babyhood, adapted to his flesh and selfishness). The Sarkinos baby is a *true spiritual baby, constitutionally weak* and *childishly irresponsible.* The Sarkikos baby is a *tragic "spoiled brat," willfully selfish, willfully disobedient, willfully stubborn,* and *willfully weak—but still a member of God's Forever Family.* Much attention needs to be given to the carnal baby, both in our understanding of him (perhaps of ourselves), and in helping him to move from this category to a category of victory in his life. *He* may be casual about his carnality, but *God* regards it as a crisis in heaven. You see, this persistent baby in God's family is *God's biggest problem on earth.* Thus, as long as he stubbornly insists on remaining carnal, he is subject to increasingly severe chastisement and discipline from God.

These three lives may be pictured as a mirror facing in different directions. The "Natural Man" is like a mirror pointed only to the *earth.* He is "of the earth, and earthy" (I Cor. 15:47). The "Spiritual Man" is like a mirror pointed only to *heaven.* He is "of heaven, and heavenly" (I Cor. 15:48). The "Carnal Man" is pointed to the *horizon,* and his reflection is divided. He reflects both *heaven and earth.* He is "double-minded" (James 1:8; literally, *dipsukos,* or *"two-souled"),* and the Bible says that He is "unstable in all his ways."

Finally, let me share the popular illustration of these three categories of men, which I merely repeat from a book by author Dan Baughman, entitled, <u>The Abundant Life</u>. In a chapter entitled, "Starting to Walk," Baughman presents the three kinds of men in a very-easy-to-understand illustration. I have simply added interpretations of the characters. Here is the illustration:

Once there was a wealthy man (he represents God) in whose family there were two sons ("carnal" and "spiritual"). The father loved his sons and wanted the very best for them. So he hired a special teacher (the Holy Spirit) to train and teach and take care of the children. The father had particular jobs for which he wanted his sons trained.

Next door lived a neighbor boy (the "natural man") who often played with the sons, but the teacher never tried to instruct him because he had not been hired to do that. The neighbor boy did not want to learn anyway and considered the things being taught as a lot of foolishness. The less time the sons spent playing with the neighbor boy the more they seemed to learn.

In this family there was a difference in the attitude of the two sons. The one son, named *carnal*, never did like the teacher. He wanted to do things his own way, and was not interested in the lessons which the teacher had been asked to teach. He was always fighting and getting into trouble. He envied the other boys. He was always joining "gangs" and seemed to enjoy the neighbor boy's company more than his own family.

About all the teacher could do was the try to keep him out of trouble. The only time he seemed to listen was when he was in a "jam" of some kind and he needed help. *Carnal* never thought of anyone but *himself*. So, as soon as he was out of trouble, off he would go to find something to amuse himself.

The other son's name was *Spiritual*. He loved his father very much and wanted to please him. He realized that his father had an important position for him and remembered all the wonderful things that had been done for him in the past. He believed that his father had his best interests at heart, so he decided he would do whatever the new teacher wanted him to do. He wanted to cooperate in every way to learn the lessons and skills that his father wanted him to know. He knew that in this way he would be able to help his father sooner and assume the responsibilities and position awaiting him.

Spiritual was not a perfect child. He sometimes had to be reproved and corrected, but he had the right attitude and wanted to do what was right.

The Christian's life may be illustrated by a father who sends his son for a walk. No human father would send out his little son by himself, and neither has our heavenly Father. Jesus said just before he returned to Heaven: "I will pray the Father, and He shall give you another Comforter, that He may abide with you forever" (John 14:16).

The words "another Comforter" in the original language are full of meaning. "Another" could be translated "another just like me, of the same sort, with the same characteristics" (as Jesus). Comforter, from the Greek word *paraclete*, means "one called alongside to help." So the Holy Spirit may be called upon by the Christian at any time to give His Personal assistance in any situation.

Suppose the father asks his son, named *Spiritual*, to go to the store and buy a $5 can of paint. He gives him a $20 bill and says that 50 cents will be his to keep but to bring back the change.

He tells his son he can spend the 50 cents for anything he likes except something to eat, because it is almost dinner time. He also instructs the teacher to go along.

The storekeeper (who represents Satan) is not honest; he is only interested in getting people's money. He tries to make people think he is kind to them so he can trick them into spending more money.

There happens to be a "special" on paint <my note: isn't there *always* some kind of "bargain" dangled by Satan in front of us?> and the storekeeper wants to sell the boy three cans for $11. He tries to convince him that his father will be very proud of him for taking advantage of the bargain. *Spiritual* only buys one can, however, because his teacher reminds him that his father had said, "Buy one can of paint."

The storekeeper, eager to get more of the boy's money, suggests that he might like to visit the candy counter. *Spiritual* is getting very hungry, and he does have a quarter that belongs to him. But the teacher says, "Remember your father said not to get anything to eat." So the boy turns to the toy counter, eager to spend his 50 cents.

There are many toys he would like to buy. After a few helpful words from the teacher he selects a nice toy and is ready to return home.

The storekeeper is not going to give up so easily. He calls his own son to one side and tells him to help persuade *Spiritual* to spend more money.

The storekeeper's son comes and says, "Say, have you seen the new footballs Dad has? Why don't you get one? Your father is rich and he wouldn't care." *Spiritual* had been wanting a football all summer. The storekeeper, seeing he is interested, becomes almost insistent. This scares *Spiritual* and he is glad his father sent the teacher along. He steps a little closer to him, then tells the storekeeper, "No, my father said I should bring the change back to him!" The storekeeper quickly mutters an apology and does not try to sell him anything else, for he is afraid to make *Spiritual's* father angry.

As the boy passes the candy counter on the way out, he stops just to look. His stomach seems very empty and he knows if he stays any longer he will have to buy some. He turns to ask the teacher what to do, but he is at the door already, holding it open for him. *Spiritual* grabs his paint and runs out the door. On the way home he passes an apple tree loaded with beautiful red apples. He would like to steal one but a word from his teacher reminds him that it is wrong to do this.

Upon arriving at home, the boy delivers the paint and money to his father. Upon learning of his experiences, and the way he has resisted temptation and accomplished his assigned mission, his father is very proud of him and gives him a special reward.

Dear friend, which of these kinds of men are you? Which will you wish you had been on earth after you have logged your first thousand years in pure eternity? These are very serious questions, and they hold out to each person the happy possibility of being involved in the Greatest Venture, the Greatest Relationship, the Greatest Romance, the Greatest Life of Contribution, the world has ever seen.

!!
!!!!!!
!!!!!!!!!!
!!!!!!!!!!!!!!!!!

Chapter Six

THE INFINITE IMPORTANCE OF ILLUMINATION

Ephesians 1:15-23:

"Wherefore I also, after I heard of your faith in the Lord Jesus, and love unto all the saints, Cease not to give thanks for you, making mention of you in my prayers; That the God of our Lord Jesus Christ, the Father of glory, may give unto you the spirit of wisdom and revelation in the knowledge of him: The eyes of your understanding being enlightened; that ye may know what is the hope of his calling, and what the riches of the glory of his inheritance in the saints, And what is the exceeding greatness of his power to us-ward who believe, according to the working of his mighty power, Which he wrought in Christ, when he raised him from the dead, and set him at his own right hand in the heavenly places, Far above all principality, and power, and might, and dominion, and every name that is named, not only in this world, but also in that which is to come: And hath put all things under his feet, and gave him to be the head over all things to the church, Which is his body, the fulness of him that filleth all in all."

Studies in the Person and Work of the Holy Spirit

The publishers of my Bible have added editorial paragraph summaries to the text of Scripture, attempting to help the reader discern the theme of the coming paragraph in each instance. Just before the text recorded above, they added the explanatory words, "A Prayer for Knowledge and Understanding." This assessment is reasonably accurate. I believe these words to contain the most important single prayer that any human being can pray for any other human being at any time. I simply do not believe that it is possible to pray a more important prayer for yourself or for any other human being.

Notice the mood that Paul was in when he prayed this prayer. The word "wherefore" (verse 15) indicates that he was in a very *thoughtful* mood. The word "wherefore" is a connecting word. When we read such a word in a text of Scripture, we should ask, "What is the *wherefore there for?*" In this case, the answer is absolutely overwhelming. When we inquire about the preceding thoughts and words, we discover that the Apostle Paul has just written *the greatest single sentence ever written*. It is an incredibly long sentence. So long, in fact, that it probably would not pass any grammatical structure test in any classroom on earth. But remember, Paul is not interested in grammar; he is only interested in grace! As far as I know and have been able to research, this is the longest sentence ever recorded in literature. The sentence is *twelve verses long* in the Biblical text, and some of the verses are lengthy by themselves! Paul has just written a celebration, a kind of hymn, of the Christian understanding of the grace of God. He has just verbally celebrated grace as the source, the reason, the cause, the producer, of our salvation.

The written celebration (verses 3-14) is divided obviously into three parts. The first part is made up of verses three through six, and ends with the refrain, "To the praise of the glory of His grace." The second "stanza" is made of verses seven through twelve, and ends with the chorus, "That we should be to the praise of His glory." And the third stanza is comprised of verses thirteen and fourteen, and ends with the refrain, "Unto the praise of His

The Importance of Illumination

glory." So the hymn has three stanzas, and they all end with essentially the same chorus.

The respective themes of the three stanzas are a delight to explore. The subject of the first stanza is the work of *God the Father* in accomplishing our redemption. And the "smaller" subjects in this stanza are fathomless. Paul writes of such things as "the heavenly places," "election," holiness, justification, the love of God, "predestination," "adoption," and the will and pleasure of God. No wonder his mind is soaring when he comes to our text. But he goes higher yet before he records the prayer of our text.

The subject of the second stanza is the work of *Jesus the Son of God* in securing our salvation. Such terms as "redemption," "his blood," "the forgiveness of sins," "the riches of His grace," His abounding wisdom and prudence, and the inheritance we have in Christ, comprise the themes of this second stanza. Paul's soul seems to soar right out of prose into spiritual poetry! He ascends the ladder of the stars as his spirit explodes in celebration, yet he is solid and deliberate in his verbal expression of these great treasures.

Stanza three presents the work of *the Holy Spirit of God* in securing our redemption. After Paul has given the order of the "saving steps," he writes about the Holy Spirit as a "seal" and an "earnest" in applying and protecting our salvation. He says, "you heard the word of truth, the Gospel of your salvation," and "you believed and trusted in Him," and then you were "sealed with the Holy Spirit of promise," and given "the earnest of our inheritance until the redemption of the purchased possession." And remember, the truths of these three packed stanzas form one single sentence. I say again: It is the greatest single sentence ever written! Paul ponders these great things, and then writes them down. No wonder he is in a thoughtful mood, and no wonder it leads him to pray this prayer for spiritual understanding. It is possible even to hear and read about such truths as this — and be absolutely sterile of understanding. But Paul is mystical and meditative in heart and thoughtful in mind as he ponders and presents these great truths.

Then, Paul is in a *thrilled* mood, also. He says to the Ephesian Christians, "I heard of your faith in the Lord Jesus, and love unto all the saints." What a testimony! What a tribute to the Ephesian Christians! There is no pastor on earth who would not be absolutely ecstatic with joy and celebration if he could see these two things growing and abounding among his people—"faith in the Lord Jesus, and love unto all the saints." Note several things. Note the word, "Lord," in referring to Jesus. The Ephesian Christians did not fragment Jesus into parts which could be dealt with separately. They had received a whole Christ to match their whole need. They did not think of dealing with Jesus as Savior at one time, and as Lord at another. They had "faith in the Lord Jesus." And note the order of the two features of Christian experience which are mentioned. "Faith in the Lord Jesus" preceded "love unto all the saints." These two features have a cause and effect relationship in the Christian life. They are mutually inclusive and mutually exclusive in the Christian life. If one is present, they both will be. If one is absent, they both will be. Only the person who is *rightly related to the Lord by faith* will be *rightly related to others in love.* Faith in the Lord Jesus always leads to love unto all the saints. The presence of one indicates the presence of the other. Faith is the vertical relationship of the Christian life, and love is the horizontal relationship of it. So Paul is thrilled as he celebrates with the Ephesians the abundance of these things in their lives.

And Paul is in a *thankful* mood, also. He writes, "I cease not to give thanks for you, making mention of you in my prayers." The Greek word translated, "I give thanks" ("eucharisteo") is used twenty-three times by Paul, and only 14 times in the rest of the New Testament. *What a statistic!* Here is one of the gigantic secrets of Paul's incredible Christian life and influence. While everybody else thought, planned, prayed, and lived the Christian life *for themselves,* Paul's constant thought and conduct was *"for you."* While they lived "outside-in," Paul lived *"inside-out,"* always toward *someone else.* He was constantly praying and thanking God *for others.*

What an introduction to the greatest of all possible prayers! Paul was in a *thoughtful, thrilled, and thankful* mood.

The Importance of Illumination

I. THE SEQUENCE OF THE REQUEST, VERSES 3-14

First, we will look at the sequence, or spiritual progression, which is climaxed by this great prayer. Note again the "wherefore" of verse 15. What is the "wherefore" there for? Paul has been straining at the leash of language, piling words on top of words, and all superlatives, to tell us that all that God is—Father, Son, and Holy Spirit—is totally implicated in our total salvation. So the great truth of the Trinity is on high profile in verses three through fourteen. The doctrine of the Trinity is a high and holy mystery, just like God is. But it is a vital and indispensable mystery. The idea of the trinity is far more relevant than we can imagine.

A book like <u>Great Expectations</u>, for example, may be regarded as a *trinity*. First, there was the essential idea in the mind of Charles Dickens. Nobody else knew the ideas at the beginning, apart from perhaps friends with whom he might share some of his ideas. <u>Great Expectations</u> thus existed as *concept*. But then, the book was published, and you could hold a copy in your hand and say, "This is <u>Great Expectations</u>." Now you have a manifestation or a *concrete expression* of the concept that continues to exist in the author's mind. Thus, you now have *two* <u>Great Expectations</u>, each of them distinct from the other, but both of them may be described as being <u>Great Expectations</u>. Finally, people read the book, the concepts of it are *communicated personally*, people grasp the concept, and may seek to put it into practice. Now, you have a *third* <u>Great Expectations</u>, this time in person and in practice. The concept still exists, the book still exists, but now the concept manifested in the book finds *realization*.

I bear personal testimony at this point. When I read Dickens' great novel, I saw that all fleshly and selfish expectations must be refined into gentleness and unselfishness, and that this likely takes place only through a process of suffering. So the author's idea, published in a book, became a means of insight and change in my life. Notice that all three have to exist—the book in *conception*, the book in *publication*, and the book in *action*. Any two would be insufficient by themselves. You must have a trinity.

Studies in the Person and Work of the Holy Spirit

A trinity is found in everything. In everything, there is a hidden inner nature (the *inner essence*), an exterior form (the *outward expression*), and a result (the *ongoing effect*).

Suppose that I hold my fountain pen in my hand; suppose that you also hold your own fountain pen in your hand. Suppose that mine is a Parker and yours is a Schaeffer. They have the same inner essence in that they both are fountain pens. But they have a different outward expression in that each has the distinctive manufacturer's form and trademark. And they both have an ongoing effect—you can write or mark with them. In fact, I could use my pen to sign my name on a piece of paper, mail the paper to central Africa, and the pen might still be held in my hand in Memphis, Tennessee. Understanding the limits of any finite illustration in addressing infinite truth, the inner essence of God is God the Father; the outward expression of God is God the Son, and the ongoing effect of God is the work of God the Holy Spirit.

Salvation has been called "the house that Grace built." The *Architect* who provided the blueprint was God the Father; the *Contractor* who has purchased and supplied all the materials is God the Son; and the *Carpenter and Builder, the Constructor* who makes all applications to "materialize" the Finished Product, is the Holy Spirit.

Horace Bushnell was a teacher at Yale University before he became a famous preacher. Later he wrote, "When the preacher touches the mystery of the Divine Trinity and logic shatters it all to pieces, *I'm glad I have a heart as well as a head.* My heart wants the Father; my heart wants the Son; my heart wants the Holy Spirit—and one just as much as the other. The Bible has a Divine Trinity for me; my heart says that I need that Trinity—and I mean to hold by my heart." Give careful attention to the word "heart" in this statement. I have just completed the reading of a book by Peter Kreeft entitled, Heaven, the Heart's Deepest Longing. In his book, the author says, "Our desires go far deeper than our imagination or our thought; the heart is deeper than the mind." Blaise Pascal, the French philosophical and technological genius, said, "The heart has reasons that reason knows not of." We must learn to trust the

The Importance of Illumination

innate, natural, God-implanted instincts of the heart. When these are taught by Scripture, we find the deepest needs within us addressed and met through the truth and work of the Divine Trinity.

So the Apostle Paul has just celebrated the truth of the Trinity, and has shown us his mood as he ponders it and the Ephesian Christians. Now, he will record the prayer he prays for them in light of this great celebration. Remember the marginal title: "A Prayer for Knowledge and Understanding." Actually, it is a prayer for *spiritual illumination.* And what an incredible prayer it is.

II. THE SIGNIFICANCE OF ILLUMINATION, VERSE 18

Next, we will attempt to see the *significance* of spiritual illumination, which is the subject of this great prayer. The effectiveness of any truth in our lives depends on our apprehension or understanding of it. If a truth only "sits there neatly arranged on the shelf," it won't move us very far. Television has a "Discovery Channel," but the Bible is the greatest "discovery channel" in the world. But just as a TV set must be turned on, tuned in, and flooded with light for us to appreciate what the Discovery Channel reveals, so it is in our relationship with the Bible. It is not possible for the unaided human mind, regardless of its natural brilliance, to understand the mind of God in Scripture without the miracle of Divine illumination. Note this carefully; it is an absolute dogma. There is no understanding of the mind of God at any time without the miracle of illumination!

A family was entertaining another family of friends in their home for an evening of food and fellowship. After a good meal, they were all seated in the family den, visiting. The little four year old was playing quietly with toys in the floor. There was a lull in the conversation, and the four-year-old spoke into the silence, repeated something he had heard his older brother say as he was reciting his arithmetic assignment. "Two times two is four," the little boy said thoughtlessly. Suddenly, everyone gasped when they heard this erudite recitation from a four-year-old. The mother just knew that they had a child genius! She said proudly, "What did you say, dear? Say it again." The little boy, surprised at the attention he was receiving, said, "Two times two is four." And the two families expressed their amazement that a child so young could know so much. But suddenly, while they were discussing his brilliance, he interrupted and said, "Mommy,. *what's a two?"* You see, he had *information without illumination,* and this is precisely the problem with most of us.

Many of the sophisticated cameras of today have two shutters. One covers the lens, the other covers the film. To open one is to prepare the camera for use. To open the other is to snap the immediate picture. *The one corresponds to the new birth, the other to illumination.* The new birth is only the beginning. It gives the spiritual eyes, and prepares them for use. Thereafter, we need accurate understanding of every "immediate picture" that God brings before us. And this ongoing understanding comes to the individual exactly the same way the new birth comes — by a miracle of Almighty God produced in the heart of the person. John Calvin said, "Illumination is like a pair of spectacles. Without it, our visions may be blurred, but with it, we can see clearly."

The Psalmist said, "In Thy light shall we see light." Go into a great cathedral at night. You can't see the astounding beauty of the windows because of the absence of the light. Go again at noon. The light makes the windows show their splendor. You had the power of sight before, but no light. What the sun is to those windows, the Holy Spirit is to the student of the Word of God. To see, we must have *both sight and light.* If we have sight but no light, we cannot see. But if we have light but no sight, we still cannot see. Both sight and light are indispensable for us to see.

A policeman saw a man crawling around on his hands and knees under a street light, searching with his hands through the grass. The policeman approached, spoke to the man, and discovered that he was drunk. "What are you looking for?" the policeman asked. "I lost my wallet," the drunk man replied. The policeman joined the pitiful drunk and began searching with him. After a considerable time of fruitless search, the discouraged policeman asked, "Sir, are you sure you lost the wallet here?" "Why, of course not," mumbled the drunk. "I lost it back down the street." "What!" exclaimed the policeman, "Then why are you looking for it here?" "Because there ain't no light back there!" the drunk sighed. Whatever his folly, his reasoning was accurate. You need light as well as sight in order to see. At the new birth, God issues to his newborn child a "new set of eyes." Then, at each occurrence of illumination, he turns on the light so those eyes can see clearly. So this prayer of Paul is crucial if we are to understand the things of God.

*Only **God** can reveal **God**!* There are three indispensable factors in God's Divine disclosure of Himself: 1. Revelation (some call it "manifestation"), in which God discloses Himself; 2. Inspiration—the *recording* of revelation; and 3. Illumination. Revelation and Inspiration are objective; Illumination is subjective.

Unaided intelligence gives you your point of view; illumination gives you God's point of view.

III. THE SOURCE OF ILLUMINATION, VERSE 17a, b.

Next, Paul identifies the nature and *source* of illumination. Verse eighteen uses the word "heart." The King James Bible translates it "understanding," but the Greek word is "kardia," from which we get our word, "kardiac." This does not merely refer to man's intellectual understanding. It refers to "the eyes of the heart." Misguided by our everyday use of the word, we have forgotten that *in the Bible, "heart" means every area and function of the personality.* Paul uses a remarkable phrase in Ephesians 1:18: "the eyes of your *heart.*" So every believer has two pairs of eyes. One pair is in his head, and the other pair is in his heart. He received the eyes in his head at physical birth, and he received the eyes of his heart at spiritual birth. But just as the eyes of his head must be trained and developed after birth for proper use, the eyes of the heart must be trained and developed after the new birth. Our hearts have eyes by which we are to see (all things) from the depths of our personality. But this "seeing" requires spiritual illumination.

Paul reveals the *source* of this illumination of the heart in verse 17. He tells the Ephesians that he is praying for them, "That the God of our Lord Jesus Christ, the Father of glory, may give unto you the spirit of wisdom and revelation." "Wisdom" is the *understanding and appropriation* of Divine truth. "Revelation" is the disclosure, the "unveiling," of God and His truth. Note the order of these words in the text. Why this order? You might expect that revelation would be mentioned first, then wisdom, but such is not the case. In Genesis one, God created light before He created the material universe. Why? Because, no matter how many worlds He created, no matter how many eyes He made, there would have been no sight without light. The same is true in spiritual experience. He gives wisdom with which to understand (the *means* to see), then He begins to bring His revelation (the *thing* to see) before us.

IV. THE SUBJECT OF ILLUMINATION, VERSE 17c

The *subject* of this illumination is "the knowledge of Him." There are three kinds of knowledge: 1. "I—it" knowledge, which we may call *scientific* knowledge; 2. "I—you" knowledge, which we may call *social* knowledge; and 3. "I—Thou" knowledge, which we may call *spiritual* knowledge. The *basic, ultimate, eternal* knowledge is **relational knowledge**, one's knowledge of God, himself, and others. This is reflected in the "great commandment," the duty to "love God with all your heart, mind, soul, and strength," and the second great commandment, which is to "love your neighbor as yourself."

The greatest knowledge of all is the knowledge of God through His Son, Jesus Christ. In fact, Jesus said, "This is life eternal, that they may know Thee, the only true God, and Jesus Christ, Whom Thou hast sent" (John 17:3). To know God **personally** is **salvation**; to know God **progressively** is **sanctification**; and to know God **perfectly** is **glorification**.

"Ready information is everywhere;
Relational insight is all too rare."

V. THE SUBSTANCE OF ILLUMINATION, VERSES 18b-23

Now we come to the most incredible part of the prayer. Now we will see why this matter of illumination is so vital and urgent. Now we will see the *substance* of Divine illumination. Verse 18 says that the purpose of this illumination, or "heart-seeing," is "that you may know." The word "know" is "oida," which is distinctively *not* the word for intellectual or academic knowing, the knowing you do by the use of your mind, your brain, your reason, your intelligence. The word "oida" means "*to know by seeing.*" This is the intuitive spiritual seeing of the heart, and requires that the eyes of the heart be opened and flooded with Divine light, a miracle of the Holy Spirit. When this occurs, *a **blind** person can accurately say, "**Oh, I see!**"* Helen Keller was likely referring to this when she said, "I would rather be blind the way I am blind, and see the way I see, than to see the way many people do, and be blind the way they are blind." Think over these words carefully. A reporter asked Miss Keller, "Is there anything worse than to be without organic sight?" She quickly replied, "Oh, yes, there is one thing much worse, and that is to have *sight without vision.*" But remember, true vision is an absolute miracle of God!

And what does the illumined person "know by seeing"? Verses 18 and 19 have been called "the prayer of the three 'whats.'" When the eyes of my heart are opened by a miracle of God, I discover that: 1. I don't have to *protect* myself—because God has provided *perfect security* for me; 2. I don't have to *prove* myself—because God has provided *perfect significance* for me; and 3. I don't have to *provide* for myself—because God has supplied *perfect sufficiency* for me. These insights are conveyed through the three "what" clauses of verses 18 and 19. We will now attempt to examine and explain the content of these three "what" clauses. These three "whats," these three objects of the prayer for illumination are the greatest and most vital areas of human life, and the answer to this prayer solves the three greatest problems in a believer's life.

Studies in the Person and Work of the Holy Spirit

A man is lost in a forest. He is in darkness and danger. A storm shatters the silence, and the lightning illumines the darkness. *The fool will look at the lightning; the wise man will look at the road that lies illuminated before him.* The quest for illumination has its own peculiar and massive dangers—the dangers of egocentricity and superiority—the dangers of diabolical pride. Psalm 119:130 says, "The entrance of Thy words giveth light; it giveth understanding to the simple." So we must ask God for this "simplicity" of heart and spirit, and for the proper "entrance of His words" into our minds and hearts, and *for the light that will enable us to see and appreciate* these three incredible "whats."

The telescope was "accidentally" discovered by a Dutch spectacle maker. Spectacle making involves handling lenses which need to be checked and this involves looking through them. It was during such an examination that the spectacle maker found himself looking through not one, but two lenses. To his surprise the magnification of the lens combination was much greater than that of a single lens. In placing the two lenses at opposite ends of a tube, the telescope was invented. Again, the "accident" "happened" to a careful and diligent researcher (!!). In spiritual matters, the "serendipities," or "happy surprises" ("accidents"?!), happen to the diligent researchers, also. The two indispensable ingredients are *heart-hunger* and **humility**. John Baillie wisely said, "I am sure that the bit of the road that most requires to be illuminated is *the point where it forks.*" Much damage is done in the community of believers because we rush ahead roughly and crudely, without illumination, at the forks of the road—the forks of dispositional differences, doctrinal differences, etc. So we must approach this great territory boldly, but *humbly*. First, Paul prays that God may open the eyes of the heart and flood them with light, so that the Christian may know by seeing *"what is the hope of his calling."* At first glance, these words sound so very innocent. They evoke a yawn and a "Ho, hum." But once you examine them thoroughly and carefully, you see why the reader needs illumination. This is a vast treasure, but it appears at first glance to be of little worth. There are two words which require attention and definition and interpretation. One is the word

The Importance of Illumination

"hope," the other is the word "calling." In both cases, *these words do not mean in the New Testament what we mean when we use them in everyday conversation today.* For example, consider the word, "calling." Today, a "calling" is an inviting, or a vocation. But in the New Testament, the word "calling" is the all-inclusive word for Divine salvation. So we see immediately that this first "what" is infinitely bigger than it first appeared to be. Then consider the word, "hope." Again, the word is vastly bigger and more meaningful than even our big word "hope." To us, hope is wish-projection, or wishful thinking. It is the desire for something projected into the future. But in the New Testament, the word "hope" has another dimension to it. It is identified in the New Testament as *"a sure and certain* hope." So there is no degree of uncertainty in the New Testament use of the word, "hope." But uncertainty is a very significant part of our modern word "hope." So the New Testament word would be accurately translated, "guarantee," or "assurance." Eureka! What a serendipity this is!

So the prayer of Paul is that the eyes of the believer's heart will be opened up and flooded with light, in order that He may "know by seeing" how absolutely guaranteed his salvation is. Think of this: It is God's intention that every believer have absolute, unconditional, perfect assurance of His salvation. Do you see now why I earlier said that the believer no longer has to prove himself, because God has provided perfect, inviolable, invulnerable, invincible security for him! The reason for this is vital. *Only secure people will ever serve God.* Insecure people cannot serve God; they must serve themselves, seeking the security that eludes them outside of Christ. Every person outside of Christ is a nobody seeking to make of himself a somebody, but every person in Christ (though many don't know it) is everything to the most important Person in the universe; thus, he can easily volunteer to be nothing, because he cannot lose what he has in Christ. Once he is truly in Christ, he is perfectly secure! So this prayer is a petition that each Christian will realize His perfect security in Christ. But look around you. It is easy to see that most Christians (yes, truly born-again people) act regularly out of insecurity instead of security. Why? Because the first "what" has never been deeply and richly illuminated to the eyes of their hearts. Is this an important prayer—or what?

Now, look at the second "what" in this prayer. Paul prays that the eyes of your heart may be flooded with light, that ye may "know by seeing what are the riches of the glory of his inheritance in the saints." Again, careful consideration must be given to the words, and Divine illumination must disclose their meaning to our hearts (see II Timothy 2:7). Question: what "inheritance" is being considered here? Be very careful. Our first tendency would be to answer: The believer's inheritance in Christ, or what I received when I became a Christian. But that is not what the verse says! In fact, the believer's inheritance in Christ has already been discussed in the preceding verses of Ephesians one (verse eleven). No, the inheritance here is God's inheritance in the saints! You see, Christ and His estate are the believer's inheritance, but the Christian is God's inheritance. Study the Old Testament, and note how many, many times His people are identified as God's "portion," God's "lot," God's "treasure," God's "inheritance." This is the idea here. Christians are God's inheritance, God's treasure. From God's viewpoint, He came into possession of something extremely valuable when He saved you.

So what did God get when He got you? Can you believe it? *He says that He got **rich**!* Paul speaks of the "riches of the glory of His inheritance in the saints." You, dear Christian, are *God's precious treasure*. Now, the Christian who looks at himself and thinks only with his own mind will say, "You gotta be kidding! I am the most worthless creature in the universe. The God who would become rich by getting me must not have much of an inventory!" But again, we must put on the lenses of Heaven. We must think with the mind of God. We must see with the eyes of Christ.

Just how much is a Christian really worth, anyway? Are you ready to get blown clean away? Every Christian on earth is *exactly equivalent in value to Jesus Christ Himself—in God's eyes!* How do we know that? Because *that is exactly what God paid for me—Jesus Christ Himself!* Now, none of us could make the claim that we are inherently as valuable as Jesus is. And if we made such a claim,

The Importance of Illumination

nobody would believe us. But this is the whole point. The value referred to here is *conferred value*, not mere inherent value.

Suppose that I am very, very rich. I assure you, that is a supposition! Then suppose that you own a grocery store. That, also, is likely a supposition. Then suppose that I walk into your store today and say to you, "I have come in to buy a Classic Coke—and I am prepared to pay twelve million dollars for it." What should you do? Certainly! Ask me if I would be interested in a six-pack of Cokes at the same rate, or an entire case of Cokes! As stupid as the illustration is, it enables us to consider a vital truth. The value of an article is not determined by the price-tag that appears on it on the shelf; it is determined *by the willingness and capability of the purchaser.* When God showed Himself willing and able to pay Jesus Christ to purchase me to Himself, He conferred upon me an unbelievable value. Ephesians 1:14 refers to the believer as God's "purchased possession," and verse seven tells us that the price of purchase was the life, yes, the *death*, the *blood*, of Jesus Christ Himself. So God has conferred on every Christian the exact value of Jesus Himself.

Several years ago a painting entitled *Irises* by Vincent van Gogh sold for $53.9 million. Now the canvas and paint were barely worth $10 by today's standards, yet Alan Bond, an Australian financier, was willing to pay an incredible price for this work of art. Yes, incredible!

At another auction, Pablo Picasso's *Acrobat and Young Harlequin* was bought for $38.46 million. It was purchased by a Japanese buyer who became quite emotional over the acquisition. Well, I would have gotten emotional, too, but for an altogether different reason! The buyer was so excited to have this wonderful masterpiece that he paid that vast price without questioning it.

Would you think any differently of yourself if someone very famous and important regarded you as a treasure of incalculable value, like a great work of art, a masterpiece? Dear Christian, that is the you God sees! Ephesians 2:10 says, "You are God's workmanship." The word is "poiema," a work of art, a masterpiece!

But wait a minute! Isn't God looking through blind eyes when He confers such worth on someone like me? Is God realistic when He buys me at the cost of Jesus? Remember, dear friend, that this is *conferred* worth. By the transaction of purchase, God confers on you the value of Jesus. But God is certainly not stupid. He knows that you are not inherently as valuable as Jesus. So He confers on you the value of Jesus by the purchase of Calvary — *and then, in order to justify His investment,* **He sets out immediately after you come into His possession to make you like Jesus!** What a *Gospel* this is!

Suppose you inherit a gold mine. You're absolutely elated. You love that gold mine. But the first time you go out to inspect your new treasure, the gold says to you, "How can you possibly love me? I'm all dirty. I'm all mixed up with that awful iron ore, and I have that filthy clay all over me. I'm contaminated with all kinds of alloys and mineral deposits. I'm ugly and worthless." "Oh, but I do love you," you reply to the gold. You see, I understand what you can become. I know you have all these imperfections, but I have plans for you. I am not going to leave you the way you are now. I am going to purify you. I am going to get rid of all that other stuff. I see your real worth, though it only appears now as potential. I know that the alloys and mineral deposits are not the true you — you are just temporarily mixed up with them. I warn you, it won't be easy. You will go through a lot of heat and pressure. But look at this piece of gold jewelry. Isn't it beautiful? That's what you are. Left to yourself, you would remain in this dark place, buried in the dirty ore. But I know how to change you from what you are now to what you can be. *I will make you beautiful, and you will make me rich!*" Now, dear Christian, read the second "what" again, being sure to put on the "God-glasses" of illumination first.

Do you see why I earlier said that *I don't have to prove myself any longer, because God has provided me with perfect significance.* I am His cherished treasure! So this prayer is a petition that each Christian will realize his *personal significance* in Christ.

The Importance of Illumination

Now, we come at last to the final "what" of Paul's prayer. "I pray that the eyes of your heart might be flooded with light, that you may know by seeing *what is the exceeding greatness of God's power toward us who believe.*" So the third "what" of this prayer has to do with *personal sufficiency*. It has to do with "God's power" in our lives. Paul shows that this power is *defined* power (verse 19) and *demonstrated* power (verses 20-23). In defining God's power that is to be operable in our daily lives, Paul uses four words in verse nineteen. He speaks of "the exceeding greatness (the word means to "throw immeasurably beyond," a picture of great magnitude) of God's power toward us who believe, according to the working of God's mighty power." One word for power in this verse is the Greek word, *dunamis*, from which we get our English word "dynamic." This word essentially means capability or potential. A second is the word *energeia*, which gives us our words "energy" and "energize." This word means effective or operational power. A third word is *kratos*, which refers to power that is exercised in resistance or control. And the final word is *ischuos*, which indicates inherent, vital power. So again, Paul strains at the leash of vocabulary to show us how great is the character dynamic that is available to the believer in Christ.

But Paul doesn't stop with mere words which define God's power. He also points to certain events which *demonstrate* God's power. You see, when the Bible wants to impress us with the *love* of God, it points us to the Cross of Christ. When it wants to impress us with the *power* of God, it points us to the Resurrection and Exaltation of Christ. So Paul says that God's power was "wrought in Christ" when God *enlivened Him from the dead* and *exalted Him in glory.* In his words, this power was wrought in Christ "when God raised Him from the dead, and set Him at His own right hand in the heavenly places, far above all principality, and power, and might, and dominion, and every name that is named, not only in this world, but also in that which is to come, and has put all things under His feet, and made Him to be head over all things to the church, which is His Body, the fullness of Him that fills all in all." So He declares that the same power which elevated Jesus to a position of glory is available to elevate us to a life of Divine sufficiency. I emphasize again that this power is available to us for the sake of building our own character and exerting character impact upon others.

Do you see why I said earlier that I don't have to *provide* for myself because God has supplied perfect *sufficiency* for me? So this prayer is a petition that each Christian will realize his *powerful sufficiency* in Christ. However, again we must sadly admit that these expressions of power are foreign to the experience of most Christians. And we must again guess that one of the primary causes for the dearth of power is a lack of illumination. Most Christians are sadly blind to the great character power that is available to them.

Dr. C. I. Scoffield related an illustrative story from his preaching ministry. He was in a Bible Conference in the city of Staunton, Virginia, many years ago. The week had been especially busy, with two services daily and a round of other activities. On Friday night, a kind layman invited Dr. Scoffield to visit his workplace on Saturday in order to have a little relief from the press of people and the pressure of communication. He accepted the invitation and went with the man the next morning. He discovered that he was being taken to a mental institution which the layman managed. They casually toured the grounds, visiting along the way, then they entered the main building. As they walked down the long central hallway through the building, a heavily muscled man came toward them, though he was walking with the shuffling gait of a mental patient. As he came near, Dr. Scoffield stepped aside to let him pass, marveling at the muscled strength of his body. When he was out of earshot, Dr. Scoffield said to his host, "Man, you must have a real problem when *he* gets angry and goes on a rampage! It has been a long time since I have seen such a strong man." But the manager's answer surprised the preacher. "Oh, no, Doctor Scoffield," he replied, "that man is no problem at all. You see, as strong as he is, he is in this institution because he has the illusion of weakness. He thinks that he is so weak that he can't even lift a spoon full of food or a glass of water to his lips. Someone else

The Importance of Illumination

must do it for him." Later that day, the Holy Spirit spoke to the preacher about the visual parable he had seen that morning. "My child, you have just seen a picture of the typical Christian of today, and the typical church. While the great power of God is perfectly available to those who believe, instead *they struggle under an illusion of weakness."* Friends, the primary difference between the Christian suffering under the illusion of weakness and the Christian functioning in the efficiency of God's power is the *miracle of illumination.*

Christian, *what you see is what you will be*—within the limits of God's revealed truth. *What you behold is what you will become.* I repeat, this is the most important prayer that any Christian can pray for another, and when this prayer is answered in a Christian's life, he has just become the recipient of the first great blessing toward total victory in Christ. By means of the miracle of illumination, the problems of *insecurity, insignificance, and insufficiency* are solved for the believer.

The Psalmist said to God, "In Thy light shall we see light." "The entrance of Thy words giveth light; it giveth understanding to the simple" (Psalm 119:30). As God gives us grace to see, *His story becomes ours, His vision becomes ours, His concerns become ours, and His vocation becomes ours.* So illumination is a continual necessity in disciple-making. Lord, you have given sufficient light; now, give us sufficient sight.

Chapter Seven

THE CONVICTING WORK OF THE HOLY SPIRIT, THE NECESSARY PREPARATION FOR SALVATION

John 16:7-11;

"I tell you the truth; It is expedient for you that I go away: for if I go not away, the Comforter will not come unto you; but if I depart, I will send him unto you. And when he is come, he will reprove the world of sin, and of righteousness, and of judgment: Of sin, because they believe not on me; Of righteousness, because I go to my Father, and ye see me no more; Of judgment, because the prince of this world is judged."

Jesus said two very peculiar things in introducing this great truth of the convicting work of the Holy Spirit. He said, "I tell you the truth; It is expedient for you that I go away."

Can you imagine Jesus ever prefacing anything He ever said by saying, "I tell you the truth"? When a friend of mine casually says, "I'm going to tell you the truth," *I wonder what he has been telling me the rest of the time!* Preachers often say in sermons, "I want to be honest with you," but when they say that, my question is, What were they in the *rest of the sermon*? No, they don't mean that *this only* is the truth, but that *this particular* truth bears special emphasis. When Jesus preceded our text with these words, He was indicating that the following truth was especially important—and indeed it was.

The other peculiar thing He said was, "It is expedient for you that I go away." The disciples might have answered in dismay, "Say what?" You see, the word translated "expedient" means "beneficial" or "to your advantage." "It is actually *beneficial* to you that I depart from you." "It is *to your advantage* that I leave you." There is absolutely no way at this point that His disciples could have possibly understood or believed that statement. However, there is absolutely no uncertainty about the actual meaning of the word translated "expedient." It is found several times in the Gospels, and it always has the same meaning. So what did Jesus mean when He daringly said, "It is to your advantage that I leave you"? He meant that it would be better for Him to be removed from their sight and apparently from their presence than for them to become more locally involved with Him only by hearing His words and observing His works.

Every novice Christian has wished he could have seen Jesus in the flesh and enjoyed His near Presence on earth. A child's hymn says, *"I think when I read that sweet story of old, When Jesus was here among men, How He called little children as lambs to His fold, I should like to been with them then; I wish that His hand had been placed on my head, That His arms had been thrown around me, And that I might have seen His kind look when He said, "Let the little ones come unto Me."*

These words and the emotions they reveal are very deep, so Jesus must have had reasons for disappointing such a deep, poignant, universal, sacred feeling in human hearts. What were His reasons? In what senses would His *absence from them* be better than His *presence with them*? First, He knew that He would still be with them even after His departure, though in a different way. Second, He knew He would be nearer after He departed than He had ever been before. Third, He knew that upon His departure He would be

The Convicting Work of the Holy Spirit

universally near to *all* believers, and not merely *locally* near to *some*. Fourth, He knew that they would continue to walk only by sight if He remained with them, and that they would know "a better way," *to walk by faith*, only if He departed. Last, and most important here, He knew that He had to go away before the Holy Spirit would come, and the coming of the Holy Spirit was an enlarged advantage over His physical presence. Christian, we must remind ourselves until it reaches our deepest heart that we have gained much in Christ's departure from earth and the following descent of the Holy Spirit to continue His work. *In fact, the disciples of Christ did not really, fully, deeply, truly know Christ **until** the Holy Spirit came, and neither will we really, fully, deeply, truly* know Christ until the Holy Spirit is fully known, honored and obeyed in our lives. You see, man's confidence in himself—his morality, his capability to please God, his ability to save himself—must be shattered if the Spirit is to be allowed to do His saving work in and through God's people. And that shattering work begins in the convicting work of the Holy Spirit.

Our text contains one of the most crucial truths ever spoken. It describes one of the most important works done by the Holy Spirit, Whom Jesus promised in this great section of John's Gospel (John 14-16). In these chapters, Jesus calls the Holy Spirit *"the Comforter"*—and then He proceeds to tell us that His introductory work in a sinner's life, His foundational work in making eternal salvation personal, is a work of *discomfort*. Furthermore, this convicting, convincing work of the Holy Spirit is *so* crucial that, if this work were to suddenly cease, that is, if the Holy Spirit never convicted another sinner in line with this statement of Jesus, *no sinner would ever be saved again*. So what did He mean when He said that the Holy Spirit would come and "reprove the world"?

I. THE MEANING

First, we will consider the *meaning* of this particular work of the Holy Spirit. What did Jesus mean when He said, "When He has come, He will reprove the world"? It is important, first, that we examine the exact meaning of the word "world." The word is used in three senses in the New Testament. First, it means the created world. Then, it is used to describe the Godless world system that prevails on earth. And finally, it is used for the entire populace of planet earth. In the text, Jesus was speaking of the populace of planet earth. The reproving work of the Holy Spirit would be directed toward the entire populace of the human race. I personally believe that this work of the Spirit is taking place to one degree or another in the hearts of men all the time all over the world.

The most important word in the text in understanding this work of the Spirit is the word translated "reprove" in the King James Bible. This is a very strong and full word. It combines in itself the two ideas of *convicting* and *convincing*. One translation uses the word "confute," which combines both meanings. This work is actually done in three great areas, all of which involve very important factors in human experience. The three are "sin, righteousness, and judgment." Without the convicting and convincing work of the Holy Spirit, there would not be a single Christian on earth. In convicting of "sin," the Holy Spirit powerfully convinces us that we are sinners in desperate need of salvation. In convicting us of "righteousness," He shows us the only basis for salvation. And in convicting of "judgment," He shows us what we deserve and how He has acted to save us from it.

The convicting work of the Holy Spirit is the shining of the light of Divine truth into the hearts of sinful human beings, revealing their sins and seeking a response of faith from them. This shining of the light of God's truth is going on all the time, as silently and as certainly as the shining of the sun. The Holy Spirit does not merely convict of sin on special occasions. No, there is no time that is "out of season" for the Holy Spirit. If we have not admitted our sins after seeing them clearly in the light of God's truth, it is not because He is ambiguous in revealing the awful truth about us, it is likely because we are not willing to admit this truth to ourselves, to others, or to God. Since the Spirit's voice is usually very soft and gentle, it is easy for sinners to avoid the conviction He brings.

The root form of the word translated "reprove" means "to scorn," "to pour contempt," and "to convince." So this is both a *severe* and a *saving* ministry of the Holy Spirit. It is the means by which the sinner is convicted of his sins and convinced of his need of a Savior. This is, indeed, a crucial and indispensable work of the Holy Spirit.

II. THE MEANS

Second, we will consider *the means* by which this convicting, convincing work is done. In considering the means, we will look at the *agent* of this conviction and the *activity* that is performed.

The *agent* of this conviction is identified by Jesus as "the Comforter" (verse 7), and "the Spirit of truth" (verse 13). The word "Comforter" is the familiar Greek word, *paracletos*, or *Paraclete*. This is a rich and wonderful word, surely intended by Jesus to reveal how great is the Person Jesus described. The word means "guardian," or "ally," or "fortifier," or "champion." Probably its widest use is to refer to a "counselor, a defender, a lawyer, an advocate." According to the New Testament, the Christian economy has *two Paracletes*, or two Advocates. Thus, the Christian system is like a Law Firm with two branches, each being "manned" by a Lawyer. One branch with one Lawyer is on earth, the other branch with the other Lawyer is in heaven. The One above is Jesus, Who is *our Lawyer in heaven* (see I John 2:2). The One here is the Holy Spirit, Who is *Christ's Lawyer on earth*. Jesus pleads and wins our case in heaven, securing on the basis of His Finished Work on the Cross and by His Resurrection our justification from all factors that might condemn us. And the Holy Spirit pleads and wins Christ's case in the hearts of men on earth.

Heaven is a prepared place for a prepared people. While Jesus is in Heaven *securing the place for the people of God*, the Holy Spirit is on earth *securing* the *people of God for the place*. So while *Jesus* stands alongside of God in heaven securing *our* case there, the *Holy Spirit* stands alongside of sinners securing *Christ's* case here. You see, the Holy Spirit makes final dispatch of sinners in His dealing with them. He will either convict them in such a manner that will finally lead them to salvation and heaven, or He will *convict* them as fully guilty and they will go to damnation and hell. The Holy Spirit of God is the Agent of the Spirit's conviction.

Second, the text points out the *activity* by which this work is done. Consider again the word "reprove." The word could be translated "contradict." "The Holy Spirit will contradict the world." This activity is not flattering to unsaved men, because it tells us that, without exception, all lost people are always wrong about the three most important things in human experience—sin, righteousness and judgment. Natural men are so inaccurate in their assessment of these factors in their lives that the Holy Spirit must flatly contradict them if they are ever to be convinced about them. And without this work of the Holy Spirit in their hearts, sinful human beings will remain wrong forever. I repeat, the convicting work of the Holy Spirit is indispensable for man's welfare and God's glory.

The New Testament contains no clearer picture of the effectiveness of the agency of the Holy Spirit in convicting and convincing men than in the order of events in the group of Jesus' disciples immediately before the coming of the Holy Spirit on the Day of Pentecost and immediately after He came. Just before Pentecost, ten committed and honest disciples told Thomas the Doubter that they had seen Jesus alive after His Death on the Cross. Thomas had probably never had a reason to doubt the testimony of any one of them or all of them, but he still stubbornly said, "Dead men don't rise from the dead! Unless I see the print of the nails in His hands, and can put my hand into the scar in His side, I will not believe." *Ten honest men could not convince one man before the Holy Spirit came.* But on the Day of Pentecost, Peter preached the Gospel and explained what was happening, and *one man convinced 3,000 to believe "impossible" things and to make an "impossible" surrender!* What was the difference? The ten depended on human persuasiveness, while Peter was empowered by the Holy Spirit!

III. THE MANNER

Next, we will look at *the manner* in which the Holy Spirit convicts and convinces sinners. The text points to three cardinal

The Convicting Work of the Holy Spirit

points on God's spiritual compass. The three points are "sin, righteousness, and judgment." "When He (the Holy Spirit) has come, He will reprove (convict and convince) the world of sin, and of righteousness, and of judgment." Then Jesus explained His meaning: "Of sin, because they believe not on Me; of righteousness, because I go to my Father, and ye see me no more; of judgment, because the prince of this world is judged." All three of these factors may appear very strange at first glance, and the explanations even stranger, but a little "unraveling" will reveal the glory of this statement. If we could see from God's perspective, we would recognize that, until these three matters are satisfactorily settled, there are simply no more important things in existence than these three. Sin is an extremely influential and important reality on earth, and unless men are saved from it here, they will never escape it or its penalty forever. Righteousness is an extremely important and influential reality in heaven, and unless men gain a righteousness that matches that of heaven, they will never be saved. And judgment is the means by which righteousness wins over sin.

Note that these factors are all sinner-related *and* Savior-related. That is, all three have to do with sin and God's dealing with it in order to save sinners, and they also have to do with the Savior and what He has accomplished and provided for our salvation. Thus, they all expose some facet of our salvation. Look with me at the statement.

First, the Holy Spirit "reproves the world of sin." This is designed to cause men to see the *absolute necessity* of being saved. In order to convince man of his dire need of God's salvation, the Holy Spirit exposes to Him the real and deadly nature and consequences of sin.

We have already said that this work of the Spirit is necessary because the natural (unaided) human being is *always wrong about sin.* It is a pathetic reality and an incredible contradiction that human beings have an immense *history* of sin, but almost no *sense* of sin. In fact, little scrutiny is necessary to see that human beings *deliberately avoid* a consciousness of sin (or at least an admission of it). They are like a person who constantly sponges an indelible stain, but it simply will not go away.

You can poll any number of natural human beings at any place, and you will never secure from them an adequate or accurate view of sin. Some will tell you that sin doesn't even exist at all. Just as Adolf Hitler labeled sin "a fiction of the synagogue," so sinners renounce the Biblical revelation of the existence and seriousness of sin. One man said to me, "I don't go to church because all they want to do is tell you how bad a sinner you are." Well, that assessment is simply not true, but it does remind me of a man with a cancer who refuses to go to the doctor because he might *inform him of his problem*. He only faces the problem when it is too late to do anything about it—just like *sinners* who won't admit the poison that spreads its death throughout their lives. They will face the problem, but for many it will be too late to apply The Cure God has provided.

Others concede that sin may be real, but it is after all unimportant. When I asked a lost neighbor what he did with his sins without a Savior, he wryly replied, "Oh, I do just what everybody else does; I make the best of a bad situation." I replied, "No, not everybody; I know many people who have dealt with their sins by giving them over to the Savior who died for them." Some people even testify that sin is a very charming part of this world, but ask them in another hundred years.....

Still others glibly think of sin only in terms of shameful moral excesses. Murder may be sin, rape may be sin, assault may be sin, but "the small mistakes *I* make are not worthy of consideration." Drunkenness and adultery, maybe, but not my mild stumblings! I even heard a public speaker say on one occasion, "*My* family *had* no sinners in it." Presumably, he meant that there was no record of his ancestors or relatives being alcoholics, murderers or convicted criminals.

You see, the world is completely in the dark concerning the truth about sin, and it is not an easy matter to adequately and accurately convince the world of sin. However, conviction of sin is necessary for man's highest welfare.

The Convicting Work of the Holy Spirit

Now, note Jesus' explanation of "sin." "The Holy Spirit will reprove the world of sin, because they believe not on Me." We are suddenly alerted to the truth that accuracy about sin is a profoundly intelligent matter and requires a shift of paradigm from man's guesswork to God's wisdom. This is the work of the Holy Spirit!

I said earlier that sin is a sinner-related word (obviously) and a Savior-related word (also obvious, because man would not need Jesus *as a Savior* if it were not for sin). Now, we can begin to see why Jesus added His seemingly strange explanation of sin. "He will convict the world of sin, because they believe not on me." The one damning sin is unbelief with regard to Christ. Unbelief is the mother sin, the father sin, the parent sin, of all sins. Unbelief is sin at its worst. No other sins would be committed without the catalytic sin of unbelief. "He who does not believe God has made Him a liar, because he does not believe the witness that God gave of His Son. And this is the testimony, that God has given to us eternal life, and this life is in His Son. He who has the Son has life, but he who has not the Son of God does not have life" (I John 5:10-12). "He who believes on Jesus is not condemned, but he who believes not is condemned already, because he has not believed in the name of the unique Son of God" (John 3:18). So the "sin-question" is actually a "Son-question." It is finally the sin of rejecting Jesus Christ the Son of God that dispatches the fully responsible sinner to hell. You see, unbelief is not only a sin in itself, but it prevents the forgiveness of all other sins. So the Holy Spirit takes the blinders off of the eyes of sinners and shows them their dire and desperate need of Jesus. When the Spirit does this work in the hearts of sinners, it is as if they saw their state of sin mirrored in the rejection and crucifixion of the Son of God. In that act, the sinfulness, lostness and madness of the human race is exposed.

Second, the Holy Spirit convicts and convinces sinners of the *authentic possibility* of salvation. "He will reprove the world of righteousness, because I go to my Father and you see me no more." The key word here is the gigantic word, "righteousness."

Again, the world of unsaved men is *always wrong* about righteousness. Everyone has some concept of sin, and everyone has some concept of righteousness. As usual, the world is vague as well as inaccurate, engaging in remarkable guesswork about what it takes to be "right" with God.

First, it declares that if a man is "sincere" in whatever he may believe about right and wrong, or about God, or in his moral conduct, God will admit him to His holy heaven. But it is possible, even likely when everything is based on uncertainty, that the person will be *sincerely wrong* in his view. This may not matter much with regard to some things, but it is all-important when it concerns God, eternity and the eternal destiny of human beings. The Bible says this about this dangerous course: "They, being ignorant of God's righteousness, and going about to establish their own righteousness, have not submitted themselves to the righteousness of God" (Romans 10:3).

This old facetious poem was born in a science laboratory:

*"Poor Willy, he has gone from us, His face we will see no more,
Because what he thought was H_2O, Was actually H_2SO_4."*

Willy sincerely thought that sulphuric acid was water—but drinking it proved his mistake, though he never lived to analyze his error! This is facetious, but that same kind of mistake is made with regard to eternal salvation by innumerable hordes of self-centered human beings is not! Sincerity is not adequate!

Others suggest that sinners can (and must) earn God's salvation and a place in His heaven. Let me adapt a story Jesus told, creating a revision of it: a certain man owed a $20 million debt and had maybe $20 to pay on it, but he vainly said, "Give me time, and I will pay all." When the average laborer's daily wage was about a penny a day, one wonders how anyone could think in this manner, but sinners vainly do the same thing quite glibly. The false view of man's supposed ability to earn salvation shows a total ignorance or a deliberate disregard for the Biblical truth of the nature of sin, the nature of God, the terms for salvation, and all the other things that derive from these. No man will ever be able to declare in heaven that he deserves to be there. No sinful human being can earn God's salvation.

The Convicting Work of the Holy Spirit

Note the order of the three factors that are listed. First, sin, then righteousness. Righteousness corresponds to the consciousness of sin. When a person is awakened to his sins, he wants an answer to this question, "Is it possible for somebody in my condition to be right with God?"

Let me create a brief running commentary on the word "righteousness." First, consider the *reality* of righteousness. There is such a thing as *real* righteousness, or "righteous righteousness," and the Holy Spirit convicts the sinner of it. Then, consider the *necessity* of righteousness. Without perfect righteousness, no man will get to heaven, and the Holy Spirit convicts the sinner of that problem. Then, consider the *availability* of righteousness. Though among men "there is none righteous, no, not one"(Romans 3:10), "now the righteousness of God without the law is manifested....even the righteousness of God which is by faith of Jesus Christ unto and upon all them that believe" (Romans 3:21, 22). And the Holy Spirit convinces the sinner of it. Finally, consider the *integrity* of this righteousness. Many raise the questions, "How can it be just for one person to be held accountable for the sins of all men, and even if it were just, how can one person pay for the sins of all men. The very idea is immoral, unjust and impossible." Or, "How could a perfect God maintain His perfection if He allowed real sinners into His Heaven?" These questions are answered in a classic argument by Paul in Romans 3:9-26, which should be read and studied carefully. Paul says that, because of God's Perfect Settlement of the sin-problem through the Perfection of Jesus (His *passive* righteousness) and His Perfect Payment for sin on the Cross (His *active* righteousness), and His own Perfect Endorsement of His Son's Payment through the Resurrection, God can now be both *"just* and the *Justifier* of the sinner who believes in Jesus" (Romans 3:26). So salvation is authentically possible! Righteousness is what God *is*, what God *has*, what God *demands*, and *what God **provides**.* What a Gospel! What a Savior! What a salvation!

We have not yet examined one small clause in this context. "The Holy Spirit will convict the world of righteousness, because I go to My Father, and you see Me no more."

What does this mean in this setting? It is a reference to the Ascension of Christ, but how does it explain "righteousness," or how does the Holy Spirit use the truth of the Ascension of Christ to convict the world of righteousness? This simply means that the Ascension of Jesus back to Heaven ("I go to My Father") and His continuing Presence there ("and you see Me no more") prove to the awakened heart the truth that *there is one standard of righteousness, that of Christ Himself, that is perfectly acceptable to God and indeed, already perfectly accepted in Heaven.* And remember, this righteousness has been made available to sinners through the convicting work of the Holy Spirit. So we know that if we trust Christ to save us, His righteousness immediately becomes ours, and we are as acceptable to God as if we were Christ Himself! These are marvelous truths, almost too good to be true. It is the Holy Spirit who convinces us that these things are true, and He does this through exposure to this glorious Gospel.

Third, the Holy Spirit convicts and convinces sinners of the *assured certainty* of salvation. This He does by convicting and convincing the world "of judgment, because the prince of this world is judged."

The fact that the Holy Spirit must convince the world concerning judgment lets us know again that without this work of the Spirit, the world is *always wrong* with regard to judgment. Consider society's weak view of judgment. When it entertains the idea of judgment at all, it puts "God in the dock" and holds its own court over His reveal truth. It says that the very idea of a day of reckoning that has eternal fallout is foolish, or preposterous. The note of judgment has been reduced to near silence in today's world. However, the world must be reminded that consensus of opinion does not determine truth. Judgment is occurring in this world as I write these words, and there is yet a "judgment to come." These are stark realities, but they are not the argument of our text.

Jesus said, "The Holy Spirit will convict the world of judgment, because *the prince of this world is judged.*" What a peculiar explanation! Let me appeal to a statement by theologian/scholar P. T. Forsyth at this point: "It is very hard on the lower planes of life

The Convicting Work of the Holy Spirit

to convince the world of judgment, to persuade men that there is an infallible reckoning for all transgression, that no sin can be permanently concealed, that in the end the hidden things of darkness will come to light, and will receive their just reward. How, then, are they to be convinced of judgment? There is only one way. The judgment to which Jesus pointed in John 16:11 was that conquest of the dominion of evil which He had already commenced, and the final victory over it which He should gain on His soon-coming Cross. The German theologian Schiller made this statement famous: 'The world's history is the world's judgment.' But there is something more true than Schiller's famous phrase. It is not the world's history, but Christ's history, that is the world's judgment. And especially is it Christ's Cross." Dear Christian, read this paragraph until it reaches you. In the *Person* of Christ (His *passive* righteousness) and the *performance* of Christ (His *active* righteousness), Jesus judged and conquered sin. *The Cross of Christ was the crisis of earth's history, and the judgment and overthrow of the "prince of this world."* The Death of Jesus was the apparent moment of Satan's greatest conquest, but it was actually the moment of his greatest defeat. That same moment was apparently the moment of Christ's greatest defeat, but it was actually the moment of His greatest conquest. That was the moment of the judgment of the prince of this world, Satan. Without full and final judgment being enacted against sin and against its sponsor, Satan, there would be no complete settlement of the massive problem from which we need to be saved, and thus no assurance of salvation. With that full and final judgment accomplished at the Cross, the sin-problem is resolved, trusting sinners are saved, and perfect assurance of salvation may be theirs.

Of course, "the prince of this world" is Satan, and Jesus used a perfect tense verb for the judgment enacted against him. "Now does the prince of this world *stand forever judged.*" Jesus made a precisely similar statement in John 12:31: "Now is the judgment of this world; now shall the prince of this world be cast out." Forget at the moment the *date* for *coming* judgment, and remember the *state* of *complete* judgment, that *the world, sin and*

Satan have already been fully and finally judged—at and through the Cross of Christ.

According to Jesus, this judgment of the world, sin and Satan has already been passed and executed through His Death on the Cross. This judgment is not future; it is already finished, accomplished, completed! Thus, a person taking refuge from his sin and its judgment in the Cross of Christ and His judgment there for our sins, is forever freed from judgment. Jesus said, "He who hears My words, and believes on Him Who sent Me, has everlasting life, and shall not come into judgment, but has already passed out of death into life" (John 5:24). Paul later echoed, "There is therefore now no judgment to those who are in Christ Jesus."

In the early history of our country, pioneers traveling west had to cross the broad prairies of the Midwest. Occasionally, they had to face raging prairie fires that were driven at high speed by the strong winds of the prairie country. There was no way for them to outrun such a fire when caught in the open prairie, but they learned a tactic from the Indians which rescued them from the danger. They learned to set backfires around them when they saw a fire approaching in the distance. They would burn out a circle in the high grass, then station themselves and their wagons in the middle of the charred circle and wait for the fire to burn its way past them. They knew that another fire could not burn where the flammable material had already been burned. What an illustration of God's accomplishment for us through His Son at Calvary. He fully exhausted His justice, His wrath and His judgment against sin at the Cross, and now when a sinner comes to the Cross and trusts Christ and His Work there, God can fully and justly extend His saving Mercy to the trusting sinner.

Judgment upon the sins of a sinner who trusts Christ has already been exhausted upon Jesus, the sinner's Substitute, and God will not exact justice twice for the same crimes. You, dear heart, may have full assurance that you have eternal salvation from sin and its consequences through the Finished Work of Christ. It is the Holy Spirit Who convinces men of these things, and this is the manner in which He does it.

IV. THE MANIFESTATION

Fourth, we will look quickly at *the manifestation* of the Holy Spirit's conviction.

The truth of the convicting and convincing work of the Holy Spirit deserves much more investigation and exposure in the Christian community and in our teaching, preaching and witnessing than it generally receives. It is very closely related to the level of our Christian living. The neglect of this truth and our poor expectation with regard to the Holy Spirit's conviction has left the quality of Christian living in our day much lower than it should be. It is a general rule that *grace tends to grow strongest in the experience of the believer in whom conviction of sin has pierced deepest.* So how much conviction is necessary in a true salvation experience?

In I Corinthians 12:6, Paul wrote that there are "different kinds of working (of the Spirit), but the same God works all of them in all men." Some, like John Bunyan and Martin Luther, had a prolonged season of incredible agony in conviction of sin before the light of "Christ our righteousness" burst upon them. Personally, though I had an experience of conviction and conversion that was somewhat like theirs, mine was still considerably different. Others, like Lydia in Acts 16, experience a quiet persuasion and act accordingly. My wife had this kind of experience, but I have seen every reason to be convinced that she is a true born-again believer with a vital and spiritual walk with Christ (and I have seen no reason whatsoever to question that). Many others had varying degrees of conviction somewhere between those extremes.

I personally believe that three things may determine the depth of the conviction. One, the degree of sin's entrenchment in the sinner's life may account for the degree of conviction he receives. If he is a rebel (like religious Paul was), the Holy Spirit may treat him very roughly to prepare him for salvation. Two, the purpose God may have for him after conversion may determine how God prepares him for it through conviction. If he is being prepared for an exceptional fruitful ministry, or a ministry in a very hard place, God may "tighten the vise of conviction" more fully on him in order to give him special equipment through his salvation. Third, the nature of his temperament and personality may determine the apparent degree of conviction he receives from the Holy Spirit. If he is mild-mannered, it is not likely he will receive a lightning and thunder conviction. But if he is a volatile personality, he may be shaken with conviction more than others. If this assessment is accurate, we may be sure that we can count on the All-wise God to give the suitable degree of conviction that is required is each individual case. An old Puritan adage says, "God suits the north wind to fit the shorn lamb." That is, "the different kinds of working" of the Spirit will fit the necessity of each person. So the manifestation of the Spirit in convicting sinners may vary widely, but I do not believe that a sinner is ever saved *without* the convicting work of the Spirit preceding his salvation and preparing him for it.

Just as Joseph in the book of Genesis spoke roughly to his needy brothers to bring them to a confession of their former sin before revealing himself to them in reconciliation, so the Holy Spirit reproves first of sin in order to lead sinners to repentance and salvation. It is the hungry man who values bread, and it is the guilty man who values pardon. The sinner is very likely to receive the degree of conviction that will make him willing to give up his sins and long for Christ as his Savior. Whatever the degree of conviction, the Holy Spirit does convict lost people of their sins, thus convincing them of their radical need of God's salvation.

V. THE MEDIATORS

Fifth, consider *the mediators* of this convicting work of the Holy Spirit. One feature is usually overlooked in this text, but we must not be guilty of that oversight. Look again at Jesus' introductory words: "I tell you the truth; It is expedient for you that I go away: for if I go not away, the Comforter will not come unto you, but if I depart, I will send him unto you. And when he is come, he will reprove the world....."

In my entire early ministry, I was guilty of the usual oversight. I thought that the text meant that the Holy Spirit would

The Convicting Work of the Holy Spirit

"come" into the world on the Day of Pentecost, and would go directly to lost sinners and convict them of sin. Now, He may do that, but this text suggests a different course. Jesus said that the Holy Spirit will "come unto you," that "I (Jesus) will send Him unto you." Note the recurring references to the recipients, "unto you." Read the seventh and eighth verses of the text again, each time emphasizing the word, "you." Then take the same word and insert it in verse eight to get the meaning of the verse. "I will send Him (the Holy Spirit) unto you. And when He has come (unto *you*), He will convict the world...." The Holy Spirit is apparently not coming to the world as such; He is coming to you, the Christian. And when He comes to the Christian, He will convict the world of sin and of righteousness and of judgment. In fact, Jesus had earlier said specifically to His disciples that when the Spirit of truth would come, the world would not be able to receive Him. It does not receive Him, and cannot, because it neither sees Him or knows Him (John 14:17). But He does come to us, and when He is allowed to operate in and through us as He desires, He will have this threefold effect upon the world. Apparently, it is from this "sounding board" (you, your life, your character, your witness) that the Holy Spirit will do His convicting work.

In everything Jesus Christ does on earth, and in everything the Holy Spirit does on earth, both the Son and the Spirit seek to enlist and use the Church, the Body of Christ, to accomplish the work. The individual Christian might be called "God's middleman," or "God's contact man." I have not been able to find one case in the New Testament where a sinner was won to Christ without the Holy Spirit using at least one believer as His agent of contact, conviction and conversion. *The Holy Spirit goes by way of the saint to get to the sinner!* In some cases, the Holy Spirit went to great measures to get the saint to the sinner, but in each case, the sinner was not converted until the saint arrived. Just think of Philip riding beside the Ethiopian eunuch on his chariot, or Simon Peter in the house of Cornelius, and remember that the Holy Spirit took great pains in each case to get the saint to the sinner to lead him to Christ. In the case of Peter and Cornelius, an angel coordinated the contact, but the angel did not tell Cornelius how to be saved. Apparently, neither God nor the angel would do the work that the Christian is supposed to do! The same is surely true today. The responsibility for the lost man belongs to the evangelizing Christian.

Some years ago, I read a sermon entitled "The Vanishing Sinner." The article was a lament that the consciousness of sin seems to have disappeared among sinners across the United States. The article mourned the inactivity of the Spirit in doing the convicting work that leads people to salvation. Several reasons were suggested to explain "the vanishing sinner." I see one reason suggested by our text that was not mentioned in that article. It is my firm conviction that the reason for the vanishing sinner is *the vanishing saint!* If Christians grasped their identity in Christ and lived accordingly, if Christians recognized their inventory in Christ and lived accordingly, if Christians admitted their responsibility to tell lost people about Christ and lived accordingly, more and more sinners would be convicted of their sins and convinced of the Savior. I am persuaded that, in spite of our loud protests that sinners are not willing to respond to the Gospel, they are more willing to *hear* the Gospel than we are to *share* it with them. It should be said of each believer that "from him sounded out the Gospel...." (see I Thessalonians 1:8). Each individual Christian is to be the mediator of the Holy Spirit's work of conviction.

VI. THE MERCY

Finally, a word about *the mercy* God exercises when He sends the Holy Spirit to convict us of sin and convince us of the Savior. The fact that there is even one Christian on earth today is because of the mercy of God in commissioning the Holy Spirit to do this work.

I have known many, many friends who had serious and major surgeries on something defective or diseased in their bodies. Again and again I have heard this testimony after those surgeries, "I feel better today than I have for years, or than I have in my entire life." When the pain and uncertainty of the surgery were over, the person was only regretful that he had not had the surgery sooner.

The Convicting Work of the Holy Spirit

Conviction of sin is like major surgery. You have an uneasy feeling that something is wrong, then a diagnosis is made, then you submit to the surgeon. On the day of the surgery, you go down into the shadowy land of unconsciousness, very concerned about your return. Because of the need, you place your entire life in the hands of another, go down to death's door, allow the cutting removal or repair, and then awaken to a joyful life on the other side. So it is when you experience the convicting work of the Holy Spirit. It is painful, but it is the preparation for eternal life now and forever. *What a mercy!*

AN ADDENDUM

I live in the city of Memphis, Tennessee. Memphis rests on a notorious earthquake fault called the New Madrid Fault. We are constantly being reminded of this, and often warned of the coming "big one." I would know none of this personally, nor would you without the same help I have. We depend on the knowledge and testimony of skilled experts to know where the fault is, and how serious it is.

In the same manner, I am unreliable in recognizing my own faults, and you are equally unreliable in knowing about your faults. The sinful self-curl each of us suffers from prevents our being truly objective and fully honest about our own faults. You cannot be trusted to tell me the full and accurate truth about my faults, and I cannot be trusted to tell you the full and accurate truth about your faults. A skilled expert is required.

The only Expert skilled enough to tell us the "whole truth and nothing but the truth" about us and our faults is the Holy Spirit. (Source undocumented)

Dwight L. Moody once saw a man in the streets of Chicago almost asleep in a winter blizzard. It was apparent that the man unaided would freeze to death. Moody could not just talk this man into warmth. He pulled him up roughly and began to pound the man's body with his fist until the man was awake—and angry. The man began to flail back at Moody with his arms, and then he stood

Studies in the Person and Work of the Holy Spirit

up on his own and weakly began to run after Moody, with the preacher just staying a step ahead. Thus Moody saved the man's life. The conviction of the Holy Spirit is like this. A concerned Christian may be the agent of the Holy Spirit's "pounding," as Mr. Moody was. He may have to be willing to be "rough" with the prospect, and may need to stay in contact long enough to see life (LIFE) begin to exhibit itself. (My adaptation and explanation; source undocumented)

I hold in my hand a threaded sewing needle. Think of the combination. A rent garment cannot be repaired by the thread without the needle, or by the needle without the thread. The thread does the actual repair work, but without the piercing needle leading the way the thread cannot get into the rent place to repair it. Also, the needle alone would simply pierce the fabric but would do no repair work without the thread. *Christians must never purposely 'needle' people because of some negative emotion in themselves.* But we will often find that the truth in our testimony will always needle those who are in sin and error. This needling of the Holy Spirit, and perhaps assisted by the Christian telling the truth, is necessary for the repair (redemption) of the sinner.

In the illustration, the needle represents the piercing, painful conviction of the Holy Spirit, without which a person cannot be saved. The thread represents the saving Gospel, that makes the rent sinner "whole." The sewer represents the Christian, who is the agent being used to skillfully use both the needle and the thread. (Source undocumented; my adaptation and explanation)

"In true conviction, the sinner sees *himself* for what he really is, the *world* for what it really is, the *law of God* for what it really is, *death* for what it really is, *hell* for what it really is, *Christ* for Who He really is, *God* for Who He really is, and also what *judgment* is. Without this true conviction, no one will ever know God." (John Bunyan, who after a history of slave-trading and *being* a slave himself both of men and sin, was awakened through conviction and brought to the Savior. This conviction proved to be the "grace that taught his heart to fear," and led him to the "grace that fear relieved.")

The Convicting Work of the Holy Spirit

Several years ago, I went with a group of men to an eastern European country on a short-term mission/training trip. I taught and trained pastors in a seminary setting for five days, and the other team members either taught with me or engaged in various evangelism activities during the week. When we departed on KLM Airline, we landed in Amsterdam with a full day of R and R to negotiate. We gave great attention to the possible activity for the day, then we decided to go downtown, through Central Station and into the downtown canal district of Amsterdam. It was during the time when drugs were legal, prostitution was legal, and every attending activity was evident on the streets. When we stepped from the airport-to-downtown train, we walked out through a plaza where all of these things were clearly visible. We went through the plaza to get to the downtown streets. About a half a block from the plaza, one of the team members, a very excitable and emotional type of guy, stopped us in the doorway of a store and said, "I don't think I can take this. These are the last things I will see on this trip, and they will leave images in my mind. This will ruin every good memory I have of the trip." A candid statement! So we gathered around him, joined hands and prayed for a miracle. "Lord, please give to _____ a miracle that will erase the memory of these sinful activities we have seen." We hardly knew what we were praying for! Most of the group decided to catch a trolley out to the Van Gogh Museum, about a two-hour trip, but this emotional man decided to stay downtown, "waiting for the YWAM (Youth With a Mission, a radical missions organization) office and bookstore to open in just a short while." So we left him and told him where and when we would return. About 2 to 3 hours later, we rode the trolley back downtown. We were to leave the trolley at the corner just beyond the YWAM office. When we passed the office building, we saw this emotional man engaged in animated conversation with a man on the street. We got off the trolley and stood at the corner of the building, watching as the two of them engaged in excited conversation. Finally, I became impatient and said, "Let's go and see what is happening." We hurried over to these two men. When our team member saw us coming, he fairly shouted to me, "Herb, you're not going to believe this! You've got to hear this man's story." While the two of them were talking (just before we arrived on the trolley), a man had approached them, inquiring about the "red-light district" of downtown Amsterdam. Our man said, "Sir, you don't need a prostitute; you need something a lot better than that"—and he shared Christ with the man. After a few minutes, the man went over to the wall beside the sidewalk, knelt with these two men, and received Christ! Installment Number Two of the miracle we have requested for this man! But the First Installment was equally incredible. While my emotional team member was standing outside the YWAM building waiting for the office to open, a stranger walked up and joined him in waiting. They began to talk, and it was disclosed that this man had been a top-drawer drug runner for the China Drug Cartel, one of the biggest drug traffickers in Amsterdam. One Friday night, he was at a brothel-bar in downtown Amsterdam, and was seated at a table where a stripper was dancing. As she was dancing, she was mocking various religions. She roughly mentioned Buddhism, Hinduism, Islam, and then she said viciously, "And of course, everybody knows that Jesus loves you!" The man at the table heard that—and could not get it out of his mind. Suddenly, his drinks were tasteless and his pleasure was not so enjoyable any more. Finally, he jumped up from his seat, miserable, and ran out of the place. He had a difficult time sleeping that night, and remained troubled by that sentence throughout the next day. Saturday night was also a miserable night. So he did the only thing he knew to do. He got up on Sunday morning and ventured out to find a church. It just "happened" that he attended the best evangelical church in Amsterdam that morning! Primed and ready, he responded brokenly to the invitation and gave his heart to Christ. When I approached him and my emotional fellow team member on the street, and after this story was repeated, the former drug runner said, "Tell me how to explain that. I didn't remember anything that stripper said about Confucianism, Buddhism, Hinduism or Islam, but when she said, "Jesus loves you," I couldn't get it out of my mind. Why?" I waited for my team member brother in Christ to

The Convicting Work of the Holy Spirit

answer, but he stood silent. I called him by name and said, "_____, give the man an answer!" He looked dumbfounded, so I said, "Tell him why he only remembered that sentence. The reason is, Confucius doesn't have a Holy Spirit, Buddha has no Holy Spirit, Mohammed has no Holy Spirit! When she mentioned Jesus, she gave His Holy Spirit a tool to work with, and look at the results!" (A true story which occurred at my fingertips in downtown Amsterdam in the Netherlands)

The only way any human being can ever be saved is to (actually, not theoretically) know that he's lost. Jesus said, "They that are whole don't need a physician, but those who are sick." A well man doesn't need a doctor. Only sick people need doctors. The person who doesn't know he is lost doesn't feel any need for a Savior. It's only when a man becomes burdened by his sin and realizes that the worst thing he's ever done is to turn his back upon Jesus Christ , then he can turn to Christ and find peace and joy in his heart. Only the Holy Spirit can convict a man of this need. (Roland Leavell)

One of my favorite newspaper comic strips is one about two goofy characters named "Frank & Ernest." Of course, the title is taken from the names of the two main characters. In today's "Frank & Ernest" cartoon, our truth is illustrated. Frank and Ernie are approaching the club house on the golf course after playing 18 holes of golf. Frank is holding a score card in one hand as he carries his golf clubs in the other. He says to Ernie, "I never realized what a bad golfer I was until somebody else kept score." Think of it. It is easy to cheat, to be dishonest, to not be objective about yourself, if you keep your own score. But golf is played by rigid rules, and the score is to be kept in rigid honesty and accuracy. If you keep your own score, you can "hit 5, shout 4 (fore!), and write down 3." But if an objective scorekeeper keeps the score, the truth will be told.

Even so, if sinners keep their own score, playing by their own rules and matching themselves against their own standards, they will think they are good folks. But if God keeps the score, that's a different story. Well, the Holy Spirit is the Scorekeeper, and He holds you to God's Perfect Standard, that of absolute holiness, and convicts you of your sins when you fail. This is the first necessary step to Divine salvation. (Mine)

Chapter Eight

GOD'S GREAT POWER WORKING IN US
Or
AVAILABLE POWER FOR AVAILABLE PEOPLE

Ephesians 1:15-23

> "Wherefore I also, after I heard of your faith in the Lord Jesus, and love unto all the saints, Cease not to give thanks for you, making mention of you in my prayers, That the God of our Lord Jesus Christ, the Father of glory, may give unto you the spirit of wisdom and revelation in the knowledge of him: The eyes of your understanding being enlightened; that you may know what is the hope of his calling, and what the riches of the glory of his inheritance in the saints, And what is the exceeding greatness of his power to usward who believe, according to the working of his mighty power, Which he wrought in Christ, when he raised him from the dead, and set him at his own right hand in the heavenly places, Far above all principality, and power, and might, and dominion, and every name that is named, not only in this world, but also in that which is to come: And hath put all things under his feet, and gave him to be the head over all things to the church, Which is his body, the fullness of him that filleth all in all."

Elsewhere, I have called the prayer of Ephesians 1:17-19 "the prayer of the three 'whats'." "I pray . . . that you may know *what* is the hope of His calling, *what* (are) the riches of the glory of His inheritance in the saints, and *what* is the exceeding greatness of His power." The first and second, properly understood, are transcendent in their glory, but they mock us without the third. In fact, the transcendant glory of the first two sharpens our doubt: "Could I ever hope to reach *that*?" The third "what" answers our problem: the transcendent glory of the first two "whats" is to be experienced and implemented only *by the power of God!*

The three "whats" of Paul's great prayer presuppose that man has very real problems that cannot be answered, very great needs that cannot be met, except through the answer to this prayer. One of these problems is the problem of man's insufficiency, man's impotence, man's inadequacy. This problem immobilizes men everywhere, and Christians are no exception. If they never realize the power of God and appropriate it into their lives, they will be as powerless as lost people. Indeed, a candid examination of the church will show that Christians are often as fearful and as impotent, if not more so, than the lost world around them. Christians, though without excuse, succumb to the external pressures of the world, the internal pressures of the flesh, and the infernal pressures of the devil, just like lost people do. So Paul is praying that Christians will have the eyes of their hearts opened and flooded with spiritual illumination that they might "know by seeing" the greatness of the Divine power that is available to them.

But is this power truly available to a believer in Christ, and is it *equally* available to *all* believers?. What kind of power is Paul speaking of? *How* is it available to each believer? How is it manifested in our experience? Paul seems to address such questions as these in this great statement about the power of God.

I. THE WORDS THAT EXPRESS THIS POWER

First, we must study the *words* which Paul uses in verse 19 to express God's power. No single word is sufficient to describe the power of God. So Paul borrows several words from the vocabulary of dynamics to describe the power which God employs on our behalf. He marshals an impressive array of words in one verse to define and describe God's power. Paul seems to be straining at the leash of language to picture God's power. Even though he was moved by Divine inspiration, Paul was taxed to find words to express the indescribable power of which he was writing. As someone has said, the words seem to bend under the weight of a giant idea.

The four root words he uses for God's power are *dunamis, energeia, kratos,* and *ischos*. Though there are many dimensions to these four Greek words, they essentially define outward and active power (*dunamis*); the efficient working of energy (*energeia*); the mastery that rules and subdues (*kratos*); and inner, residing power (*ischos*). Commentator Dale Moody said that "*dunamis* is the general word that includes the totality of the other three, *energeia* is the power as it goes forth in action, *kratos* is the power applied to the task and accomplishing it, and *ischos* is inherent power." These words are like ocean billows that keep sweeping in upon the beach of our minds with new content. No wonder that the English Bible calls it "God's mighty power"! And this power became ours (both actually and potentially) when we became Christians! It came into our *possession* through the incoming and indwelling of the Holy Spirit, but it must be translated from potential to *practice* through our full and regular dependence upon the Holy Spirit at every moment of our lives.

I have before me a Bible that is loaded with study notes that have resulted from my own personal Bible study. If you were to receive my Bible, you would receive all the notes that are in it, too. When you received the Person of Jesus Christ into your life, you received His power, also. But just as you would have to exploit the use of the notes in my Bible before they could be beneficial to you, you must exploit the power He has given *before it can be beneficial to you*. And it must be exploited on His terms, not yours or mine.

Several years ago, while a Rose Parade was in progress preceding the Rose Bowl football game in Pasadena, California, a brightly decorated flower-covered parade float suddenly stopped, halting the movement of all the vehicles behind it. Mechanics worked feverishly to discover the problem. It was discovered that the vehicle was out of gas. To make matters worse, the float was sponsored by a major oil company! Those who had the most fuel available, and knew best how to deploy it, had simply failed to appropriate that fuel to their own need. We will say more about this in the final point of this message, but this is often true of Christians today. Even while on parade, and while advertising the available power, they may themselves not use, or abuse, or misuse, that power.

II. THE WORKS THAT EXPOSE THIS POWER

Second, we will examine the works that Paul mentions to reveal God's mighty power. The works, respectively, are the resurrection, ascension, and exaltation of Christ. That Jesus Christ was **enlivened** from the dead, **elevated** to the heavenlies, and **exalted** above all, are demonstrations of God's mighty power, the power that is active in the lives of Christian believers.

Each of these is a demonstration of the kind of power that has been made available to every believer. The three great facts about Christ that are stated here present the pattern-works of the power that is operating in all Christians. Look at Jesus *as* He was and *where* He was, then lift your eyes and look at Him where He *is*. The kind of power that brought Him from where He was to where He is, is the kind of power that is available to every believer.

The power that made the greatest change for Jesus was *resurrection* power, and the same is true of us. Now, resurrection power is different; it is not like any other power. It isn't the power of a strong personality nor of an educated mind. It isn't the power of a good family background nor of money, numbers, or leadership ability. It is the power that raised Christ from the dead and thus is able to bring life out of death. Resurrection power works best in a cemetery atmosphere where death reigns (cf. Ephesians 2:1). I repeat, *resurrection works best in a graveyard!* If you are living in the spiritual and moral equivalent of a cemetery, if everything around you is dead and dull and lifeless, you need this power. Indeed, if

Available Power for Available People

everything *within* you is dead toward God, it is this resurrection power which is necessary to save you and give you His Life.

Resurrection power is not deterred or defeated by obstacles or impossibilities. Furthermore, resurrection power requires no outside support. It needs no vote of confidence. It can operate alone, completely alone, if necessary. And it makes no noise or display. Publicity is not necessary to support resurrection power; it supplies its own publicity. When resurrection occurs, it combines all lesser miracles—the healing of the blind, the deaf, the crippled, etc. When a person is dead (the major condition), he is also blind, deaf, etc. (minor symptoms). When the major condition is corrected, the lesser symptoms are corrected, also.

The same power is required to convert a sinner which is demanded in raising the dead (cf. 1:20 & 2:1); indeed, the regeneration of a sinner *is* a resurrection from the dead.

Also, the power that is available to every Christian today is a *reigning* power. "God seated Jesus at His own right hand in the heavenlies," the text says. The Person who was treated like a criminal on earth was elevated by God to the throne of the universe. His redemptive work was finished. He had defeated sin, death and Satan. Verse 21 tells us that He is elevated "far above all principalities, and power, and might, and dominion"-- whatever else these words mean, they certainly mean that He is far above any power that may be considered. The leaders of this world, the leaders of the underworld, Satanic forces, demonic hordes, good angels and bad—He is above them all. And the power that accomplished His elevation is resident in us!

Paul ascends toward his climax and conclusion when he says, "God has put all things in subjection under His feet." Jesus walks over everything you and I fear, and what Jesus walks over, we don't have to walk under. If you are in His Body, you are at least as high as the feet, because the feet are the lowest parts of the body. And He has put everything under His feet! People have been known to pay unbelievable amounts of money to sit beside someone whom they think to be great. Christian, what should we think of our seat of privilege, power, purpose, etc., with Christ in the heavenlies (see Ephesians 2:5-6)?

So the resurrection, ascension and exaltation are the pattern-works that reveal the kind of power that is available to believers in Christ. But the question still remains: How is this power activated in our lives?

III. THE WAY TO EXPERIENCE THIS POWER

According to verse 18, each believer can "know" this power. There is a specified *way* to receive God's power. Two ideas are brought to mind: (1) Christians *must* know this power if they are to be a credit to the God who has saved them. Remind yourself again that no Christian can live the Christian life or perform as a Christian is supposed to perform in his own power. In his own strength, any Christian is too feeble for the conflict he is called upon to engage in. His understanding is too limited. His heart is too cold. Trying to be a mature, loving, serving human being *on God's* terms while using only human energy is like trying to power a luxury cruise liner with two "C" batteries. No Christian can live the true Christian life with such a limited, inherently deficient, power source.

In his useful book, <u>A Guide to Spiritual Success</u>, Pastor Tony Evans declares this truth by means of this illustration:

> Suppose you went to Sears and purchased a new refrigerator, the top of the line. This model has all the bells and whistles and cost you a hefty $6,000. On your way home you stop at your local grocery store to purchase the food for your new appliance. Later that afternoon your refrigerator is delivered and installed, and you fill it with all the goodies you purchased – your favorite chocolate chip ice cream, chocolate milk, and fresh corn on the cob. You retire for the night, but when you come into the kitchen the next morning, you experience the shock of your life. Ice cream is all over the floor! The milk is sour, and the vegetables are changing color! It is quickly evident that your brand new, top-of-the-line refrig-

Available Power for Available People

erator isn't working! Angry and disgusted you call Sears to give them a piece of your "Christian mind" for selling you a dud. The salesperson who sold you the refrigerator is aghast at the news. He asks you to pull open the freezer door to see if the light comes on. You do so. No light. He then asks you to put your ear to the bottom of the refrigerator to see if you hear the low hum of the motor. You do so. No hum. Finally, he asks you to look behind the refrigerator and see if the electrical cord has been plugged in. You do so. Lo and behold the cord is lying on the floor, unplugged! You return to the phone and inform the salesman that the refrigerator is unplugged but that shouldn't matter. You argue that for $6,000 it should work—plugged in or not!

The salesman then explains a very important principle to you – namely, refrigerators are dependent appliances. They were never made to work on their own. They are built with certain specifications that can only be realized when they have been energized by the power of electricity. While all the necessary parts are there, they will not work until they get the necessary electrical juice to enable them to be and do what they were created to do. In this regard, Christians are like appliances. We are dependent creatures. When you receive Christ as Savior, He gives you the requisite parts necessary for you to live a victorious Christian life. But you will not be able to do so until you are plugged into God's power source, the Holy Spirit.

As Pastor Evans said, each Christian is like machinery that stands idle until the electric current is turned on. When it is, power is released into the working parts. Great forces are then set in motion. When we recognize and receive the power that God waits to release in and through us, our lives will be powerful and productive for Him. But how? How do we receive this power? Not by intellectual perception alone, but by contact and relationship. This is "acquaintance power," thus it is character power, not cataclysmic power.

(2) Christians *may* know this power, and *the means of appropriation is faith*. Paul tells us in verse 19 that this power is exercised by God "toward us who believe." Note that Paul places himself on an equal footing beside his Ephesian brothers and sisters. So this power is not exclusive or elite power. It is available (& necessary) for even the simplest believer. The key word in this verse is the word "believe." "Faith" is the noun, and "believe" is the verb, and both convey the same idea. Following the "machinery" analogy of the previous paragraph, faith is the "switch" we push to release the power of God in and through our lives. Doubt, fear, and skepticism will short-circuit that power in us. It is available to faith alone, and must be appropriated by faith alone. So it is essential that we understand what faith is.

Faith is the faculty of taking God into the heart and accommodating Him there. Faith is *God-receptiveness*. Faith appropriates the nature of God into the human heart, and enables Him to transform the believer's character and conduct (I John 4:8). Faith, like a narrow channel, conveys God's ocean fullness into the lagoons of human need.

If you should take a boat up the Nile River to central Egypt, you would often see simple farmers with homemade irrigation devices, lifting water from the Nile by buckets affixed on a horizontal pole, which in turn is affixed atop a vertical pole. As the horizontal pole is rotated, each bucket is filled with the water of the Nile and is manually revolved to be emptied into the ditches of the farmer's field. So the mighty Nile River fills an irrigation ditch! Even so, through the simple "irrigating" device of man's receptive faith, the mighty power of God will flow into and through a Christian.

The late great pastor and author Ray Stedman has this paragraph in one of his books:

Available Power for Available People

"I've been doing a bit of electrical work in an addition to my home, and I've discovered that electricity follows a pattern of its own and takes no notice of how I feel at the moment. That can be a *shocking* experience! Electricity is not in the slightest degree impressed with my position as a pastor of Peninsula Bible Church. It doesn't hesitate to retaliate for any violation of its laws that I commit. It is up to me to discover how it works, and then to respect it if I want to use it."

The same is true of God's great power. It will remain totally indifferent to me and aloof from me if I don't discover what it is, what the laws of its operation are, and how to adjust myself to those laws and thus to receive His power. But if I do learn the "laws" of the Holy Spirit's operation and adapt myself to Him by means of those "laws," I can experience His power and can be a channel through which it flows into the world.

So each Christian is not only to be a point of *reception* of God's power; he is also to be a point of *release* for God's power. According to verse 15, Christians are not storage batteries for God's power as much as they are relay stations for it. "According to your faith be it unto you." You can (will) have all the power of God that you will make room for. The only limit is the capacity of your faith. Wherever faith links the believer to the Lord Jesus, His nature begins to flow in to the waiting, expectant heart, and then to flow out toward all the saints and toward the surrounding world of lost people. May God grant that more and more of His people will awaken to their privileges and their responsibilities with regard to God's mighty power.

.

.

Chapter Nine

THE SPIRIT-FILLED LIFE

Ephesians 5:18;

"And be not drunk with wine, wherein is excess, but be filled with the Spirit."

To be filled with the Holy Spirit is the ideal condition of a Christian believer in this life on this earth. Thus, our text is as important for living the Christian life as any single verse in the Word of God. Not only is the fullness of the Holy Spirit the *ideal* condition of a Christian on earth, it is also absolutely *indispensable* if we are to live the life, walk the walk, talk the talk, and fulfill the many obligations of a Christian. There is simply no way to do these things without the enabling of the Holy Spirit. Without His fullness, we are thrown back upon our own weak resources, our own poor intentions, and our own weak and stumbling ways. No one is to think that we are peculiarly unable and that we are morbidly down-playing, bad-mouthing and self-deprecating ourselves. Oh no, we are just like the universal lot of mankind—helpless and hopeless without God's salvation and the filling of the Holy Spirit.

Let me remind you of the location of our text. It is found in *Paul's letter to the Ephesians,* a New Testament book that has as high a reach of spiritual revelation and theology as any book in the Bible. The occurrence of our text in this setting indicates that the fullness of the Holy Spirit is the best (*only*) means of *understanding* God's revelation and the best (*only*) means of maximizing that revelation. Furthermore, the letter to the Ephesians is divided into two equal parts, the first three chapters being devoted primarily to *Christian doctrine,* and the last three chapters to *Christian duty.* Chapters 1-3, the Christian *proposition*, chapters 4-6, the Christian *practice.* Chapters 1-3, the Christian *concept*, chapters 4-6, the Christian's *conduct.* This outline is not artificial, but actual.

Then let me further remind you that our text is located *at the very heart of the practical section of Ephesians.* Ephesians 5:18 is midway in chapters 4-6. Ephesians 4-6 is a masterpiece in exploring the dimensions and demands of Christian living. It is full of teaching about our responsibility as Christians. However, anyone who has ever attempted such things as this without the endowment of heaven (basically, that is *religion*) knows how hopeless his effort is. Without the fullness of the Holy Spirit, a human being is left to his own sterile effort (and resulting frustration), to his own erratic intentions and commitments (and the resulting mosaic of failure), and to the stark and cold practice of legalism (and the resulting burdens of it). In short, he would be left to draw from the empty well of the "flesh." *So verse 18 is indeed as important as any verse in the Word of God for living the Christian life.* If I made a list of verses that contain essential counsel for the Christian, Ephesians 5:18 would be one of the two top verses on my list. So we will explore it as carefully and extensively as possible in one brief study.

I. THE CONCEPT

First, we will examine *the concept* of being filled with the Holy Spirit. What does the Bible mean when it speaks of being filled with the Holy Spirit? Without a careful and candid investigation of Biblical revelation about the fullness of the Holy Spirit, I am left to surmise, opinion and guesswork in this matter. And that is

The Spirit-filled Life

precisely what has happened in a substantial portion of the Christian community, resulting in much confusion, much unexamined belief, and much malpractice with regard to the Holy Spirit.

To put it simply (and yet even this statement must be given much thoughtful attention), the fullness of the Holy Spirit means that the indwelling Holy Spirit is having His way unimpeded, ungrieved and unquenched in the life of the individual Christian, and that the believer is therefore fulfilling his role in the plan of God for him at that moment. It means that the believer immediately agrees with God when the Holy Spirit reveals a "new" area of truth to him, or checks him in some area of disobedience or shortfall. Thus, the believer yields to the Holy Spirit *at every intersection of life*, deferring his poor perception and practice to the wise and capable Holy Spirit.

The above paragraph *describes* the fullness of the Holy Spirit, but we have yet to *define* it. So let me attempt a definition of the fullness of the Holy Spirit. The fullness of the Holy Spirit is the condition that prevails in a believer's life when *the Holy Spirit of God has inner possession, mastery and control of the human spirit of man. The fullness of the Holy Spirit means that all the faculties and powers of personality are brought into subjection to and under the supervision of the Holy Spirit of God.* Of course, this condition can only occur in the life of a Christian, because no lost man is indwelt by the Spirit of God.

Lest I take too much for granted, let me use a paragraph to identify and explain the Person of the Holy Spirit. Let me emphasize that the Holy Spirit *is* a *Person*. The Holy Spirit is not a mere impersonal force or influence. He is a *definite* person—just as you and I are definite persons. Also, He is a *Divine Person*, a personal member of the triunity (Trinity) of God. He is co-equal, co-essential, co-existent, and co-eternal with God the Father and God the Son. Each is a Person. Furthermore, the Holy Spirit is a *dynamic* Person, possessing the full dynamism of God. That is, He is Omni-competent or Omni-capable; He possesses the full capability of the All-powerful God. He is also Omni-intelligent, with the full knowledge and wisdom of the All-knowing, All-wise God. Again, (and this is a crucial understanding to a Christian), the Holy Spirit is a *delightful* Person. He is innately a fulfilled, happy Member of the Godhead. He is as loving (and as Holy) as God the Father and God the Son. He is often pictured in the Bible as very gentle and very sensitive with regard to moral and spiritual things, and thus is bent on the destruction (another characteristic of the entire Trinity) of that which would destroy *Him and all that He loves.* So, while He is delightful and dynamic in supporting spiritual reality in your life, He is equally and dynamically destructive of that which opposes the Divine purposes in your life. So it must be finally and decisively stated that the Holy Spirit is also a *destructive* Person, always engaged in aggressive warfare within "the castle of man's soul" against sin in all of its multi-form expressions.

Read the above paragraph again, and remember that it is this Person who wants to fill your life, and will do so with your agreement, cooperation and permission. The word "filled" is the translation of the Greek word, *plaroo,* which means to fill full, so full that there is no part left empty. So we are talking about a Christian life that is wholly possessed by and filled with the Holy Spirit, and thus is utterly absorbed with the life and fullness of Jesus Christ. The Holy Spirit is simply the agent and channel through Whom Christ enters, possesses and operates in the yielded heart. This consolidates the entire Christian life into a great simplicity. The Christian's will must be totally surrendered to the Holy Spirit and then Jesus (mediated by the Person and Presence of the Holy Spirit) "takes over" and reproduces His own life in all the diversified experiences and activities of our seemingly "complex" life. The Holy Spirit is occasionally identified in the New Testament as "the Spirit of Christ," and this is the reason why. There is nothing which God requires of a human being, or which a human being can ever need in the varied experiences and emergencies of life but that Christ possesses it for us, and we may have it in exact fulfillment of our every need by simply "receiving" and "negotiating" Him. "Of His fullness we all have received, and grace for grace" (John 1:16), and the Administrator of this fullness is the Holy Spirit.

The Spirit-filled Life

In defining the fullness of the Holy Spirit, it is essential that we give careful attention to Paul's exact words. What does the word "filled" mean in the New Testament. Occasionally, it is used to describe a vessel that is filled with a substance, like water filling a jar. Unfortunately, this is the way many Christians understand the fullness of the Holy Spirit. Being filled with the Holy Spirit does not mean that the believer is partially filled at one moment and then additionally filled later. The Holy Spirit is not received by degrees or in doses. He is a Person, and He came into the individual believer as the Mediator of Christ and His salvation at the very moment he trusted and received Jesus Christ into his life. Furthermore, once the Holy Spirit is in a believer, it is a matter of permanent residence. Remember that Paul said to the terribly carnal Corinthian Christians (note the chiding sound of his words), "Know ye not that ye are the Temple of God, and that the Holy Spirit dwells in you?" Two terms bear major emphasis in that question, the terms "Temple of God" and "in you." In both occurrences of the pronoun "you" in that verse, the plural form is used, meaning "all of you." Paul is referring to the entire (carnal) Corinthian church! Then, in I Corinthians 6:19, he repeats the idea, but here he used the singular form, which means he is now referring to the individual (carnal) Corinthian Christian. Note, too, that his chiding sound intensifies when he addresses the individual (Paul is saying in effect, 'you should know this as the first truth in your Christian life, and if you know it, why are you living as if you don't?)' I Corinthians 6:19 says, "What? Know ye not that your body is the Temple of the Holy Spirit Who is in you, which ye have of God and ye are not your own?" Paul does not say, "Be clean and spiritual so that the Holy Spirit will fill you"; rather he says, "Let the Holy Spirit fill you so that you will be clean and spiritual." Thus, being filled is not an additional reception of the Holy Spirit, but a maximizing of the Person Who dwells within every believer. As you commit to Him (surrender to His Person), He consecrates you (sanctifies, or sets you apart, to His Person and His use). Also, because He is a delightful Person, you should learn to progressively "delight yourself in" Him, and He will progressively give you "the desires of Your heart."

This point can be summarized by three subsidiary points. (1) To be "filled" carries the idea of possession, or total control. We will return to this point later in the study. (2) To be "filled" carries the idea of penetration, or permeation, or pervasiveness. Thus, to be "filled with the Holy Spirit" means exactly that.

The Greek word used here (*pleroo*; the 'e' is pronounced with a long 'a' sound) is used in John 12:3 to describe the result of Mary's breaking of the alabaster flask of costly ointment to pour its contents on the feet of Jesus. The text says, "The house was filled with the perfume of the ointment." That is to say, the fragrance was all-pervasive, filling every nook and cranny of the enclosure. In the same way, our lives are to be permeated with the Holy Spirit.

More than merely being indwelt, I am interpenetrated (with no "compartment" of me left excepted, exempted or excluded) by the Holy Spirit just like my body is interpenetrated by the blood that flows throughout. This is one of the major problems in the usual Christian life. The believer assumes everything is top-notch in his life, though there are numerous provinces or compartments of his life that are carelessly ignored. One such "problem province" is his mind, which for many believers is a passive compartment that is merely kept conveniently neutral but never generates any of the dynamic planning and acting the New Testament calls for, or their minds are like a garden patch which grows many weeds, or a playground for vagrant and evil concepts. Another is his will, which is often allowed to remain passive and idle and thus sins of omission galore fill his life (that Christian simply drifts into "won't" because of a passive will). The list goes on and on, and usually unchallenged. One of the great Greek philosophers said, "The unexamined life is not worth living," and if that is true for a pagan philosopher, how much more true is it for a Christ-indwelt Christian! The list includes the use of the believer's tongue, the use of his eyes, the use of his capacity for discipline in devotion to the one overwhelming mandate and model of Jesus to "make disciples," the use of his feet (both in the areas of where he goes and especially in the area of his refusal to consider 'going' the full distance in the world-call of Jesus **for him as for every Christian**). In short, the typical Christian seems to see the Christian life more as a vacation to be operated at his leisure and for his pleasure, than as a vocation to be developed under the vocational Lordship of Jesus for total obedience to the mandate of Heaven and the total glory of the All-worthy God. Instead, all areas, provinces and compartments of the believer's life are to be consciously yielded to the Holy Spirit so they can be fully penetrated, permeated and pervaded by Him. What a place this world would be, or the church would be, if this were true of all Christians! The dynamic and delightful Holy Spirit would spread His delight, His satisfaction, His pleasure, His gratification throughout each believer's life, throughout the Church, and throughout the world! May God hasten that day! Why not begin today, with yourself, as you read these words? (3) To be "filled" carries the idea of propulsion. Get a concordance and check the use off the word "filled" in the narrative accounts of the New Testament. The person "filled" always acted or spoke under the propulsion, the enablement, the empowerment, the enduement, of the Holy Spirit. Often he was "carried along" or "driven," and the recorded results (where he was carried to, where he was driven to, where he went, what distances he traveled, what he said, what he did) provide an education for the studious believer in the intended outcome of the Spirit-filled life.

This, then, is the meaning of being filled with the Holy Spirit of God. More needs to be said about the word "filled," but we will return to that later in the study.

II. THE COMMAND

Second, we must note that our text places the "be filled" verb in the imperative mood. Thus, it is a command of God, a command of equal force to any positive or negative command God ever gave. Christian, realize at this moment that you are clearly commanded by Almighty God to "be filled with the Holy Spirit."

It is instructive to investigate the relationship of the Holy Spirit to every believer. Let me mention several "relationship realities" that the Holy Spirit has produced in the life of each believer. First, every believer is *born* of the Spirit (John 3:5). When a person is saved, he is regenerated by the Spirit, or quickened from spiritual death in sin to spiritual life in Christ. Then, every believer is *assured* by the Holy Spirit. Paul said, "The Spirit Himself bears witness with our spirit, that we are the children of God. This is the inner assurance possessed by every born again person that he has been accepted by Christ, and can never lose his salvation. This assurance is wrought in the human spirit by the Holy Spirit. Then, every believer has received both the *sealing* of the Spirit and the *earnest* of the Spirit. The sealing guarantees the ownership of the believer by God and the believer's security in salvation. The earnest is the "down payment" given to the believer by God to guarantee his inheritance until he acquires final possession of it. Fourth, every believer (*every* believer) has been once-for-all (aorist tense verb; I Corinthians 12:13) *baptized* into the body of Christ by the Holy Spirit. The baptism of the Spirit is the means by which He takes independent and isolated believers and incorporates them into the church as the very body of Jesus Christ. Fifth, every believer is *indwelt* by the Holy Spirit. "If any man have not the Spirit of Christ, he is none of His" (Romans 8:9). "Your body is the Temple of the Holy Spirit, who dwells in you" (I Corinthians 6:19). It is the indwelling Presence of the Holy Spirit that provides the potential for the victorious Christian life. But that victory is not automatic; it depends on the fullness of the Holy Spirit.

All of these relational results that the Holy Spirit produces in the believer's life occur simultaneously at the moment of salvation. Thus, *no believer is ever commanded in Scripture to be born of the Spirit, or assured of the Spirit, or to seek the sealing or the earnest of the Spirit, or to be baptized by the Spirit, or to be indwelt by the Spirit.* I repeat, all of these "relational benefits" are *automatic by-products of being born again,* and thus there is no need for a believer to seek them later. There is not a single verse in the Bible that commands Christians to seek any of these experiences. However, the fullness

The Spirit-filled Life

of the Holy Spirit is not automatic and thus the believer is commanded to "be filled with the Holy Spirit."

There are fourteen references in the New Testament to the fullness of the Holy Spirit. Four of those are before the Day of Pentecost and all four are recorded in the Gospel of Luke (the book of the Humanity of Jesus, which was always perfectly filled with the Holy Spirit, as ours *should* be). Ten of the fourteen New Testament references concern occurrences on or after the Day of Pentecost. Nine of these are *descriptive* of experiences of the fullness of the Holy Spirit, and one (our text) is *directive* (that is, it commands the fullness, and suggests directions for receiving it). Our text is literally a directive, giving a clear command to every believer to be filled with the Holy Spirit.

Look at the grammar of the word translated "be filled." Every Greek verb has five parts inherent in it. They are tense, voice, mood, person and number. Each is a lesson in itself. This verb is a present tense, meaning that it applies in every believer's life at this very moment. Thus, it involves continuation through every second of every day. There is never a moment after salvation when a Christian is not to be filled with the Spirit. This involves daily, moment-by-moment surrender to the Holy Spirit's control. Thus, no past filling is adequate for this moment, and no present filling will be adequate for tomorrow. The present tense forbids carelessness in my Christian walk, and also means that if I do sin away the fullness, I am responsible to immediately do what is necessary to get it back. Because it must be maintained and may be broken, the fullness of the Holy Spirit may (and must) recur many times in a believer's erratic daily walk. Without assuming anything, I am to be filled now.

This verb is also a *passive voice* verb. Some translations say, "*Let* the Holy Spirit fill you," and this captures the passive voice. The passive voice means that the recipient does not receive the fullness by self-effort or by engaging in activities that entice the Spirit to fill him. The fullness of the Holy Spirit is something that is done for us and to us, not something we can do ourselves. This implies that our primary "contribution" is *emptiness,* and the primary condition for receiving the fullness is *faith*. The fullness of the Holy Spirit is not an *attainment*, but an *obtainment*. It is *received*, not *achieved*. You were saved by grace through faith without works, and you are filled with the Holy Spirit the same way.

This verb is also an *imperative mood* verb. "Be saved" is not a suggestion, or an invitation, or a hope, or a wish, but a command. It is not a luxury which a Christian may take at his leisure; it is a command. The fact that it is a command stresses the idea that God is urgently concerned about the spirituality of His people. The fact that it is a command clearly means that it is a serious sin for a Christian to not be filled with the Spirit. Because fullness is available to all and expected of all, emptiness is now a sin. The Christian community needs a fresh persuasion and conviction of this truth. The positive side of the command is that "God's commands are His enablings." If He says *must*, that necessarily includes *may*. If you are *commanded* to be filled, you *can* be filled!

This verb is also a second person plural verb. The second person plural means "you," and the plural means "all of you." Too many Christians have the mistaken notion that the fullness of the Holy Spirit is reserved for pastors, evangelists, missionaries or others who have a more prominent place in the Lord's work than they. This is a fatal fallacy. Each Christian has the same responsibility as any other Christian.

Remember, dear Christian, that at this very moment, God has commanded you to be filled with the Holy Spirit. In the very same verse of the very same paragraph of the very same chapter of the very same book of the very same Bible in which I as a Christian am commanded to "be not drunk with wine," I am commanded with equal force and authority to be "filled with the Holy Spirit."

Several years ago, a layman in a Midwestern U.S. city was entertaining Billy Graham in his home while Mr. Graham was preaching a crusade in that city. In the course of their conversation, the layman said, "We had a very sad experience in our church recently. We had to dismiss a leader from membership because he came to church drunk." Mr. Graham quietly answered, "What does your church do to members who attend church not filled with the Holy Spirit?" The puzzled man asked what Graham meant, and Billy answered, "The same verse that commands a Christian to not be drunk with wine also commands him to be filled with the Holy Spirit. If you dismiss a member for getting drunk, should you not also discipline members for not being filled with the Spirit?" Mr. Graham certainly was not suggesting a legalistic discipline imposed on a believer for failure in an area of inner appropriation, but his point was well taken and extremely serious. For you as a Christ to ignore this command would be absolutely disastrous to your Christian life.

III. THE CONTRAST

It is obvious that our text contains a *contrast* between two factors. One is "wine," the other is the "Spirit," that is, the Holy Spirit of God. Two stimulants are mentioned in the text. One is a *superficial* stimulant which is ingested from the outside. The other is a *supernatural* stimulant which is resident within. One is *diabolical*, the other is *Divine*. Wine makes a man *less of a man*, not *more*; the Holy Spirit makes a man *more of a man*, not *less*. To be drunk with wine tends to make a man totally *irresponsible*, but being filled with the Spirit causes the believer to act *responsibly* in all matters. Being drunk with wine is *disabling*; to be filled with the Spirit is *enabling*. To be "drunk with wine" is to be *devil*-intoxicated; to be "filled with the Spirit" is to be *Divinely* intoxicated.

Another contrast is hidden in the text itself. Note the parallelism of the verse:

> "*Be not drunk with wine,*
> *But be filled with the Spirit.*"

But the verse has an additional phrase which throws it out of balance. After the words, "Be not drunk with wine is the additional phrase, "wherein is excess," but no such addition is made after the words, "But be filled with the Spirit." The phrase, "wherein is excess," means that wine-drunkenness involves extravagant excess. One cannot become drunk with wine without consuming too much wine. Drunkenness means debauchery. But the Spirit's fullness never produces debauchery or excess. *It is not possible to have an excess of the Spirit's fullness.*

Furthermore, drunkenness means a loss of self-control. A man is not truly "drunk with wine" unless he has lost control of himself, but one of the fruits of the Holy Spirit is "self control" (Galatians 5:23). A Christian who is filled with the Spirit is never transported beyond himself where he can no longer control his actions.

So there is contrast suggested in our text between being "drunk with wine" and being "filled with the Spirit."

IV. THE COMPARISON

It is obvious to me that the text also intends to suggest a *comparison* between being "drunk with wine" and being "filled with the Spirit." Let's pursue the suggestion.

In three different New Testament texts, there is a suggested parallel between being drunk and being filled with the Spirit. Of John the Baptist it was said, "He shall be great in the sight of the Lord, and shall drink neither wine nor strong drink; he shall be filled with the Holy Spirit" (Luke 1:15). In a veiled parallel, Jesus Himself, filled with the Spirit, was called "a winebibber" (Matthew 11:19). On the day of Pentecost, the observers said, "These men are full of new wine," but Peter replied, "These are not drunk, as you suppose," and then he explained the filling of the Holy Spirit (Acts 2:13-16). In our text, a possible comparison is drawn between being "drunk with wine" and being "filled with the Spirit." What are the possible points of similarity?

First, when a person is drunk, he has *lost control of himself, and cannot hide his drunkenness.* The first test a police officer gives a person suspected of "driving under the influence" is a walking test. In both conditions, the person's walk is affected—his physical walk in the case of drunkenness and his moral behavior in the other instance. In being "filled with the Spirit," a believer has voluntarily surrendered the control of himself into the control of Another, and doesn't even attempt to hide the fullness. In both conditions, the person is under a power from outside himself that has entered

The Spirit-filled Life

into him. Both stimulants, the "wine" and the "Spirit", completely master the person whom they control.

Second, when a person is drunk, he is either *empty of everything else, or soon will be*. How many times have drunk people "emptied themselves" of everything in their stomachs! Even so, a person who is "filled with the Spirit" is willing to be self-emptied.

Third, a person who is drunk with wine *has boldness to speak, though he might be very timid when he is not drunk*. Both his speech and his song are freed from normal restrictions. Numerous texts show the relationship between the fullness of the Holy Spirit and the freedom to speak for Christ. Luke 1:41 says, "Elizabeth was filled with the Holy Spirit, and she spoke out with a loud voice." Luke 1:67 says, "Zacharias was filled with the Holy Spirit, and he prophesied." Acts 2:4 says, "They were all filled with the Holy Spirit, and began to speak." Acts 4:8 says, "Then Peter, filled with the Holy Spirit, said unto them…" Acts 4:31 says, "They were all filled with the Holy Spirit, and they spoke the Word of God with boldness."

Fourth, when a person is drunk with wine, he *"jus' luvs everybody,"* though he may care for no one when he is sober. The first-named "fruit of the Spirit" in Galatians 5:22 is "love." When a person is filled with the Spirit, he loves everybody.

Fifth, when a person is drunk with wine, *he just wants one thing—more wine*. Even so, when a Christian is filled with the Holy Spirit, he has lost his "taste" for lesser stimulants and wants more and more of the control of the Spirit and the results of that fullness.

Sixth, when a person is drunk with wine, he may lose a lot of friends, but he also gains a lot of new, different friends. Other people with similar tastes will linger at the same bar and drink out of the same bottle. Even so, when a Christian is "filled with the Spirit," he loses a lot of old acquaintances who do not understand his new interest, but he will also gain a lot of new and different friends, those who have the same taste for the Spirit's fullness which he has.

Seventh, when a person is drunk with wine, *he is animated by an extraordinary fervency*. This is what confused the observers on the day of Pentecost. The fervency produced on that day by the Holy Spirit within Christians was mistaken for that produced by new wine (Acts 2:13).

Halford Luccock was once the professor of homiletics at Yale Divinity School. One day, a policeman approached him at the intersection of city streets in Boston and asked him this question, "Dr., what do the letters 'D.D.' mean after a minister's name?" Dr. Luccock replied, "Those letters mean that the person has a conferred 'Doctor of Divinity' degree from a college or seminary. Why do you ask?" "Well," replied the policeman, "I noticed in the newspaper this morning that a minister with the letters 'D.D.' following his name was coming to speak at our church. One of the charges we inscribe after a person's name at the police station is abbreviated into the letters 'D.D,' and that is the charge of being 'Drunk and Disorderly.' You can imagine what I thought when I saw those letters after a minister's name." Dr. Luccock said he reached his home before the implications of the conversation reached his heart. "Why, these are the very charges that were brought against the believers who were involved in the Coming of the Holy Spirit on the Day of Pentecost. They were charged with being 'Drunk and Disorderly' because of the difference the Holy Spirit made in their lives." Then the thought came, "Wouldn't it be a wonderful thing today if Christians made such a similar difference in their communities that they, too, were charged with being 'drunk with the new wine of the Spirit's fullness,' and 'disorderly in the trouble they cause Satan'?" Wonderful, indeed!

In summary, strong drink is known to make quiet men talkative, to make mean and selfish men generous, to make timid men bold, to make mournful, sad men to be filled with joy for a little time until the intoxication wears off. Is the comparison not obvious? Dear Christian, do these symptoms of the fullness characterize you?

V. THE CONDITIONS

Next, we need to consider *the conditions* for being filled with the Holy Spirit. The command in the text indicates that the fullness

The Spirit-filled Life

of the Holy Spirit is not automatic. Certain conditions must be met before the individual believer is filled with the Holy Spirit. Let me suggest some conditions that must be met in order for you to be filled with the Holy Spirit of God. I am going to place these conditions into two categories, *suggested* conditions and *Scripturally stated* conditions. Actually, both are Scriptural, but one is gleaned from the general interpretation of several texts, while the other is the specified list of three conditions extracted from a single text.

Let me begin with the *general* or *suggested* conditions gathered from several texts.

First, you must *acknowledge the need to be filled, and realize that God wants to fill you.* If He has commanded you to be filled, He is intensely interested in your fullness. God knows that we cannot fulfill any responsibility we have as Christians, or serve Him according to His will, unless we are filled with the Holy Spirit.

Second, you must *check your motive for seeking the fullness.* Many Christians annul their own request for the Spirit's fullness by seeking an experience instead of the pleasure of God, by seeking self-satisfaction instead of the will of God, by seeking the respect of others that comes by their fullness instead of seeking the smile of God.

Charles Spurgeon showed the importance of motive in these picturesque words: "I looked at Jesus, and the dove of peace flew into my heart, but then, I looked at the dove of peace—and it flew away." That is, if my motive is Jesus Himself, Jesus and His glory, Jesus and His pleasure, Jesus and His purpose, Jesus and His will, the Holy Spirit will fill me and fulfill my motive which is merely an echo of His motive. Paul said, "My will is that Christ may be glorified in my body, whether it be by may life or my death." The Holy Spirit will never fill us to enable us to gain celebrity, or for personal comfort. The Holy Spirit can only fill those believers who are willing to be united with Him in His purpose of glorifying Christ.

Third, you must *renounce and forsake all know sin.* After all, He is not named the *Holy* Spirit without having a definite bias against sin and unholiness. Psalm 66:18 says, "If I regard (give favorable place to) sin in my heart, the Lord will not hear me." The old Puritans said, "If we get hold of God at all, we must take hold of Him by the handle of our sins." That is, confession and repentance of sin will "clear the decks" for the fullness of the Holy Spirit in our lives.

Fourth, *ask God to fill you and trust Him to do so.* Agonizing prayer is not necessary in order to be filled with the Holy Spirit, but it may be necessary to prove your desire to be filled. Ephesians 5:18 commands us to be filled, thus clearly revealing the will of God for us. I John 5:14-15 says, "This is the confidence that we have in Him, that if we ask anything according to His will, He hears us. And if we know that He hears us, we know that we have the petitions that we desired of Him." The first of those two verses informs us that it is God's will to fill us, and the second one informs us that if we ask anything in prayer that agrees with His will, He will grant the request. So we may accept the fullness of the Spirit by faith on the basis of our agreement with God's revealed will. Remember, *just as you were saved by grace through faith without works, you are also filled with the Spirit by grace through faith without works.* You simply *acknowledge* your need, *ask* Him to fill you, *accept* the fullness by faith, and *act* in keeping with the revealed purposes of the Holy Spirit. Consider the alternatives—to not admit the need to be filled, to not approach Him with an admitted need, to be indifferent to the Holy Spirit and His fullness, and to disobey God at the point of His revealed will.

Fifth, you must *continue abiding in Christ, continue obeying Him, and continue feeding on His Word.* I have developed the habit of closing all correspondence with these words: "Keep praying, praising, trusting, studying and teaching His Manual, and *building disciples. One day, you will be very, very glad you did."* This could also almost be a formula for the fullness of the Holy Spirit.

Finally, *be willing to reveal Jesus Christ in every situation you may be in.* I once asked an electrician, "Is it true that electrical current will not continue flowing into and through a conducting wire after that wire becomes saturated with the current? That is, it will not continue to fill that which it can't get out of? Is that true?"

The Spirit-filled Life

His answer was, "Yes, that is true." The Holy Spirit will not long flow into a person whom He cannot flow through and out of in blessing someone else.

Let me conclude with the *Scripturally stated* conditions extracted from a single text about the Person and Work of the Holy Spirit. The text is John 7:37-39, and it explains both the *requirements* for being filled with the Spirit, and the *results* of the fullness in a believer's life. Here is a brief exploration of both the specified requirements and the stated results. First, the requirements or conditions for the Spirit's fullness.

"In the last day, that great day of the feast, Jesus stood and cried, saying, "If any man *thirst*, let him *come unto Me* and *drink*. He who believes on Me as the Scripture has said, *out of his innermost being shall flow rivers of living water*. (But this spake He of the Spirit, Whom they that believe on Him should receive: for the Holy Spirit was not yet given, because Jesus was not yet glorified"). Note that when Jesus spoke these words, the Day of Pentecost was still future, and would only come after the Death/Resurrection/Ascension/Glorification of Jesus. And notice that every true believer in Christ would "receive" the Spirit through his/their believing.

The three conditions for the fullness of the Spirit according this text are stated in two symbolic terms and one very literal term.

First, "if any one *thirst*." Step number one in Jesus' conditions is that there must be in the believer's life *a consuming recognition of need for the fullness of the Spirit.* There must be a dominating thirst for Christ, His Truth, His Life, His service, etc. Now, there is a big difference between *emptiness* and *thirst*. The cup in the kitchen may be empty on the shelf, but it is never thirsty for the coffee that may soon fill it. The gasoline tank of your automobile may be *empty* but it is not *thirsty* for gasoline. No lost person is thirsty for the fullness of the Holy Spirit, and tragically, the same is true of multitudes of professing Christians.

When I became a Christian (over 61 years ago!), the very first verse God magnetized to my heart was this precious verse from the Sermon on the Mount: "Blessed is the man who hungers and thirsts after righteousness, for he shall be filled." I found out much later that, in the Greek text, the word translated "hunger" is a word which means to "hunger for the whole loaf of bread," and the word translated "thirst" means to "thirst for the whole bottle of water." I asked God to give me this hunger and thirst—and He has been answering that prayer ever since!

How does a person become thirsty for Christ and righteousness. S. D. Gordon, the great devotional preacher of the past, answered the question with this wise advice, "Look at the Fountain!" Focus on Jesus will make us thirsty for Him and His living water.

Before we leave the "thirst" condition, let me tell you that the verb translated "thirst" is a *present active subjunctive* Greek verb. The present tense means that it applies at this very moment. The active voice means that you have a very specific and important role to play in this—that is, that the thirst is your responsibility. The subjunctive mood must be understood. In Greek, the subjunctive mood is the mood of *potential*. It clearly reveals again that this is not an automatic occurrence in a believer's life. It is evident that, for one sad reason or another, not all believers have this overwhelming thirst for Christ and His fullness. This thirst is *potential* and the fullness of the Spirit is *conditional*. So this thirst is not to be taken for granted. As Gordon suggested, *look at The Fountain (Jesus) until your thirst rages for Him.*

The second condition for the fullness of the Holy Spirit is, *"Let him come unto Me."* Give special attention to this important feature, which I will show by putting the three conditions in an isolated column:

"Thirst"
"Come unto Me"
"Drink"

You can clearly see by this column that the second condition is the only one of the three in which the verb is followed by an object. "Unto Me." Jesus is the focus and the force behind the Holy Spirit's fullness. The Holy Spirit does not publicize Himself. Jesus said, "When He has come, He will take the things of Mine and

The Spirit-filled Life

show them unto you." We must come (and keep coming) to Jesus Christ Himself if we are to be filled with the Holy Spirit and maintain that fullness. Thus (condition # two), there must be *a complete and continuing reliance upon Jesus Christ.* The word "come" in the text is a *present active imperative* verb. That is, it is a command that is in force at this very moment, and you are expected to do what this command tells you to do—keep on coming to Jesus Christ. We are not commanded to come to a conference, or to a meeting, or to a service, or to an activity for Christ. None of these must be allowed to displace personal relationship with Christ Himself. A great lady in Texas once said before a great conference, "The Christian life is one gigantic 'Yes' to Jesus, followed by a lifetime succession of 'Uh-huhs.'" Yes, indeed! Our happy assignment is to give Jesus Christ complete freedom in every province of our lives. *His* freedom in *me* will give *me fullness* in *Him.* He must be free to fill me and to flow through me. The product of His flow through me is often called "fruit."

The final condition specified in our selected text is, " Let him come unto Me and *drink."* We must approach Christ, and appropriate His gift of the Spirit's fullness. Charles Howard, evangelist and Bible teacher of a past generation, often said, "We are to drink, not just gargle. We are to drink, not just sip a taste." The tense of the verb indicates continual appropriation. "Keep on drinking," the text says. Thus, there must be *a constant reception and accommodation of the Spirit's fullness* in each of our lives.

When a thirsty person drinks water, that water instantly begins to be assimilated into the cellular structure of his body. It is absorbed into the body, and refreshes and replenishes his entire physical existence. The same is true of our appropriation of the Holy Spirit's fullness. When a person drinks water, he does not see the inward assimilation that always occurs, but his obliviousness does not prevent the assimilation. Even so, the Christian will not see most of the "transaction" when the Spirit fills him—but he knows that his thirst has been quenched, he is satisfied, and good health and much fruit are the by-products of the right intake of the Water of Life!

Studies in the Person and Work of the Holy Spirit

One final thought about the requirements for fullness before we briefly examine the results of the fullness of the Holy Spirit in a believer's life. A good channel is always receiving, always ready to flow, and thus always full. Are you (am I) always receiving the Holy Spirit's fullness? Are you always ready to flow? Are you always full?

Now, let's examine the *results*, or the *consequences*, of the fullness of the Holy Spirit. Again, the text does not give an exhaustive list of the results, but the result it does give is overwhelming.

Jesus indicated in the text that when the *fullness* is *experienced*, a *flow* will be *expressed*. A *flowing* will follow the *filling*. In fact, the quickest way to abort the filling is to cease to seek and find and use outlets for the Spirit's flow. *If He cannot flow out to produce fruit, He will quickly cease to flow in to produce fruit.* Jesus said that when a believer meets the conditions for fullness, "out of his innermost being shall flow rivers of living water" (verse 38b).

Herein lies the greatest problem of the typical Christian and the typical church—they are ingrown, introverted, imploding, instead of outgoing, outflowing, world-impacting. One only has to contrast the *implosion* of the typical church today with the *explosion* that produced the Book of Acts. You see, when water is unimpeded in its movement, it tends to flow out from its point of release. The Biblical direction is *OUT*. Jesus specified the locational assignment when He said, "....both in Jerusalem, and in Judea, and in Samaria, and unto the uttermost part of the earth." Note that the concentric circles suggested (Acts 1:8) are *outgoing* and *enlarging*. This is the strategy a believer (or a church) is to follow in impacting the whole wide world.

Note the specifics of the product. First, the fullness and flow of the Holy Spirit will produce a *living* supply. "Out of his innermost being shall flow rivers of *living* water." "Living" water is distinguished in the Bible from still, stagnant, stinking water. What a word to describe the Holy Spirit's impact—everything lives where He freely fills (see Ezekiel 47). Question: is your inner life foul and stinking because of some residue of sin there? Or is it merely *nice* and *neutral*? I wonder what it is going to be like when

The Spirit-filled Life

Jesus tells us that the Christian *niceness* and *neutrality* which constitute the "norm" we often see among Christians in church were, in fact, radical enemies of His purpose?

Second, the fullness and flow of the Holy Spirit will produce a *large* supply. "Out of his innermost being will flow *rivers* of living water." It is not "trickles," or "brooks," or "rivulets," or "streams" of living water. It is not even a "river," but *rivers*. The word translated "rivers" is the very word Jesus used in Matthew 7:25, 27, when He described the two houses, one built on rock and the other on sand. In each case, "the rains descended, the floods came, and the winds blew, and beat upon that house." The house built on rock withstood the storm, while the house built on sand collapsed under the assault of the storm. The word translated "floods" in that text is the same word translated "rivers" here. It is obvious that Jesus Christ intends a gigantic flow of His life through each of His children. It is obvious that Jesus Christ intends that this flow extend "*OUT*"—to "the uttermost part of the earth." It is obvious that Jesus intends vast fullness, freshness and fruitfulness to characterize the lives of His followers. How am I doing at this point? And you?

As I write these words, I hold in my hand, before my eyes, a common little plastic conduit called a soda straw. It is about eight to ten inches long, and it has a very small channel. Its purpose is to convey liquids to the mouth of the user (though it may be used for a few other purposes).

Some time ago, my wife Judy and I went to Scotland on a sight-seeing and learning trip. I learned that the southwest shore of the country and the shores of some of the western islands of Scotland are covered with plush (almost tropical) vegetation—yet this is the most northernmost country of Europe! Why? Because the warm flow of the Gulf Stream flows upon the southwest short of Scotland and upon the western shores of Scotland's western islands.

Has it ever occurred to you that the Gulf Stream can flow through a soda straw? Well, it *can!* Oh, not *all* of the Gulf Stream, to be sure, but the Gulf Stream can flow through the little soda straw that I hold in my hand. Of course, there are certain conditions. What are they?

One, the soda straw must be *in the element*. The straw must be placed in the water where the Gulf Stream flows. Even so, a Christian must be in the Divine element. He must "live in the Spirit" (Galatians 5:25). Have you been "born of the Spirit"? (John 3:3) Are you consciously "living in (the sphere of) the Spirit"?

Two, the soda straw in the element must be *parallel to the flow* of the Gulf Stream. If the soda straw is in the Gulf Stream, but "cross-current" to its flow, the straw will be filled with the water, but the stream will not flow through it. What an insight! A Christian can seek to be filled with the Holy Spirit for his own advantage, for his own experience, for his own improvement as a Christian—without the Spirit having full freedom to *flow out* through him. It is only as the Christian serves parallel to the purposes of the Spirit (be very careful here, pondering all the dimensions of the purposes of the Spirit)—*certainly including OUT to the uttermost part of the earth, and with total world impact as the goal*—that the Spirit will fully and freely and fruitfully flow through him.

Three, the soda straw must be *open and unobstructed* if the Gulf Stream is to flow through it. Take the straw in both hands, and bend it with the fingers of one hand. It will bend shut and close the conduit. Better yet, put both hands around the straw as fists and twist the straw in different directions. Now, it has twists and contortions throughout its length, and they may remain even when you release the straw. Again, what Biblical insights await us in the illustration!

There are four basic words used in the Bible to explain and define sin. One is the common word, "sin", which means "to miss the mark." "All have sinned (missed the mark) and come short of the glory of God (the intended target)." "The glory of God" is the manifest perfection of God's character. Thus, *to be a sinner is simply to be less perfect than God is*. And we all qualify—miserably! Another Biblical word for "sin" is the word "trespass", which means to weakly fall out of God's revealed "way". A third word is "transgression," which means to deliberately and willfully step across God's moral and spiritual boundary lines (lines which God has lovingly established for your safety and protection). A fourth word for "sin" is the word "iniquity," a specialized word which defines the inner character twist(s) or distortion(s) which are common to every sinner. As long as "iniquity" continues uncorrected *inside a Christian's life*, the flow of the Spirit's Life and power will be obstructed.

Several years ago, I visited Yellowstone National Park for the first time. Since that first visit, I have eagerly returned several more times. I find the Park to be a place of great mystery and intrigue as well as a place of breath-taking beauty. On my first visit, I was especially fascinated with the Geyser Basin in the Park. Over fifty geysers erupt out of the ground in the basin. Boardwalks have been constructed through the basin so that tourists can get very close to these geysers. Of course, the most famous geyser is "Old Faithful." "Old Faithful" erupts about 110 feet into the air, and it is so regular ("faithful") that the time of each eruption can be calculated within a few seconds. In fact, the eruption times are posted on a large board at the nearby lodge, and a cloud of steamy white water gushes out of the earth, dispersing its thin spray all around the column.

Many people do not know that all fifty of the geysers that erupt in the basin come from the same underground source—and thus have force equal to Old Faithful. However, the next highest eruption is less than fifty feet high. Then the eruptions "drop" in height so that a few don't even reach the surface of the ground; an observer must look down into a hole to see the bubbling stream. Why, if all the geysers come from the same source, and with equal force, does Old Faithful go so high and the rest do not? *The difference is in the shape of the cone through which each geyser flows.* Old Faithful's cone (or "pipe") is straight and smooth, and the flow of the hot steam is unobstructed. But the cone of the others is crooked and erratic, and thus the force of the steam is destroyed by the crookedness of the rock cone.

Studies in the Person and Work of the Holy Spirit

What an illustration of a Christian's life! If there is iniquity hidden beneath the surface in his life, the flow of the Spirit's Life will be prevented or hindered! The day he was saved, God *covered* his hideous inner crookedness with the perfect righteousness of Christ and hid it from His sight, thus perfectly justifying the sinner. However, God will not finally be guilty of a mere bookkeeping transaction that takes dirty sinners to heaven, merely *covered* by the perfect righteousness of Christ. The moment the *crisis* of justification occurs, God also begins the *process* of sanctification. Having counted you "straight" in Christ, God now begins to "hammer" on the iniquity, the remaining character distortions in your inner life, to make you like Christ—and to allow the free flow of the Spirit's Life through you.

There is one other item about the particular soda straw I hold in my hand which I want to mention. This straw has a place in it which is *designed to be bent*. Did you hear that? This straw is actually *made to be bent*. It has some ruffles in its structure about two inches from the top that allow it to be bent. Why was it manufactured to be bent? Here is a lesson! This straw was designed to be bent *for the convenience of the user.* Christian, God designs to bend you—to fit His convenience, to best accommodate His use of you.

Like the open soda straw, in the element, parallel to its flow, open and unobstructed, and available to the User to be bent for His use, the Gulf Stream of God's Life will flow through you.

Finally, the fullness and flow of the Holy Spirit will produce a *lasting* supply. "Out of his innermost being will flow rivers of living water." The verb translated "flow" is a present tense continuous verb, which means, "will keep on flowing." If the believer keeps on thirsting, keeps on coming to Jesus, and keeps on appropriating the fullness He supplies, the believer will keep on flowing with rivers of living water.

Dennis the Menace stood on a chair at the kitchen sink as his mother was preparing to wash the dishes. Water was flowing freely from the faucet in the sink. The puzzled Dennis asked his mother, "How does such a little faucet hold so much water?" I'm sure Mrs. Mitchell explained the connection between the faucet and the reservoir, and the necessity of turning on the faucet to allow the water to flow. As God works in your life and you honor the conditions of Christ's invitation, the world (and the *church*) may one day ask, "How does such a little person hold so much 'Water'?"

Someone sadly lamented, "Most Christians are like a bucket which is half-full and trying to overflow." The invitation of Jesus holds the answer to that lament. Another wisely said, "The surest sign that you are carrying a full bucket is that your feet get wet." When wet, those feet will carry you—and Him—OUT...out to the uttermost parts of the earth. And wherever you go in His fullness, you will leave a trail of new containers and conduits behind, each of whom wants to be filled with His Spirit and overflowing with a ceaseless stream of His Life.

We have looked solidly together at one of the great commands of the Bible, the command to "be filled with the Spirit." In conclusion, would you join me in going prayerfully to the Holy Spirit and courteously saying to Him, "I offer to You the only thing I really possess, my capacity for being filled by You. I bring the capacity, You bring the supply. Would You now fill me and control me from within, then communicate the Lord Jesus to others through me?"

AN ADDENDUM

Theologically, the study of the Person of God the Father, typically called "the First Person of the Divine Trinity," is technically called, *Theology*. The study of the Person of God the Son, typically recognized as "the Second Person of the Trinity," is technically called, *Christology*. The study of God the Holy Spirit, recognized as "the Third Person of the Trinity," is technically call, *Pneumatology*. This latter word derives from the Greek word for "spirit."

It is more than a lingual fascination to say that the Greek word, *pneuma*, has a three-fold meaning. The word itself has *three* dominant translations. The single Greek word, *pneuma*, means either "wind," or "breath," or "spirit." And one should begin to get suspicious of "Divine Sovereignty, Divine Providence, and Divine rigging" when he sees that this is true also in the Hebrew language. The same Hebrew word, *ruach*, is translated by the same three dominant meanings, "wind," "breath," and "spirit." So the word in each language that is coupled with the word "Holy" to give us our Name for the Third Person of the Trinity equally translates by the words, "wind," "breath," and/or "spirit."

Several Biblical concepts are explained and interpreted more completely by this recognition. "God *breathed* into man the *breath* of life, and man became a living soul." "Thus saith the Lord God unto these bones, Behold, I will cause *breath* to enter into you, and you shall live." "Then said He unto me, Prophesy unto the *wind*, prophesy, son of man, and say to the *wind*, Thus saith the Lord God, Come from the four *winds*, O *breath*, and breathe upon these slain, that they may live." "It is not by power, nor by might, but by My *Spirit*, saith the Lord of hosts." "And when he (Jesus) had said this, He *breathed* on them, and said unto them, Receive ye the Holy *Spirit*." This verse is enhanced in meaning when we recognize that the word translated "receive" is *an imperative mood* verb, making this a strong command from the lips of Jesus. Christian, pause and ponder. When Jesus *breathed* on them, He said, "Take ye the Holy *Spirit*." Linger prayerfully over this a long time, until The Teacher begins to explain this line of His Textbook to you. When one begins to realize the meaning, he sees that it is little wonder that Campus Crusade For Christ calls its technique of practice for maintaining the fullness of the Holy Spirit by the title, "Spiritual Breathing." Breathing is comprised of two simple exercises, *exhaling* and *inhaling*, or, *the dismissal of certain body wastes* through the first exercise, and *the intake of certain body nutrients and necessities* through the second exercise. Maintaining the fullness of the Holy Spirit requires both sides of this "spiritual breathing" process. I John 1:9 explains the exhaling function, and Ephesians 5:18 and other related "fullness" passages explain the inhaling function. This is a school of discipleship all by itself, and should be studied again and again.

It has been very captivating to me that "when the Day of Pentecost had fully come" (how much energy and power had their

The Spirit-filled Life

release point on that Day!), "suddenly there came a sound from Heaven as of a rushing mighty *wind.*" This is the first of three "audio-visual symbols, symptoms or effects" of the release of the Holy Spirit on the Day of Pentecost. The three were wind, fire, and speech. To me, the wind is the sign of the Spirit's *coming.* Wind always enters a "place" and *displaces the atmosphere that prevailed there previously.* Every activity or reality of the Christian life, whether individual or corporate, begins with *displacement.* As an example, conviction was necessary before conversion in the life of every saved person in order that the Life of God might displace and replace the selfish, sinful life of the lost person.

Pentecost is a strong suggestion that the first requirement in powerful evangelism, or corporate worship, or church life in general is the displacement of the stinking, carnal atmosphere that will prevail in any situation until it is displaced. It also seems very significant to me that Satan is called "the prince of the power of the air" in Ephesians 2:2. Why? What is the significance of that title in such a crucial passage? It seems that Satan is basically quarantined to the ozone belt around planet earth, and that he has temporary permission to usurp the position of the rightful ruler of the world in order to fulfill Divine purposes. In a remarkable book about Satan, Pastor Irwin Lutzer has a great chapter named, "The Serpent, God's Servant." The Pastor is right! Satan is finally God's servant, and a part of his "service" is to arouse us to militancy, urgency and warfare according to the revelation of Scripture. A part of the vocation of a Spirit-filled Christian is to take the assigned measures to "clear the air" of Satan's control in any situation.

Let's return for a final look at the three translated meanings of both the Greek word, *pneuma,* and the Hebrew word, *ruach.* They both translate by the words, "wind," or "breath," or "spirit." The word, "spirit," when used of the Third Person of the Trinity, of course refers to the Holy Spirit. This is the Name by which we identify His *Person.* The other two words, "wind" and "breath," are pictures of His *work.* "Wind" has to do with *His enabling power,* and "breath" has to do with *His indwelling and equipping Presence.*

In a Dennis the Menace cartoon, Dennis and his little friend, Joey, are wearing jackets and caps and wrapped in a scarf, which is blowing in a strong wind. Dennis repeats the question Joey has apparently just asked him. "You asked, 'What is wind?' Well, Joey, *wind is air that's in a hurry!*" Wind is irregular and exceptional, just like the work of the Holy Spirit. And wind may be extremely powerful and very dangerous—just follow the news of the hurricane season in the southeastern United States! These images remind us of the *enabling power* that the Holy Spirit wants to entrust to His people.

"Breath" and "breathing"—a picture of the indwelling Presence of the Holy Spirit in a believer, as He wishes to interpenetrate every part of the believer's life, just as the oxygen taken in by breathing is translated into energy for every cell in his body.

Jesus said to Nicodemus, "The *wind blows* where it wants to, and you hear the sound of it, but you cannot tell where it came from or where it is going; so is every one who is born of the Spirit of God." Another giant verse that must not be taken for granted! Like any statement of Divine revelation, it is over-loaded with content that demands interpretation, and with implications that are "off the map" for our personal vitality and vocational efficiency as believers.

Chapter Ten

A FORMULA FOR SPIRITUAL FULLNESS

I Corinthians 6:19-20;

"What? Know ye not that your body is the temple of the Holy Ghost which is in you, which ye have of God, and ye are not your own? For ye are bought with a price: therefore glorify God in your body, and in your spirit, which are God's."

One of the key words of the New Testament and of the Christian Gospel is the word "fullness." It is obvious from the New Testament that this word expresses one of God's greatest purposes for us. In John 1:16, the Bible says, "Of Christ's *fullness* have we all received, and grace for grace." When a sinner receives Christ, he draws by faith upon the infinite fullness of the saving grace of God. In Colossians 1:19, we read, "It pleased the Father that in Christ should all *fullness* dwell." And "Christ dwells in our hearts by faith!" Thus, the goal of the Christian life on earth is that the Christian "might be filled with all the *fullness* of God" (Ephesians 3:19). But strangely, emptiness is more characteristic of most Christians than fullness. Most Christians are living far below their spiritual means. Their potential resources in Christ are not utilized to fulfill their practical responsibilities as Christians. I am convinced that many Christians believe there is more in the Christian life, more available in Christ, than they now have, but they may not know how to enter into the fullness that is rightfully theirs in Christ.

In the nineteenth and twentieth verses of the sixth chapter of I Corinthians, the Apostle Paul wrote a massive truth which provides the foundation for a Christian to build upon in using all of his (His) resources. Here, the Apostle suggests what I have chosen to call, "A Formula For Spiritual Fullness." Let me state the steps that are suggested by this great statement.

I. REALIZE THE PRESENCE OF A DIVINE OCCUPANT

In order to experience all the fullness of God, first of all, you must realize the Presence of a Divine OCCUPANT in your life.

An immediate word of precaution is necessary. Paul as a Christian is writing these words only to Christians. These verses are true only of born-again believers in Jesus Christ. The truth here is simply not true of a person without Christ. No unsaved sinner has Christ living in his heart. There is no saving "spark of the Divine" in a lost sinner, needing only to be fanned into flame by works, character or personal improvement. He must be born again, and that occurs when Jesus Christ literally comes into him in a moment of radical faith and conversion. *"Christ in you"* is your only *"guarantee of glory"* (Colossians 1:27). So friend, let me ask you forthrightly, Is Jesus Christ in you? Does the Son of God as a living Person literally reside in your heart?

In Revelation 3:20, Jesus said, "Behold, I stand at the door and knock; if any man hear my voice, and open the door, I will come into him, and will sup with him, and he with me." What a wonder, that Jesus Christ, the risen and living Lord of the universe, should approach the door of a sinner's heart and knock to get in! If an emperor or a king were knocking, that would be very impressive. If some angel were knocking, that would be very commanding. But what should a person think and do when he begins to realize that the glorious Son of God is knocking at his heart's door?

A Formula For Spiritual Fullness

He should begin by thinking that the best body of the best and strongest and smartest man is only an empty building without the intended Occupant, and he should begin seriously considering how to receive Christ into his life.

I have read several books by a splendid Christian writer named Sue Monk Kidd. When she was a nurse in a hospital pediatric ward, she often let her young patients listen to their own hearts. One day as she carefully positioned the stethoscope for a 4-year-old named David, she said to him, "Listen. What do you suppose this is?" He listened intently for a moment, then with a smile, he reverently said, *"Is that Jesus knocking?"* Dear lost friend, Jesus *is* knocking at your heart's door. Yes, *Jesus!* He actually wants to come into you—yes, *you!* What must you do to be saved? Confess your sins directly to Him, admitting the futility of leaving Him outside and controlling your own life. Realize that He loves you, died for you, arose from the dead, and wants to enter into you as the risen and living Lord who wants to be your *personal* Lord (Master, Boss). Then, by simple faith, open the door of your heart and invite Him to come in!

The Greek word translated "dwelling place" is used only two times in the Bible, and both occurrences are in John 14. One is in verse one, where Jesus said, "In My Father's House are many dwelling places," and it speaks of *the Christian's dwelling place in Heaven*. This dwelling place will be waiting for every child of God when he/she leaves this earth. The other use of the word is in verse 23, where Jesus said, "If a man love Me, he will keep my words, and My Father will love him, and we will come unto him, and make our *dwelling place* with him." This refers to *the dwelling place of God (Father and Son) in the hearts of Christians*. Only the person who lets Christ be at home in his heart will be taken into His Home when his life on earth is over. When you receive Christ, the truth of our text is instantly true in your experience. It is the Holy Spirit who enters the new-born Christian, mediating the Presence of Christ. At the moment of your salvation, the Holy Spirit enters your heart and dwells there permanently thereafter, and thus your body is the Temple of the Holy Spirit! What a miracle!

In verse 19, Paul asks, "What? Know ye not that your body is the temple of the Holy Spirit which is in you, which ye have of God?" *Before you can experience God's fullness, dear Christian, you must grasp by faith the fact that there literally lives within you a Divine Person.* Paul repeats this fact several times in his letters to the Corinthian Christians. In I Corinthians 3:16, he wrote, "Know ye not that ye are the Temple of God, and that the Spirit of God dwells in you?" Actually, the pronouns used in this verse are plural, which means that Paul is speaking here to all of the Christians in the church of Corinth, but what is true of all is true of one. Then, in II Corinthians 6:16, Paul wrote, "Ye are the Temple of the living God; as God has said, I will dwell in them, and walk in them, and I will be their God, and they shall be my people." In all three cases (I Cor 3:16, I Cor 6:19, and II Cor 6:16), Paul used the same word Jesus used when He spoke of His own body. In John 2:19, Jesus said, "Destroy this *temple*, and in three days I will raise it up." And verse 21 of the same passage adds, "He spoke of the *temple* of His body." Now, the word that is used in all of these verses is the word for the temple as the "inner sanctuary" where God dwells. It is not the word *hieron*, which refers to the general area of the temple. Rather, it is the word *naos*, which is the special word for the Holy of Holies in the tabernacle and the temple where God dwelt among His people. The "temple" is the dwelling place of God. The temple in which God now dwells is not some tent in a wilderness, or a massive building on a hillside, but the physical body of the believing Christian. If you are a born-again Christian, your physical body is the temple (the *Holy of Holies*) of the Holy Spirit, who literally dwells in you. Christian, your body is the holiest spot on earth at this moment, the very dwelling-place of the Holy Spirit of God!

From the beginning, man was made to be indwelt. No one can ever really understand the human body or appreciate the sublime nature of its capacities until he realizes that it was created to be indwelt by the Holy Spirit. Just as the tabernacle of the Old Testament was not complete until it had been filled with the glory-cloud that marked the presence of the Lord God of Hosts, so the human body falls short of its highest destiny until it becomes

A Formula For Spiritual Fullness

completely possessed by the Spirit of God. *The human personality is never complete until God moves in to fill it with the glory of His own Presence.* A sense of something lacking—whatever you call it, emptiness, vanity, frustration—is the great problem today. There is a "cavity of emptiness" in most human lives today, and its gloom can only be dispelled by the radiant Presence of Him who has come to fill us with all the fullness of God.

Years ago, Dr. James M. Gray was the guest preacher in a church in Los Angeles one Sunday evening. His text for the sermon was Romans 12:1, which says, "I beseech you, therefore, brethren, by the mercies of God, that ye present your bodies a living sacrifice, holy, acceptable unto God, which is your reasonable service." Leaning over the pulpit, he said, "Have you noticed that this verse does not tell us to whom we should present our bodies? It is not the Lord Jesus who asks it; He had His own body while on earth, and still has it in Heaven tonight. It is not the Father who asks for it; He remains upon His throne in Heaven and doesn't need a body. However, Another has come to earth from heaven without a body. God could have made a body for Him as He did for Jesus, but He did not do so. God gives you the indescribable privilege and honor of presenting your body to the Holy Spirit, to be His dwelling-place and workshop on earth." Have you recognized this? Are you living in a conscious awareness of this exciting truth?

Perhaps someone says, "But I'm a very poor, weak Christian. Surely this is not true of me." Remember, Christian, the Corinthian letters of Paul were written to a church which had many weak, worldly, even temporarily *wicked*, Christians in it. It was a church that had some doctrinal error and moral impurity in it. I call your attention to the fact that the Apostle Paul did not say to them, "You folks straighten up so the Spirit of God will live in your lives." Rather, he reversed the order and said, "Straighten up as Christians *because* the Spirit of God lives in your lives!" Why, when Paul wrote these verses, he was talking about fornication! He says, "Flee this thing." Why flee it? Not, "in order that the Holy Spirit might live in you," but "because He already does"!

Studies in the Person and Work of the Holy Spirit

One Sunday morning, Louis Talbot addressed his congregation in the Church of the Open Door, Los Angeles, California, in these searching words: "We have a large company here. Many of you are strangers to me; nevertheless, I can say with absolute certainty that not one of you will pull out a cigarette, light it, and smoke it in this room. And yet the New Testament teaches us that it is not any earthly structure that is the temple of God, for today the Holy Spirit dwells in the bodies of born-again believers. It is right that we should have reverence for the place of worship, but why should men and women have less fear of desecrating the true temple of God?" Christian, are you living moment-by-moment in a conscious awareness of an indwelling Divine Guest in your life? Indeed, are you aware that if you defer control to Him, this Guest will become Host—in your own house! Then He will implement all of the purposes of God out of His fullness in you!

We often hear the question asked, "Should I, as a Christian, do this or go there?" Many young Christians ask, "Is this right or wrong for a Christian?" Such questions should not be difficult to answer since you, as a Christian, have the Holy Spirit in you to tell you where you should go or not go and what you should do or not do. He dwells in the heart of every believer and goes wherever the believer goes. Why not ask Him if He wants to do this or that? Ask Him if He prefers to remain at home from the house of worship on Sunday night. Ask Him if He thinks the atmosphere at a certain questionable place will be congenial to Him. If not, then don't go. Remember, if you go, He has to go. Do you understand that if you sin, He is necessarily implicated in your sin—though He Himself is not guilty! No wonder He is often deeply grieved as the indwelling Guest in the lives of disobedient Christians. You can't go off and leave Him at home until you return, for He lives in you. When He came into your life He didn't come in on a temporary camping trip. He came to take up permanent residence in your heart! If you want the abundant fullness of God, you must realize the fact of the constant indwelling of the Holy Spirit. Now, that's not the scope of the total blessing. There's more, so much more. But I don't know anything any more thrilling than that Jesus Christ is living in my heart! The realization of this fact is the first step toward spiritual fullness.

II. RECOGNIZE HIS PREROGATIVE AS THE REAL AND RIGHTFUL OWNER

After you have realized the Presence of a Divine Guest in your heart, you must then recognize His prerogative as the real and rightful OWNER of your body and your life. I have spoken about the indwelling of the Holy Spirit in the life of a Christ. Let me speak now concerning the *infilling* of the Holy Spirit, or His assertion of ownership and assuming of control within you.

Paul is suggesting something about this infilling of the Holy Spirit when he says, "You are not your own, for you are bought with a price." He says, "A Divine Guest does live in you if you are a Christian, but if you are to know spiritual fullness, He must be more than a guest—He must be permitted to be the Proprietor and Landlord! He owns the house!" Before the full force of the indwelling of the Holy Spirit can be experienced in my life, I must consent to the fact that He owns me completely. Now, let's admit that for some of us, He has been nothing more than a guest. But Paul says, "You are not your own. Having been bought and paid for at a very high price, you belong to Him as His private property." The meaning of the word "bought" is well known to everyone. When you bought an item, did the clerk put it back on the shelf? If he had, what would you have said to him? You likely would have said, "I paid you for that, please give it to me; it belonged to you before, but it belongs to me now because I bought it." In the same manner, Christian, you are bought with a price, and you are not your own. And what a price! Not silver and gold, but the price of the shed blood of the Son of God! You are the purchased property of Almighty God, bought at the exchange of His Darling Son for you, and thus you are paid (not overpaid) for.

The Cross of Christ reveals God's great claim on you. When Columbus first landed in the new world, he waded ashore carrying a cross. He stuck it in the sand and claimed that land in the name of the king of Spain and in the name of the Christ symbolized by the cross. So Christ comes into your life by means of a cross—and with a cross. He says, "I claim this life as my personal and private property by virtue of My Cross."

However, if this is to be true in your experience, you must give personal consent to this. The word I'm going to use for this consent is the word "surrender." There will be no fullness of the Holy Spirit in your life apart from full surrender to the Owner of the Temple so that He has the full "run of the house" in *and through you*. What a price has been paid for you, and I repeat, it was not an overpayment. That is true in this sense—the price Christ paid for you is not a matter of *inherent worth on your part*, but of *conferred worth on His part*. God exchanged Jesus for you, thus conferring on you the full value of His Son. Price paid determines value. God knows that you are not inherently that valuable (though you are inherently worth *far more than you know*), but He paid that price for you, thus conferring that exact value upon you. Then, once you accept the Person of Christ and the payment He made for you as your means of salvation, *God immediately gets to work in you* to make you like Jesus to justify His investment!

Have you made the Divine Occupant the declared *owner* of your life? Does He monopolize your life, so much so that He can manipulate it for any purpose He chooses? In short, *have you signed away your life to the Lord Jesus Christ, to be His possession, under His control?* The absolute, unqualified surrender of our will to God is the price of the fullness of the Holy Spirit in our lives.

I think surrender has both a *negative* aspect and a *positive* aspect. The *negative* aspect of surrender is *confession of sin*. God cannot fill with His Spirit that heart that is already full of sin. I like the suggestion made by many. Get alone with God, take a sheet of paper and a pencil, and write down every single sin of which you have been guilty. Some of us had better take two sheets—and keep writing. Just let the Spirit of God speak to your heart, opening to Him, letting Him search you and prompt you. Pray with David, "Search me, O God, and know my heart, try me and know my thoughts, and see if there is any wicked way in me" (Psalm 139:23-24). Pride, lust, jealousy, not witnessing for Christ, neglect of the

A Formula For Spiritual Fullness

Word of God, a lack of prayer, not being filled with the Spirit—write them down, one by one. And bring them to Him. Then, claim the cleansing spoken of in I John 1:9, "If we confess our sins, He is faithful and just to forgive us our sins and to cleanse us from all unrighteousness." This is the negative aspect of surrender.

The *positive* aspect is the setting of your life apart completely for God. There is no substitute for this conscious and relational aspect of surrender. It is personal surrender to a personal God. When God states a condition of blessing, no other condition, however good elsewhere, can be substituted. It will not do, in place of this, to give time, or money, or service. Thousands of Christians are trying to bribe and silence their consciences and rob God by a partial surrender. We must give *ourselves* unreservedly to Him. And God will fill anything we yield to Him. So *you can have all of the fullness of the Holy Spirit you will make room for.* God's will for all Christians is that they should be filled with the Holy Spirit. It is His will that each Christian be as full of the Spirit as a tree is full of sap when it rises from the roots and fills the uppermost branches, or as your body is full of blood. The difference is that this is the permeation throughout *your* person of Another Person who is in you. We are to be filled with the Holy Spirit until Christian fruitfulness is as natural to us as the leaf, the flower and the fruit are to be tree. But before we can know the fullness of the Holy Spirit in our lives, we must consent for the Holy Spirit to own our lives "kit and kiboodle," "lock, stock and barrel."

III. RELEASE YOURSELF TO HIS PROCESSING AS THE OPERATOR OF YOUR LIFE

There is a third and final step toward spiritual fullness. You must also *release yourself to the processing of the Holy Spirit moment-by-moment as the Operator of your life.* You must recognize the Divine Occupant who lives within you, God the Holy Spirit, and you must realize fully and practically that the Occupant is also Owner of you and your life, including everything that means. And finally, you must regularly allow the Occupant/Owner by the *Operator* of your life. You must be willing for Him to control your every thought,

Studies in the Person and Work of the Holy Spirit

every action, every movement, every word, every assignment, every deployment of resources, in your life. That is, your body and your life will be continuously used as vehicles for God's glory. *"Therefore, glorify God in your body and in your spirit, which are God's,"* says Paul.

"Glorify God in your spirit." Among other things, this means to let your disposition and temperament and attitude be Christ-controlled and Spirit-saturated. What a vocation! When this happens, Jesus Christ becomes clearly visible in a modified version of The Incarnation, the difference being that now He demonstrates His life through your body which has become His. Does Christ live through your disposition? Is He exhibited in your attitudes? Does He monopolize and manipulate your inner life, and manifest Himself through it?

English Baptist pastor F. B. Meyer said, "Instead of talking of giving up all for Christ, learn to see that Christ is in you, then take Him for all He is worth. Say, 'Thy patience, Lord! Thy love, Lord! Thy peace, Lord!'"

> "Let the beauty of Jesus be seen in me,
> All of His wonderful passion and purity,
> O Thou Savior Divine, Let Thy Nature be mine,
> And let the beauty of Jesus be seen in me."

"Glorify God in your body." Does Jesus operate your visible actions, your detectible activities? Do you consult Him about His plan for you in the most minute details of your life? For example, do you ask Him to "answer your phone calls and your doorbells," and to "drive your automobile when you are behind the wheel"? We miss so many blessings because we are not alert to the fact that Christ wants to literally operate our lives.

In London, England, two prominent buildings are Hotel Cecil and Buckingham Palace. Both are magnificent architectural specimens, but there is a vast difference between them. The Hotel Cecil is open to all who can pay for the accommodations. Rooms can be hired for lust, debauchery or vice of any kind. Not so with Buckingham Palace. No amount of money could hire a single room

A Formula For Spiritual Fullness

in it. And why? Because it is the palace of the reigning King or Queen. So it is with the human body that is completely given over to the indwelling Holy Spirit.

It was said of another residence that "it was noised abroad that Jesus was in the house" (Mark 2:1). May it be so said of *this* house, your life, this temple of God.

This is God's formula for Christian plenty and productivity. If Robert Browning came into your life, you could write poetry like he did (indeed, it could be his very poetry); if William Shakespeare came into your life, you could write dramas like he did; if Napoleon Bonaparte came into your life, you could plan and pursue military campaigns. There is no "if" about this: since Jesus Christ is in you in the Person and Presence of the Holy Spirit, you can live as a child of God!

This is God's plan for spiritual fullness. Acknowledge the indwelling Divine Occupant in your life; let the Occupant be Owner; and let the Owner be Operator—"that ye might be filled with all the fullness of God"!

Chapter Eleven

A River Runs Through It

John 7:37-39;
"In the last day, that great day of the feast, Jesus stood and cried, saying, If any man thirst, let him come unto me, and drink. He that believeth on me, as the scripture hath said, out of his belly shall flow rivers of living water. But this spake he of the Spirit, which they that believe on him should receive: for the Holy Ghost was not yet given: because that Jesus was not yet glorified."

Some of the great "fundamentals" in the teaching of Jesus came at seemingly "incidental" times. Sometimes, even the greatest of His teachings seemed to be "incidental" to a more fundamental message. For example, John 3:16 is not even the main argument of John 3; it seems to be dropped as a kind of "oh, by the way" statement into a narrative about the atoning death of Christ and the new birth. Thank God for the seemingly "incidental" teachings or sayings that Jesus dropped along the way! The text recorded at the head of this study is one such example.

The Feast of Tabernacles had reached its last day, "that great day of the Feast," as John called it. On that day a large processional of people was led by the Jewish priests, a processional from the Temple to the Pool of Siloam. Upon arrival there, the chief priest filled a large vessel with water from the Pool and poured it out on the ground. This is a symbol of the inability of earthly water to satisfy the deepest needs of the human heart. Jesus capitalized this occasion to shout a message to the entire crowd of people near Him who were closing their observance of the Feast of Tabernacles. His message conveys one of the greatest invitations He ever made. John tells us (verse 39) that it has reference to the place of the Holy Spirit in a believer's life. So this is a study about the fullness of the Holy Spirit.

I. The Invitation of Jesus States the *PROMISE* of the Spirit's Fullness

The entire invitation constitutes a Divine *promise*, a promise of the full release of Redemptive power on the Day of Pentecost (see verse 39b), and a promise of the personal fullness of the Holy Spirit which is available to all followers of Christ. However, the promise means more than the mere availability of fullness; the promise includes *personal responsibility* for this fullness. That is, each individual believer is responsible to be filled with the Holy Spirit in all the dimensions of this text of Scripture. For a full examination of God's command to be filled, study Ephesians 5:18 carefully.

Jesus constantly indicated that a *new direction* has come for the ministry of the people of God (total world impact), and here He indicates that a *new dynamic* will be available to pursue that direction. That new dynamic is, of course, the Person and power of the Holy Spirit. This text is a great foundation for exploring the Person, the Presence and the power of the Holy Spirit in the lives of individual believers.

II. The Invitation of Jesus Suggests the *PURPOSES* of the Spirit's Fullness

The very terminology that is powerfully used in Jesus' invitation strongly infers the *purposes* for the Holy Spirit's fullness.

A River Runs Through It

In His invitation, Jesus went back into Old Testament history and appealed to an event that occurred when the children of Israel were in the wilderness experiencing the guidance, provision *and chastisement* of God to encourage them in their walk with Him *and* to correct their sin and rebellion. A national calendar event in the time of Jesus was annually observed to commemorate God's work among them. That event was called the Feast of Tabernacles or the Feast of Booths. One of the great events celebrated at this feast was the miraculous way in which God supplied water to a desperately thirsty nation. Here, Jesus uses that water as a type (Greek, *tupos*), or pattern, or picture, of the fullness of the Holy Spirit. In doing so, He suggests several purposes of the fullness of the Holy Spirit.

First, He suggests that the fullness of the Holy Spirit in a believer's life is the only means of overcoming *stagnation*. Again and again, Jesus warns us about being too casual, too presumptuous, too icily regular, in living in and for Him. Satan's trick is to stagnate and neutralize our lives, to "cool us off by degrees" so that we don't notice the temperature change. Look carefully and critically at your own life right now. Is your life at present more like a *swamp* or like a *river?* Has the Holy Spirit's "flow" come to a standstill in your life? Compare the local swimming pool in your community, which only provides local refreshment, leisure and indulgence, with the mighty Nile of Egypt which is called the "life-belt" of the land, flowing for great distances and in enlarging channels, furnishing life, vegetation, fruit and sustenance wherever it flows. The pool *stows* the water, the river *flows* the water. Which better represents your life as a Christian?

Stagnation always tends to breed corruption. The corruption of self-will, of self-indulgence, of self-pampering, of self-determination, is always a threat to the believer when the Spirit's fullness is not stirring, moving, flowing and pouring through his life.

Second, Jesus suggests that the fullness of the Holy Spirit in a believer's life is the only means of overcoming *shallowness*. One of the symptoms of the maturing Christian is that he is ever-deepening in perception, understanding, application and productivity.

Studies in the Person and Work of the Holy Spirit

Years ago, I had the great privilege of spending several hours with the great Scottish Christian leader and author, Major Ian Thomas. In the course of an early-afternoon conversation, I asked him, "Major, what do you think of Southern Baptists?" (I am a Southern Baptist). He paused thoughtfully, then he paried my question with one of his own: "Do you want me to be completely honest?" I laughed and answered, "Yes, I would prefer that." He replied, "In a word, Southern Baptist's are 'shallow.' You dip converts in the tank and then drop them—in the same motion." Shallow! And he was right!

The fullness of the Holy Spirit is one of the ways God corrects the baby shallowness of a Christian's life. Enlarged fullness is a matter of enlarged capacity. Enlarged capacity is a matter of spiritual growth. Maturing in Christ enlarges our capacity for the fullness of the Holy Spirit, and the fullness of the Spirit leads to more maturity. Growth → enlarged capacity → fullness → greater growth, etc. Thus, shallowness is overcome—by the fullness of the Holy Spirit.

Third, Jesus suggests that the fullness of the Holy Spirit in a believer's life is the only means to overcome *selfishness* in the Christian life. "The flesh lusts against the Spirit" (Galatians 5:17) in every Christian—until he learns to overcome the flesh by being filled with the Spirit and daily walking in the Spirit. "Walk in the Spirit and you will not fulfill the lusts of the flesh" (Galatians 5:16). The word "flesh" can best be understood by turning the word around, "H-S-E-L-F," and dropping the "H." SELF! Flesh is the self-centered, self-pampering, self-indulging life of the self-centered believer. And flesh is deadly when in control of your life. In Romans 7:18, Paul said, "I know that in me, that is, in my flesh, dwells no good thing."

Have you ever known a self-centered person who was truly happy, or made anyone else truly happy? The answer is self-evident. Many believers quietly profess Christ while constantly indulging self, quietly going through Christian "motions" while maintaining control of their own lives, quietly engaging in church activities while feeding only themselves,.... Selfishness in a Sunday suit! The only way to overcome it is through the fullness of the outgoing, others-centered, ministering fullness of the Holy Spirit.

Fourth, Jesus suggests that the fullness of the Holy Spirit in a believer's life is the only way to overcome *sinfulness* in a believer's life. Through the flesh, the believer in Christ retains the capacity to commit almost any act of sin. It is almost automatic that if a Christian does *not* walk in the Spirit, he *will* engage in a wide variety of flesh-gratifying sins.

Let me create an illustration of this truth. Think of your conversion and Christian life in this symbolic way. Picture your life as a large tub. The day you were saved, it is as if the "hose of salvation" was turned into the tub, and the "faucet of faith" released the flow of grace (or the "Water of Life," if you please) into you. It would be just like a great supply of water suddenly rushing into a previously empty tub. Suppose that your previous sins were like pieces of debris forming a large pile in your life—like crumpled pieces of dirty paper, dirty rags, dead twigs and branches of trees, etc. These bits of debris adhered like glue to your inner life and you could not get rid of them. However, the day you were saved, the grace of God, the Water of Life, rushed into your life and covered all that debris. "Where sin abounded, grace did much more abound" (Romans 5:20). To paraphrase, where sin once overflowed, grace rose up to cover it and overflow above it. Suppose, however, that while you were rapturously "taken up" with grace, a piece of that adhering debris broke loose for the bottom of the tub and surged to the surface. When it breaks into visibility, you are horrified, hoping nobody else has seen it. Quickly, you put a hand on that piece of filth and push it back down under the water, holding it down lest it re-surface and others see it. But while you are holding it down, *another piece* of filthy debris breaks loose and surges conspicuously to the surface. You quickly put the other hand on it and push it back down. But here comes another one! You put one foot on it and push it back under, standing on it to assure that it will not surface again. The outcome? Soon, all available appendages are occupied struggling with sin in order to "overcome" it. Do you see what Satan has done? He has completely canceled all the possible fruit that may have come through your life by preoccupying you in a fight against sin. After all, the feet that are obsessed with holding down sin and keeping it "under control" can't be carrying you into paths of service and obeying the many mandates to "go." And the hands that are submerging sins cannot "do with their might" what God assigns them to do. Consider the practical outcome: you are publicizing the Christian life as a struggle against iniquity, a preoccupation with sin, an obsession with guilt, etc. Is this an accurate picture of the Christian life? Absolutely not! The Christian life is *Christ*—as the origin, the source, the focus, the power, the product, of the life. Its motto is, "To me to live is Christ" (*not,* to fight sin). To pursue our illustration, what should the believer do when the filthy debris of inbred sin surfaces in the believer's life? Go back to the hose which conveys the Water of Life! Exercise faith and turn on the faucet for more of the resources of grace. Like water rising in the rub, the floating debris will be swept out of the container on the rising tides of grace. Thus, the resources of grace and the victory that attends their use will *replace* the possibility of sinning. So the fullness of the (*holy*) Holy Spirit of God is the only way to overcome sin in a believer's life.

I have stated four possible purposes of the fullness of the Holy Spirit in a Christian's life. The list is merely suggestive, not exhaustive. If you are a thoughtful Christian, you can list several more purposes for the Spirit's fullness in your life.

III. The Invitation of Jesus Summons From Biblical History a *PICTURE* of the Fullness of the Holy Spirit

Third, there is in these verses a vivid *picture* of the fullness of the Holy Spirit. In verse 39 of our text, John adds a parenthetical and editorial comment about the invitation of Jesus. In his comment, John says, "But Jesus spoke this about the Holy Spirit, which they that believe on Him should receive: for the Holy Spirit was not yet given; because that Jesus was not yet glorified." Note several key terms in John's explanation. Note the word "receive." This receiving occurs, according to the text, at the moment of a sinner's

A River Runs Through It

believing in Christ. Be careful to note that the Holy Spirit is "received" by every believer at the moment he "believes on Him." Key on the word "receive." The gift of the Holy Spirit, like salvation itself, is not something *achieved,* but something *received.* It does not take talent, or great effort, or great understanding, or perfect faith, to receive something offered. A tramp can receive a gift—if he will just *take* it when it is offered. Some well-meaning Bible interpreters give effort-laden formulas for "getting the Holy Ghost," but these are not reflected in the Bible. The Spirit's fullness is "by grace through faith" just as salvation is.

Note, too, the expression, "for the Holy Spirit was not yet given." This is a reference to the coming Day of Pentecost (Acts 2). The Day of Pentecost marked the full release of redemptive power in the Person and Presence of the Holy Spirit. Again, the text tells us that this full release of the Holy Spirit's power would not come until Jesus was "glorified." The word "glorified" is a package word for the total redemptive work of Christ for sinners—including His Death, His Resurrection, His Ascension and His Exaltation at God's right hand in Heaven. All of these had occurred "when the Day of Pentecost had fully come" (Acts 2:1). From His position in glory at God's right hand, Jesus sent the Holy Spirit as His "ascension gift" to His people. John refers to that Gift in verse 39 of our text.

But there is much more to be seen at this point. Remember that it was "on the last day, that great day of the feast" (the Feast of Tabernacles), that Jesus extended His invitation. The two verbs used reveal great intensity: "Jesus *stood* and *cried.*" The word "stood" means that He sought a prominent place of visibility (because He did not have the attention of the people He wanted to address). The word "cried" is a strong word full of great emotion and allowing very commanding expression.

The references to the Feast of Tabernacles, coupled with His invitation concerning "rivers of living water," suggest a wilderness episode which is at the center of the festive commemoration of Jesus' day. The episode is recorded in Exodus 17:1-5 and Numbers 20:7-13, which record the story of God's miraculous supply of water in the desert for the thirsting nation of Israel. Several key features should be noted: Moses was directed to a large rock in the desert, he was to strike that rock with his rod, and water would then flow from the smitten rock (and it did). The New Testament identifies this entire account as a "type" (Greek, *tupos*, an "exact impress" or pattern) of great New Testament realities.

The *rock* in the story represents *Christ*. I Corinthians 10:4 says, "Our fathers....drank of that spiritual Rock that followed them, and that Rock was Christ." The figure of a rock suggests the majesty of Christ, the stability and serenity of Christ, and the humility of Christ (a rock was a very unlikely source for an abundant supply of water).

The *smiting* of the rock in the story represents the *violent Death of Christ on the Cross*. Remember it was the people of Israel who deserved to be smitten in the story, just as it is the sinner who deserves the judgment and death which Jesus endured. Note the dimensions of this smiting of the rock in the wilderness story: (1) The smiting of the rock was *by Divine appointment* (just like the judgment upon sin and sinners). (2) The smiting of the rock was to take place *publicly* (just like the Death of Jesus, which "was not done in a corner"). (3) The smiting of the rock was to take place *before the leaders of Israel* (just like the Death of Jesus on the Cross). (4) The smiting of the rock was to take place *by the rod of the lawgiver* (just like the Death of Jesus, who was "smitten by God" on the basis of His just Law against sin and sinners).

However, Numbers 20 informs us that Moses made some crucial mistakes in his action. When a second similar episode occurred in the wilderness, Moses was carefully instructed *not* to smite the rock a *second* time, but only to *speak* to it, and the water would freely flow. But Moses became very angry with the people of Israel and struck the rock a second time. In turn, God became very angry with Moses, and due reprisal followed his disobedience. Now, God was not arbitrary with His anger; He didn't merely "have a fit of anger" (as we sometimes do).

Don't forget this hermeneutical principle (principle of Biblical interpretation): *God is very, very (very) jealous of His types!!!* If a type is not constructed or demonstrated with absolute correctness, the one responsible to obey God (in order for God to create the type) is guilty of false advertising; He is guilty of falsely representing God and His truth. When Moses struck the rock a second time, he was declaring (whether he knew it or not, which shows why our obedience is so important, even if we don't fully understand God's command) that Jesus (the "anti-type," or fulfillment of the type, I Corinthians 10:4), would die *twice!* This is an insult to the once-for-all, perfect, all-sufficient Death of Christ for sinners. Moses' angry action said, in effect, that one death of Christ was not enough, and another was necessary. This is, in effect, what is also declared by all defective views of salvation—salvation by works, salvation which can be lost after it is possessed, etc. These doctrines declare that the Death of Christ is not sufficient and man's effort, works, holiness, etc., must be added to receive and retain the salvation God offers. Paul referred to these false doctrines taught by "Christians" as "beginning in the Spirit, but hoping to be perfected by the flesh." And he calls this attempt "foolishness" (Galatians 3:1-3).

Back to the type. The rock represents Christ, the smiting of the rock represents the Death of Christ on the Cross, and the water that flowed from the smitten rock represents the provision of the Holy Spirit. The Person of Christ, the Passion of Christ, and the Provision of the Holy Spirit—the type is exact and perfect! He came, He was glorified (through His Death, Resurrection, Ascension and Heavenly Exaltation), and then from His exalted position at God's right hand in Glory, He gave the Gift of the Holy Spirit. The river in the wilderness type represents the *flow* of God's Life, the *fullness* of God's Life, the *freeness* of God's Life, and the *freshness* of God's Life (Peter referred to the Holy Spirit's visitations as "times of refreshing from the hand of the Lord," Acts 3:19). All of these things are available to believers today through the Person, indwelling Presence, and infilling power of the Holy Spirit. So the picture summoned by Jesus from Old Testament history provides a full explanation of the fullness of the Holy Spirit.

IV. The Invitation of Jesus Specifies the *PATHWAY* to the Fullness of the Holy Spirit

Fourth, the text indicates the *pathway* to the Fullness of the Holy Spirit. Christ's invitation specifies certain conditions which must be individually intact before the believer will be filled with the Holy Spirit. The conditions are expressed in three picturesque verbs: "Thirst, come, drink." "If anyone thirsts, let him come to Me and drink." Then He captured these three actions in one phrase, "He who believes on Me as the Scripture has said…." Let's pursue His three conditions for a moment.

First, *"if anyone thirsts."* Step number one in Jesus' conditions: there must be a *consuming recognition of need.* There must be dominating thirst for Christ, His Truth, His Life, His service, etc. There is a big difference between *emptiness* and *thirst*! The cup in the kitchen may be empty on the shelf, but it is never thirsty for the coffee that may soon fill it. The gasoline tank in your automobile may be *empty* but it is not *thirsty* for gasoline.

When I became a Christian (over 61 years ago!), the first verse God magnetized to my heart was this precious verse from the Sermon on the Mount: "Blessed is the man who hungers and thirsts after righteousness, for he shall be filled." I found out much later that, in the Greek text, the word translated "hunger" is a word which means to "hunger for the entire loaf of bread," and the word translated "thirst" means to "thirst for the whole bottle of water." I asked God to give me this hunger and thirst—and He has been answering that prayer ever since!

How does a person become thirsty for righteousness? S. D. Gordon, the great devotional preacher of the past, answered the question with this wise advice, "Look at the Fountain!" Focus on Jesus will make us thirsty for Him and His living water.

The second condition is, *"Let him come unto Me."* This is the only one of the three verbs which is followed by an object. "Unto Me." Jesus is the focus and the force behind the Holy Spirit's fullness. The Holy Spirit does not publicize Himself. Jesus said, "When He has come, He will take the things of Mine and show them unto you." We must come (and keep coming) to Jesus Christ Himself if we are to be filled with the Holy Spirit. Thus, there must be a *complete reliance upon Christ.* We are not counseled to come to a conference, or to a meeting, or to a service, or to an activity for Christ. None of these must be allowed to displace Christ Himself. Our happy assignment is to give Jesus Christ freedom in every province of our lives. *His* freedom in *me* will give *me fullness* in *Him*. Thus, He is *free in me–to fill me-*and to *flow through me*. The product of His flow through me is often called "fruit."

Are you (am I) regularly approaching Jesus Himself to be filled with the Spirit?

The final condition is, "Let him come unto Me and *drink.*" We must approach Christ, and appropriate His gift of the Spirit's fullness. Charles Howard, evangelist and Bible teacher, often said, "We are to drink, not just gargle. We are to drink, not just sip a taste." The tense of the verb indicates continual appropriation. "Keep on drinking," the text says. Thus, there must be a *constant reception and accommodation of the Spirit's fullness* in each of our lives.

When a thirsty person drinks water, that water instantly begins to be assimilated into the cellular structure of his body. It is absorbed into the body, and refreshes and replenishes his entire physical existence. The same is true of our appropriation of the Holy Spirit's fullness. When a person drinks water, he does not see the inward assimilation that always occurs, but his obliviousness does not prevent the assimilation.. Even so, the Christian will not see most of the "transaction" when the Spirit fills him—but he knows that his thirst has been quenched, he is satisfied, and good health and much fruit are the by-products of the right intake of the Water of Life!

One more thought before we move to the last point of this study. A good channel is always receiving, always ready to flow, and thus always full. Are you (am I) always receiving the Holy Spirit's fullness? Are you always ready to flow? Are you always full?

V. Finally, the Invitation of Jesus Shows the *PRODUCT* of the Holy Spirit's Fullness

Jesus indicates in the text that when the fullness is experienced, a flow will be expressed. A flowing will follow the filling.

Studies in the Person and Work of the Holy Spirit

In fact, the quickest way to abort the filling is to cease to seek and find and use outlets for the Spirit's flow. If He cannot flow out to produce fruit, He will quickly cease to flow in to produce fullness. Jesus said that when a believer meets the conditions for fullness, "out of his innermost being shall flow rivers of living water" (verse 38b).

Herein lies the greatest problem of the typical Christian and the typical church—they are ingrown, introverted, imploding, instead of outgoing, outflowing, world-impacting. One only has to contrast the *implosion* of the typical church today with the *explosion* that produced the Book of Acts. You see, when water is unimpeded in its movement, it tends to flow out from its point of release. The Biblical direction is OUT. Jesus identified our geographical assignment (I use the singular word because the four areas specified form a unified package calling for equal and simultaneous emphasis) when He said, "….both in Jerusalem, and in Judea, and in Samaria, and unto the uttermost part of the earth." Note that the concentric circles suggested (Acts 1:8) are *outgoing* and *enlarging*. This is the strategy a believer (or a church) is to follow in impacting the whole wide world.

Note the specifics of the product. First, the fullness and flow of the Holy Spirit will produce a *living* supply. "Out of his innermost being shall flow rivers of *living* water." "Living" water is distinguished in the Bible from still, stagnant, stinking water. What a word to describe the Holy Spirit's impact—everything lives where He freely fills (see Exeziel 47). Question: is your inner life foul and stinking because of some residue of sin there? Or is it merely *nice* and *neutral?* I wonder what it is going to be like when Jesus tells us that the Christian *niceness* and *neutrality* which constitute the "norm" we often see among Christians in church were, in fact, radical enemies of purpose?

Second, the fullness and flow of the Holy Spirit will produce a *large* supply. Out of his innermost being will flow *rivers* of living water. It is not "trickles," or "brooks," or "rivulets," or "streams" of living water. It is not even "a river," but *rivers*. The word translated "rivers" is the very word Jesus used in Matthew

A River Runs Through It

7:25, 27, when He described the two houses, one built on rock and the other on sand. In each case, "the rains descended, the floods came, and the winds blew, and beat upon that house." The house built on rock withstood the storm, while the house built on sand collapsed under the assault of the storm. The word translated "floods" in that text is the same word translated "rivers" here. It is obvious that Jesus Christ intends a gigantic flow of His life through each of His children. It is obvious that Jesus Christ intends that this flow extend *"OUT"*—to "the uttermost part of the earth." It is obvious that Jesus intends vast fullness, freshness and fruitfulness to characterize the lives of His followers. How am I doing at this point? And you?

As I write these words, I hold in my hand, before my eyes, a common little plastic conduit called a soda straw. It is about 8 to 10 inches long, and it has a very small channel. Its purpose is to convey liquids to the mouth of the user (though it may be used for a few other purposes).

Several months ago, my wife, Judy, and I were in Scotland. I learned that the southwest shore of the country and the shores of some of the western islands of Scotland are covered with plush (almost tropical) vegetation—yet this is the most northernmost country of Europe! Why? Because the warm flow of the Gulf Stream flows upon the southwest shore of Scotland and upon the western shores of Scotland's western islands.

Has it ever occurred to you that the Gulf Stream can flow through a soda straw? Well, it *can*! Oh, not *all* of the Gulf Stream, to be sure, but the Gulf Stream can flow through the little soda straw that I hold in my hand. Of course, there are certain conditions. What are they?

One, the soda straw must be *in the element*. The straw must be placed in the water where the Holy Spirit flows. Even so, a Christian must be in the Divine element. He must "live in the Spirit" (Galatians 5:25). Have you been "born of the Spirit"? (John 3:3) Are you consciously "living in (the sphere of) the Spirit"?

Two, the soda straw (in the element) must be *parallel to the flow* of the Gulf Stream. If the soda straw is in the Gulf Stream, but "cross-current" to its flow, the straw will be filled with the water, but the stream will not flow through it. What an insight! A Christian can seek to be filled with the Holy Spirit for his own advantage, for his own experience, for his own improvement as a Christian—without the Spirit having full freedom to *flow out* through him. It is only as the Christian serves parallel to the purposes of the Spirit (be very careful here, pondering all the dimensions of the purposes of the Spirit)—*certainly including OUT to the uttermost parts of the earth, and with total world impact as the goal*—that the Spirit will fully and freely and fruitfully flow through him.

Three, the soda straw must be *open* and *unobstructed* if the Gulf Stream is to flow through it. Take the straw in both hands, and bend it with the fingers of one hand. It will bend shut and close the conduit. Better yet, put both hands around the straw as fists and twist the straw in different directions. Now, it has twists and contortions throughout its length, and they may remain even when you release the straw. Again, what Biblical insights await us in the illustration!

You see, there are four basic words used in the Bible to explain and define sin. One is the common word, "sin", which means "to miss the mark." "All have sinned (missed the mark), and come short of the glory of God (the intended target)." "The glory of God" is the manifest perfection of God's character. Thus, *to be a sinner is simply to be less perfect than God is.* And we all qualify—miserably! Another Biblical word for "sin" is the word "trespass", which means to weakly fall out of God's revealed "way". A third word is "transgression," which means to deliberately and wilfully step across God's moral and spiritual boundary lines (lines which God has lovingly established for your safety and protection). A fourth word for "sin" is the word "iniquity," a specialized word which defines the inner character twist(s) or distortion(s) which are common to every sinner. As long as "iniquity" continues uncorrected *inside a Christian's life*, the flow of the Spirit's Life and power will be obstructed. Several years ago, I visited Yellowstone National Park for the first time. Since that first visit, I have eagerly returned several more times. I find the Park to be a place of great

A River Runs Through It

mystery and intrigue as well as a place of breath-taking beauty. On my first visit, I was especially fascinated with the "Geyser Basin" in the Park. Over 50 geysers erupt out of the ground in the basin. Boardwalks have been constructed through the basin so that tourists can get very close to these geysers. Of course, the most famous geyser is "Old Faithful." "Old Faithful" erupts about 110 feet into the air, and it is so regular ("faithful") that the time of each eruption can be calculated within a few seconds. In fact, the eruption times are posted on a large board at the nearby lodge, and a crowd of people always gathers to see the next explosion. When it erupts, a vast column of steamy white water gushes out of the earth, dispersing its thin spray all around the column.

Many people do not know that all 50 of the geysers that erupt in the basin come from the same underground source—and thus have force equal to Old Faithful. However, the next highest eruption is less than 50 feet high. Then the eruptions "drop" in height so that a few don't even reach the surface of the ground; an observer must look down into a hole to see the bubbling steam. Why, if all the geysers come from the same source, and with equal force, does Old Faithful go so high and the rest do not? *The difference is in the shape of the cone through which each geyser flows.* Old Faithful's cone (or "pipe") is straight and smooth, and the flow of the hot steam is unobstructed. But the cone of the others is crooked and erratic, and thus the force of the steam is destroyed by the crookedness of the rock cone.

What an illustration of a Christian's life! If there is iniquity hidden beneath the surface in his life, the flow of the Spirit's Life will be prevented or hindered! The day he was saved, God *covered* his hideous inner crookedness with the perfect righteousness of Christ and hid it from His sight, thus perfectly "justifying" the sinner. However, God will not finally be guilty of a mere bookkeeping transaction that takes dirty sinners to heaven, merely *covered* by the perfect righteousness of Christ. The moment the *crisis* of justification occurs, God also begins the *process* of sanctification. Having counted you "straight" in Christ, God now begins to "hammer" on the iniquity, the remaining character distortions in

Studies in the Person and Work of the Holy Spirit

your inner life, to make you like Christ—and to allow the free flow of the Spirit's Life through you. Like the open soda straw, in the element, parallel to its flow, open and unobstructed, the Gulf Stream of God's Life will flow through you.

Finally, the fullness and flow of the Holy Spirit will produce a *lasting* supply. "Out of his innermost being will flow rivers of living water." The verb translated "flow" is a present tense continuous verb, which means, "will keep on flowing." If the believer keeps on thirsting, keeps on coming to Jesus, and keeps on appropriating the fullness He supplies, the believer will keep on flowing with rivers of living water.

Dennis the Menace stood on a chair at the kitchen sink as his mother was preparing to wash the dishes. Water was flowing freely from the faucet in the sink. The puzzled Dennis asked his mother, "How does such a little faucet hold so much water?" I'm sure Mrs. Mitchell explained the connection between the faucet and the reservoir, and the necessity of turning on the faucet to allow the water to flow. As God works in your life and you honor the conditions of Christ's invitation, the world (and the *church*) may one day ask, "How does such a little person hold so much 'Water'?"

In the first segment of The Lord of the Rings trilogy, entitled The Fellowship of the Ring, Galadriel says at Rivendell, "One small person can change the course of the future." If a Christian only realized what potential God has stored in his "small" life, and what power is available to flow through him, he might take more seriously God's purposes for him, both personally and *strategically*.

John Steinbeck, in his literary classic, Grapes of Wrath, puts into the lips of one of his characters, these words: "One little man, with his mind made up, can move a lot of folks." Replace the words, "with his mind made up," with the Biblical Standard, "with the mind of Christ" (I Corinthians 2:16 & Philippians 2:5). The mind of Christ is the storehouse of His truth, His purposes, His plan and His *strategy*. Let this mind prevail in you, and God will use you to "move a lot of folks."

Someone sadly lamented, "Most Christians are like a bucket which is half-full and trying to overflow." The invitation of Jesus

A River Runs Through It

holds the answer to that lament. Another wisely said, "The surest sign that you are carrying a full bucket is that your feet get wet." When wet, those feet will carry you—and Him—OUT....out to the uttermost parts of the earth. And wherever you go in His fullness, your will leave a trail of new conduits behind, each of whom wants to flow with a ceaseless stream of His Life.

Chapter Twelve

SHALL WE GATHER AT THE RIVER?

Ezekiel 47:1-12;
"Afterward he brought me again unto the door of the house; and behold, waters issued out from under the threshold of the house eastward: for the forefront of the house stood toward the east, and the waters came down from under, from the right side of the house, at the south side of the altar. Then brought he me out of the way of the gate northward, and led me about the way without unto the outer gate by the way that looketh eastward; and, behold, there ran out waters on the right side. And when the man that had the line in his hand went forth eastward, he measured a thousand cubits, and he brought me through the waters; the waters were to the ankles. Again he measured a thousand, and brought me through the waters; the waters were to the knees. Again he measured a thousand, and brought me through; the waters were to the loins. Afterward he measured a thousand; and it was a river that I could not pass over; for the waters were risen, waters to swim in, a river that could not be passed over. And he said unto me, Son of man, hast thou seen this?

Then he brought me, and caused me to return to the brink of the river. Now when I had returned, behold, at the bank of the river were very many trees on the one side and on the other. Then said he unto me, These waters issue out toward the east country, and go down into the desert, and go into the sea: which being brought forth into the sea, the waters shall be healed. And it shall come to pass, that every thing that liveth, which moveth, whithersoever the rivers shall come, shall live: and there shall be a very great multitude of fish, because these waters shall come thither: for they shall be healed; and every thing shall live whither the river cometh. And it shall come to pass, that the fishers shall stand upon it from Engedi even unto Eneglaim; they shall be a place to spread forth nets; their fish shall be according to their kinds, as the fish of the Great Sea, exceeding many. But the miry places thereof and the marshes thereof shall not be healed; they shall be given to salt. And by the river upon the bank thereof, on this side and on that side, shall grow all trees for meat, whose leaf shall not fade, neither shall the fruit thereof be consumed: it shall bring forth new fruit according to his months, because their waters they issued out of the sanctuary: and the fruit thereof shall be for meat, and the leaf thereof for medicine."

Picture your life as a large tub, like a bathtub. The day you were saved, it is as if a hose stretched from the vast reservoir of God's grace into the tub of your life, and when you trusted Jesus Christ, the hose was turned on. The life-giving, refreshing Water of Life flowed in great abundance into your life. You were absolutely "taken up" with Jesus. You thought you would only have victories throughout the remainder of your life. But what a shock it was to discover that you would have many recurrences of sin in your life, even after you were saved.

To follow the analogy, there were many bits of dirt and debris still clinging to the bottom of the tub, waiting to be dislodged and float to the surface. What an embarrassment for a Christian to have lingering filth ready to display itself at any moment! Suppose that you are enjoying Jesus when one day a piece of debris breaks loose from the bottom of the tub and comes surging to the surface. You are astounded, and quickly look around to see if anybody saw that filthy thing come to visibility in you. What you do next is crucial! You look around; then you put a hand on that dirty thing and push it back down below the surface of the water, relieved that nobody else saw it. And while you are holding it down, another dark thing comes surging to the surface! You put your other hand on it and push *it* back down, also. Then here comes *another one*! Now, you put a foot on it and hold it under. And behold, *another one*! You manage to get the other foot on it, hoping now that no more filthy things will come to the surface because you don't have any more hands and feet to use.

What does this mean? It is the picture of the typical serious Christian, completely preoccupied with the fighting of sin in his life. What is he doing? Unwittingly, he is testifying to the world that Christianity is a sin-fighting, sin-occupied religion. But it really isn't! It is actually a *Jesus-centered, Jesus-occupied, Jesus-revealing romance.* The Bible says, "Walk in the Spirit, and you will not fulfil the lusts of the flesh" (Galatians 5:16). Go back to our peculiar analogy. What should the person do when the debris comes to the surface? Agree with God that there is a serious, serious problem here, ask Him to forgive and cleanse you, and *turn on the hose again.* Become so taken up with Jesus all over again that the tub becomes brim-full of the Water of Life. Jesus called this "life more abundant," or "life that overflows" (John 10:10). Now, the debris which surges to the surface will simply be *flushed out of your life* by the rising tides of spiritual life. Thomas Chalmers called this "the expulsive power of a new affection."

You see, water is a *filling* element, a *flowing* element, a *flushing* element, a *floating* element, and a *fruiting* element. No wonder that God's Great Life is pictured so often in the Bible as water; indeed, as rivers of water. Today, we will examine the Biblical picture of one of these rivers.

I. SPIRITUAL SIGNIFICANCE

First, we will consider the *spiritual significance* of this river. There was an old saying that "Babylon has the Euphrates, Nineveh has the Tigris, Thebes has the Nile, Rome has the Tiber, but Jerusalem has no river." And it was sadly true. Jerusalem was unique among world cities in this respect. So important was this to the Jews that a psalmist wistfully wrote, "There is a river, the streams whereof shall make glad the city of God" (Psalm 46: 4). The Bible, being an Eastern book, uses Eastern images. In many places in the Middle East, water is an extremely precious commodity. It was in the Judean wilderness that stranded tourist James Pike, an Episcopal bishop, died of dehydration. I have personally seen hawkers of water on public streets of large cities, selling water — and everyone who bought drank from the same skin-bottle! The Bible recognizes the extreme preciousness of water when it uses such symbolic phrases as "springs in the valley," "streams in the desert," "wells of salvation," "showers of blessing," and "floods on dry ground." But what does Ezekiel's peculiar river represent?

It obviously represents something *supernatural.* This is quite apparently not a natural, typical, normal river. Instead, it is unnatural and miraculous.

It obviously represents something *spiritual.* It represents the life of God. It represents the love, mercy and grace of God. It represents the fullness of God. It represents the bountiful blessing of God. It represents the Holy Spirit of God. That's it! *It represents the Holy Spirit of God.* This river is the River of Life, the great stream of God's own supernatural, spiritual life. Sam Shoemaker described the experience of this river as "getting into the stream of God's life." God's life is symbolized here as a moving, flowing, growing river. This river suggests both the *environment* of the Christian life, and the *vocation* of the Christian life. This river is something each Christian is to *experience.* This river is *in us* (Christians), yet *we* are in *it.* *We* are *carried* in *it,* yet *it* flows through *us.* *We* carry *it,* and *it* carries *us.* So this river pictures the moving, free-flowing Life and mighty Power of God.

II. SUPERNATURAL SOURCE

Second, we will examine the *supernatural source* of this river. In a succession of phrases, Ezekiel tells us clearly where this river originates.

Shall We Gather at the River

According to the prophet, this river flowed from "the house" (verse 1). This is a reference to the Temple of God, or the sanctuary of God. The Temple was a sacred, separated, holy, Divine place. This clearly tells us that the supernatural stream of God's life flows from the place where God dwells, indeed, from God Himself. The Temple was the renowned place where God was enshrined and enthroned. If we would know the life pictured by this river, we must be where God is enthroned. Indeed, our very lives are to be God's Temple (I Cor. 3:16, 6:18-19). God must be enthroned in us if we are to know the power of His life.

Then Ezekiel tells us that this river flowed from "the altar" (verse 1) of the house. So the life and power of God flow from the place of sacrifice. This is true both historically and spiritually. The Holy Spirit was released in history in full redemptive power only after Jesus died on the Cross. Just as water flowed in the wilderness only after Moses had smitten the rock (Exodus 17:6, explained in I Cor. 10:3-4), the fullness of God's power was released only after Christ was smitten and broken for our sins on the Cross. You see, dear Christian, it is true both in history and in experience that Calvary precedes Pentecost. Pentecost involved "plenty cost"! All of us would like more of Pentecost in our lives, but God asks us first to demonstrate more of Calvary. It is only as we die to ourselves and our own self-centered desires that we can experience the fullness of the Holy Spirit's life and power.

Further, Ezekiel clearly specifies that the river flowed from "the right side of the house" (verse 1). In the Bible, the right side is the side of authority. We must acknowledge God's full and unconditional authority in our lives if we are to know His power and blessing.

Ezekiel also tells us that the river flowed "from under the threshold of the house." In fact, twice in verse one, he says that it proceeded "from under." It did not flow from the roof, or from a nearby hill. It didn't flow from the upper room, but from the trodden down, walked-on place. What a challenge! What a vocation for a Christian! The natural motive of all flesh in man is to elevate itself, to exalt itself, to lift itself up. But this motive must be counteracted by death with Christ if we are to know God's fullness of life. "Let nothing be done through strife or vainglory; but in lowliness of mind let each esteem other better than themselves" (Philippians 2:3).

The description of Ezekiel also tells us that the river flowed "eastward" (verse 1). To see the meaning of this important note, look at Ezekiel 43:1-2: "Afterward he brought me to the gate, even the gate that looketh toward the east: And, behold, the glory of the God of Israel came from the way of the east ... and the earth shone with His glory." If I am to know this blessing of God's life and power, I must live a life that faces, not toward my own pleasures or advantages or reputation or glory, but *toward the glory of God*.

Finally, Ezekiel informs us that "the waters came down" (verse 1). All true blessings come like Jesus did — *from above*. In fact, the higher we lift Him, and the lower we voluntarily become, the more of His life will flow upon us, within us, and through us. God's blessings come from His own Divine Presence, "from beneath the Mercy-Seat."

All of this was conspicuously fulfilled when Jesus came into the world. Through Him, God's tidal wave of Divine Life poured itself into a world that had not asked for it, and did not expect it; in fact, many didn't *want* it and wouldn't *have* it. But for those who would acknowledge the source and comply with the conditions, "out of them would flow rivers of living water" (John 7: 37-39).

III. STRANGE SIZE

Third, Ezekiel points out the *strange size* of this river. This is a peculiar river! It *grows* as it *flows*! It had no streams or tributaries flowing into it, but the further it flowed, the deeper it got! How odd! Most experiences decrease with time and distance, but *this* relationship gets *deeper, richer, fuller and bigger* as it progresses. Perhaps your own personal experience of Jesus Christ seems small and insignificant, as Ezekiel's did (*at first*). But continue to acknowledge the source and meet the conditions of the river's flow; let time and distance increase—and the results will be as-

Shall We Gather at the River

tounding. Just what does this strange enlarging size of Ezekiel's river mean for us?

It represents the *shallow, but deepening, experience* of the growing Christian. We must sadly and shamefully admit that the Christian community at large is filled with shallow believers. We must readjust our lives to get *deeper* and *deeper* into the infinite Life of God. Years ago we often sang, "Here's my cup, Lord, fill it up. Lord, and make me whole." *But if I have The River, why am I piddling with a cup?* Throw the cup away, and get fully acquainted with the flowing river! "The path of the just is as a shining light, that shineth *more and more unto a perfect day*" (Proverbs 4:18).

Then, the river represents the *submerging* of each individual believer's total life into the fullness of God's boundless life. This submerging is seen in the rising of the water of the river to progressively cover Ezekiel's body as he is led deeper and deeper into the river. First, "he brought me through the waters; the waters were to the *ankles.*" When water rises to one's ankles, his feet are covered. An old adage says, "You can tell when a person is carrying a full bucket, because his feet get wet." The first evidence of a Christian submerged in the fullness of God is that his daily walk (suggested here by his feet) is thoroughly transformed. Galatians 5:25 says, "If we live in the Spirit, let us also *walk* in the Spirit." Galatians 5:16 says, "*Walk* in the Spirit, and ye shall not fulfill the lust of the flesh." Ephesians 5:8 says, "Ye were sometimes darkness, but now are ye light in the Lord: *walk* as children of light." Wouldn't it be wonderful if all of us who *talk* like Christians *walked* like it, also? But first, we must get our feet consciously covered by God's life. Have you asked Him to so fill you that your daily walk will be absolutely transformed?

"Again, he measured a thousand (about one-fourth of a mile), and brought me through the waters; the waters were to the *knees*" (verse 4). The knees suggest the believer's prayer life. The Bible tells us that we are to pray in the Spirit (Jude 20). Praying in the Spirit means that true prayer *ends* at the throne of God with an *answer* because it *begins* at the throne of God *as a work of the Holy Spirit.* So true prayer *begins in Heaven* at the throne of God, *cycles down through the believer's heart* (with the Holy Spirit *using* that heart as *His "prayer chapel"), receives God's (right) answer,* and cycles *back* to the throne of God *in the praises of the blessed believer.* What a plan for prayer! Romans 8:26-27 needs to be explored endlessly and thoughtfully by the serious Christian. All of this is suggested by the water of Ezekiel's river reaching "to the knees."

"Again he measured a thousand, and brought me through; the waters were to the *loins*" (verse 4). The loins represent aggressive action. "Gird up the loins of your mind," Peter told us (I Peter 1: 13). *Christian, prepare your mind for aggressive action,* and do not let it "drag" through the mire and dirt of this world. The loins also represent the procreative or reproductive capacities of your life. Spiritually, the loins represent your capacity and responsibility for winning other people to Christ, the power of spiritual reproduction. If a Christian is not submerged in the energy of the Spirit, he will not maintain a faithful witness for Christ, and he certainly will not win others to Christ. It is quite obvious that *God's people need a fresh swim in the river of God,* or they will never win large numbers of people to Christ.

"Afterward he measured a thousand; and it was a river that I could not pass over: for the waters were risen, waters to swim in, a river that could not be passed over" (verse 5). *The farther Ezekiel went in this river, the less of Ezekiel was seen!* "Waters to swim in." When a person is swimming, only his head is consistently seen above water. The Bible says, "The head of every man is Christ" (I Cor. 11:3). When a believer walks in the Spirit, only the Head is seen. Jesus becomes more and more gloriously visible, and the believer is content to remain out of sight.

With regard to the *depth* of your experience with Christ, how far are you *in* the river? Three boys approached a country swimming hole on an early summer day. Each revealed a marked difference in his approach to the water. The first one walked around the bank of the stream and looked at the water, but then he decided not to go in. He remained somewhat satisfied, because *he was all the way out.* The second boy arrived at the water's edge, then cautiously waded into the water a few feet, his teeth chattering all the time. Regular exclamations and protests emerged from his lips, and he never went beyond shallow wading. He was dissatisfied, because he was *part in* and *part out*. The third boy took the aggressive approach. As he neared the water, he began to run. Reaching full speed at the edge, he gave a mighty yell and leaped as far out into the air as he could, falling with a great splash into the water. His momentum carried him below the surface of the water. When he surfaced, he let out a laugh of pleasure and satisfaction. He was perfectly happy, because *he was all the way in!*

Dear friends, even lost people may look reasonably satisfied, because *they are all the way out* —they are outside of Christ, don't know the difference, and aren't disturbed by what they are missing. Christians who are temporarily carnal are miserable, thoroughly dissatisfied because, having experienced the glory of Christ and His Life, they have destroyed their fervor by loose practice, and *they appear to be half in and half out*. This is the most frustrating position on earth. It destroys the believer's perception, his peace, his power, and his productivity. It keeps him in a state of tumult and turmoil. But the *spiritual* man! Oh, the delight and dynamic of the spiritual man! Like the third boy, he runs and leaps as much as he walks. He is *in the river as far as he can go*, and he is always moving *out* as far as possible. He is also boundlessly happy and gratified, because Jesus is proving Himself to Him at every moment of every day. How far are *you* in the river? *How far are you in the river?*

Sadly, multitudes of people sit "high and dry" on the levee of pride, occasionally watching the river's flow, but never getting in. They would tell you that they know about the river because they think they have *seen* it, but any *swimmer* knows, any *river boat pilot* knows, that you don't *know* a river by analyzing swimmers, or by observing the surface, or by reading reports of the rise and fall of the water. You don't adequately understand a river if you only stand on the bridge and look at it, or if you only cross it in a rowboat. The swimmer who enters a ten-mile kayak race on a river is much more knowledgeable about the river than the judge at the finish line who only *observes* the rules and the racers.

With regard to the dynamic of your life in Christ, how steady and joyful is your daily walk? How satisfying and powerful is your prayer life? How productive (reproductive) is your life in Christ? Are others reached for Christ because of you? How much of Christ is evident through you? Are your feet, your knees, your loins, your body, submerged. Let the cry ring out: "Come on in, the water's fine!"

IV. STEADY SPREAD

Fourth, the text points out the steady spread of the river. Verse one says that the waters "issued out." Verse two tells us that "there ran out waters." And verse eight says that "these waters issue out." Out, out, out! Jesus commanded His people to go out. The order of the book of Acts was this: the Savior went up, the Holy Spirit came down, and the church went out. Someone said, "The church that does not face outward and consistently go out will finally implode back into itself." And the same is true of every Christian. The first trained harvesters in the Lord's vineyard were called "apostles," which means "those sent away from." The command to "go" could be roughly translated, "get out." "He who believes on me as the Scripture has said, out of his innermost being shall flow rivers of living water" (John 7:38). Dear Christian, let me give you an infallible test of your success as a Christian. Your success as a Christian may be measured by the degree of your penetration for Christ's sake. A simple measurement: how far does your influence reach? Remember, you have been given a worldwide assignment — and a strategy to fulfill it! And you are seriously expected to do it personally!

This river issued *out* — but to what destination?

It flowed to the *down* place. Verse one says that "the waters came *down*." Verse eight repeats, "these waters go *down*." It is a rule that all flowing water seeks the *lowest* place. *Gravity* sends water *down; grace sends the Spirit down*. The grace of God sends the spirit of *man* down, and the same grace sends the Spirit of *God* down. And the two, the spirit of man and the Spirit of God meet at the lowest place. "Thus saith the high and lofty One that inhabiteth

Shall We Gather at the River

eternity, whose name is Holy; I dwell in the high and holy place, with him also that is of a contrite and humble spirit, to revive the spirit of the humble, and to revive the heart of the contrite ones" (Isaiah 57:15). God said,"To this man will I look, even to him that is poor and of a contrite spirit, and trembleth at my word" (Isaiah 66: 2). Also, God, like this river, seeks the place where people are at their lowest. This river flowed naturally and steadily to the down place, to the *lowest* place.

Then, it flowed to the *dry* place. Verse eight says, "These rivers go down into the desert." The desert referred to is the arid Arrabah, the famed Judean wilderness. This is the location where Bishop Pike dehydrated and died in a very short time. This water, then, flows to the languid place, the place that is parched, desolate, and thirsty. Christian, do you catch the strategy impulses of this story? If the water flows down, we should get down. If the water flows to the dry places, we should seek to minister in the dry places. Cynthia Clawson struck this note in one of her popular Christian songs:

"We need to carry the water to the desert,
Gotta stop this haulin' water to the sea."

Instead, Christians seem to be bent on strangling themselves on too much water, while the rest of the world is languishing for a drink. A viable and valid ministry should go where this river flowed, to the dry places.

This river flowed to the *dead* place. It flowed to the *lowest* place, to the *languid* place, and to the *lifeless* place. Verse eight says, "These waters go into the sea." The sea referred to is the *Dead* Sea. One elementary school boy answered the class-room question, "What is a cemetery?" with the answer, "A cemetery is a place where *dead* people *live.*" That is good humor, but it is true experience and theology to say that this world is a place where *dead people live!* "Dead in trespasses and sins" (Ephesians 2:1), dead toward God, spiritually dead. Every dead person needs the Water of Life, but that water will reach him only through someone who is already in the River of God.

Note the prophet's experience of this river. He was *"brought"* (verses 1, 2, 3, and twice in verse 4). It was God's action that brought him into the river, but when a person is caught on the current of a river, *it* takes him *wherever it* is going. If *you* are still going only where *you* want to go, you're not *in* deep enough! If you're still touching bottom (controlling yourself), you're not *in* deep enough. Since this is the River of *God*, it takes us where *He* wants us to go. It takes us *out* because *that* is where *God is going.*

V. SPECTACULAR SUCCESS

Finally, the text reveals the *spectacular success* of this river. The river had great visible and measurable results wherever it went.

Its results were reported in terms of its *penetration.* The river was continuously *moving.* Any life lived in the fullness of God will be mobile, dynamic and penetrating. It flowed "into the desert, and into the sea (the Dead Sea)" (verse 8). The success of a truly spiritual life will be measured, not by its introversion and self-improvement, but by its penetration.

Then, its success was stated in terms of its *productivity.* What happened when the river flowed into an area?

The river produced great *freshness* wherever it went. Verse 8 says, "The waters went into the sea (the Dead Sea); which being brought forth into the sea, the waters shall be healed." Verse 9 echoes, "These waters shall be healed." Fresh waters replaced mineral-saturated, bitter waters when this river flowed into the sea. When a Christian lives in the sweet fullness of the Holy Spirit, his life conveys a freshness that is evident to everyone around him. Paul said of one of his companions, "Onesiphorus has often refreshed me" (II Timothy 1:16). Some people greatly refresh you, and others greatly drain you. Gordon Macdonald called these latter people VDP (*not VIP—* this is often the view *they* have of *themselves*)—*Very Draining People.* Some people are refreshers, some are drainers, and some people are just tame and neutral! The world needs "air freshener" Christians, believers who leave the aroma of Christ lingering in the air around them. Paul wrote,

Shall We Gather at the River

"Thanks be to God, who always leads us in triumphal procession in Christ and through us spreads everywhere the fragrance of the knowledge of Him. For we are to God the aroma of Christ among those who are being saved and those who are perishing" (II Corinthians 2:14-15). Some people exude the sweetness, winsomeness, and charm of Jesus. While others have a way of making the names of God and Jesus and the Gospel hateful and repulsive, these people make these names fragrant and sweet. Some make spiritual things harsh and repellent and terrifying, but these "fresheners" make them positive, attractive, and magnetic. Wherever these waters flow, a great new freshness follows.

Every person carries a certain atmosphere. Some are stuffy, others are stale, and others are bracing and fresh. God, too, carries an atmosphere. On the Day of Pentecost, "suddenly there came a sound from heaven like a mighty rushing wind." Suddenly, the place was alive with the Presence of God, and fresh with His Life. It is tragic when the atmosphere of a Christian or a church is one of stuffiness, or staleness, or stillness, or death. When this is true, we need a fresh "dip" in God's river. A scintillating freshness goes wherever the river flows.

The river produced great *fruitfulness* wherever it flowed. Verse 7 says, "There were very many trees on one side and on the other." Verse 12 indicates the measure of this fruitfulness when it says, "And by the river upon the bank thereof, on this side and on that side, shall grow all trees for meat, whose leaf shall not fade, neither shall the fruit thereof be consumed: it shall bring forth new fruit according to his months, because their waters issued out of the sanctuary: and the fruit thereof shall be for meat, and the leaf thereof for medicine." Verse 8 says, "And every thing shall live where the river comes." What a river! Fertility, abundance of life, provision of food and medicine attend the flow of this river. And each of these has a spiritual counterpart in the Spirit-saturated life. The person who is in this river (or, just as accurately, the river is in him) will be "filled with the fruits of righteousness which are by Jesus Christ" (Philippians 1:11). He will reveal the "life more abundant" (John 10:10) which Jesus came to impart. He will convey the Bread of Life for the spiritual feeding of multitudes. And great healing of all kinds of diseases and wounds will attend him. Great fruitfulness will be in evidence wherever this river flows.

This river produced great *fishing* as it flowed. Verse 9 declares, "And there shall be a very great multitude of fish." Verse 10 adds, "And it shall come to pass, that the fishers shall stand upon it ... it shall be a place to spread forth nets; their fish shall be according to their kinds, as the fish of the great sea, exceeding many."

Jesus spoke of Gospel outreach, Christian influence, and soul-winning in terms of fishing. "Follow me, and I will make you fishers of men" (Matthew 4:19). There is life's greatest pursuit — "follow me;" life's greatest process — "I will make you;" and life's greatest purpose — "fishers of men." By this statement, Jesus pointed out the vocational calling of His apostles. Later He echoed, "Henceforth you shall catch men" (Luke 5:10). When a Christian is a channel for this river (or is carried by it), the Holy Spirit directs him to the right "fishin' hole," to the use of the right "bait," to the right fishing technique, and to the right "cleaning and preparing" of the fish once they are caught.

Wouldn't you say that this is a very remarkable river? In order to know just how remarkable it is, you must plunge in and let it carry you. Some of us have "sat on the bank" long enough. It's time we gave up our *spectator's view* and got into the *spiritual vitality* and took up a *serving vocation*. Can we sing it with new meaning just now: **"Shall we gather at the river?"**

An Addendum

Evangelist J. Wilbur Chapman, in an old book entitled Revival Sermons, tells this story:

"In crossing the United States to the Pacific coast at one time, I was urged to go by the Santa Fe Railroad and was ticketed in the special Limited Express. The journey was fine and the equipment was palatial, and all went well until we came to the desert; and then, although every ventilator was closed, every window shut and every blind drawn down to save us from the heat of the sun as it glared upon the sand, the journey was most uncomfortable.

"Opposite my section sat a man who continually raised the blind and looked out of the window. The porter quite as often drew the blind down. I went over to talk with him and complain of the journey and to say that I wished I had gone by the mountains. He looked at me as if I was bereft of reason and said, 'This is the most wonderful trip in the world.' I left him almost with disgust. My annoyance and discomfort increased as we went on, and after a while, wearied more and more by the journey, I went back to talk with him again. Among other things, I asked him his business, and, as he threw up the window blind, he said with a smile, 'I am an *irrigator*; and that is why the journey is wonderful, for *I keep seeing in my mind what could happen if I could turn the water in on this desert. I'm sure I could make it blossom like the rose.*'

"I went back to my seat, having learned my lesson: that all that God requires is to have the right of way to turn His Water of Life into and through my life, and thus it would be released into our land. I'm sure the results would be staggering."

Chapter Thirteen

FAITH'S FINEST FORMULA Or BECOMING BY BEHOLDING

II Corinthians 3:18;

"But we all, with open face beholding as in a glass the glory of the Lord, are changed into the same image from glory to glory, even as by the Spirit of the Lord."

The "formula" is found in a somewhat difficult passage to understand. The third chapter of II Corinthians contains a comparison of two covenants. These covenants were both intended as means by which man was invited into relationship with God. One is the covenant of law (the old covenant), and the other is the covenant of grace (the new covenant). In verse seven of II Corinthians three, the old covenant is called "the ministration of death," while the new covenant is called "the ministration of the spirit" (verse 8), which "giveth life" (verse 6). Verse nine speaks of the old covenant as "the ministration of condemnation" and the new covenant is "the ministration of righteousness." Verses seven through eleven declare that the old covenant was glorious, but the new covenant exceeds the old in glory. Verse eleven says that the old covenant "is done away" while the new covenant "remains."

Having drawn this comparison, Paul then says:
"Seeing then that we have such hope, we use great plainness of speech: And not as Moses, who put a veil over his face, that the children of Israel could not steadfastly look to the end of that which is abolished: But their minds were blinded: for until this day remaineth the same veil untaken away in the reading of the old testament: which veil is done away in Christ. But even unto this day, when Moses is read, the veil is upon their heart. Nevertheless, when it shall turn to the Lord, the veil shall be taken away. Now the Lord is that Spirit: and where the Spirit of the Lord is, there is liberty. But we all, with open face beholding as in a glass the glory of the Lord, are changed into the same image from glory to glory, even as by the Spirit of the Lord."

This passage takes us back to the Old Testament account of Moses' long confrontation with God atop Mount Sinai. When he came down from the mountain after forty days, Moses' face shone with the reflected glory of God. But after a short time of removal from this encounter, the glory began to fade from Moses' face. In order to hide the fading of the glory (which is another good picture of the old covenant), Moses covered his face with a veil, or a small curtain.

Using this background as his launching pad, Paul then records the verse which I call "Faith's Finest Formula." To me, this is the greatest motto verse in the entire Bible in defining the Christian life. Let me paraphrase the verse (the First Herb One and Only Version):

"But (unlike Moses, who wore a veil over his face, and the Jews, whose eyes are blinded about Jesus) all of us Christians, with uncovered or unveiled faces, going on beholding as in a looking-glass (a mirror) the glory of the Lord (Jesus), are being changed (transformed) into the same image (the spiritual character-likeness of Jesus, the One we are beholding) from glory to glory (from one stage of glory to the next higher stage of glory), even as by the Spirit of the Lord (the Holy Spirit is the only One who can produce this transformation within us)."

Let's explore this formula.

I. A PECULIAR DESCRIPTION

First, the formula contains a Peculiar Description of faith. For the living of the Christian life, faith may be described as "beholding as in a mirror the glory of the Lord Jesus."

The *method* of faith is found in the phrase, "beholding the glory of the Lord Jesus." Faith is beholding (or seeing) Jesus in His glory. This idea of faith is consistently presented throughout the Bible. Note the following references in the book of Psalms. In Psalm 25:15, we read, "Mine eyes are ever toward the Lord." In Psalm 27:4, the writer said, "One thing have I desired of the Lord, that will I seek after; that I may dwell in the house of the Lord all the days of my life, to behold the beauty of the Lord, and to inquire in his temple." This verse gives two excellent reasons for going to church: (1) To express the quest of your heart — "to behold the beauty of the Lord," and (2) to express the questions in your head — "to inquire in his temple." However, as we express the questions of our minds, we are often surprised to find that God answers them in unexpected ways. Instead of giving intellectual or academic answers (and there are fantastic intellectual answers to our questions in the Word of God!), He often answers our questions by giving us a fresh view of Jesus Christ. Notice in Psalm 27:4 that the desire "to behold the beauty of the Lord" precedes the desire "to enquire in his temple."

Some years ago, in one of my pastorates, a young girl walked down the church aisle one Sunday morning during the public invitation at the end of the sermon. She was weeping brokenheartedly. When I asked her what she was coming for, she said through her tears, "I want to be saved." After I had talked and prayed with her, I shared her decision with the church and asked the church to postpone receiving her as a member until I had visited with her parents. When the closing prayer had ended the service, I looked up to see the entire family of this young girl seated on the front row. They thought I meant that I wanted to meet with them immediately. They were a lovely family of five members. I slipped over and sat down on the prayer bench and introduced myself to them. It was evident from the beginning that the Holy Spirit of God had done a deep work in their hearts that morning. I introduced myself first to the wife and mother. Then I asked, "May I enquire about your personal relationship with Jesus Christ?" She leaned forward, broke into tears, and said, "I need what my daughter got this morning." After a few moments of sharing, she knelt on her knees and received the Lord Jesus into her life. A few moments later, I asked her husband the same question I had asked her. These were his words as nearly as I can remember them. "Years ago when I was a young boy, I attended another Baptist Church in this city. Several of my friends were joining the church on Easter Sunday, so I went with them. I did not understand anything about God and the Gospel. Joining the church seemed to be the right thing and a good thing to do. After I joined, I was baptized. I guess I would have called myself a Christian, but as I grew up, I began to have great questions arise in my mind about God, the Bible, heaven and hell, and the ideas of the Christian religion. I could not find anyone who could answer my questions, and the more educated I became, the greater the questions that were in my mind. When I went away to college, I decided that I had questions that were unanswerable. So I quietly rejected God and the Gospel and proceeded to live my own life in my own way. For over twenty years, I have almost never attended church. Then, someone invited us to this church this Sunday. When you stood to preach, you did not answer a single question I have had through these years. But something tremendous happened to me in this service this morning. In fact, it was so tremendous that I don't think I can even remember any of those questions that were so important to me before!" Do you see what had happened? God did not answer his questions academically; that would have left him merely with a convinced mind but an unchanged life. God did something far more important. He took the "wraps" off of Jesus, unveiled His Son to that dear man's

Faith's Finest Formula

spiritual eyes, and let him see Jesus in His glory. That is a great definition of faith, seeing Jesus in His glory.

Then, in Psalm 34:5, we read, "They looked unto Him, and were lightened (illuminated): and their faces were not ashamed (disappointed)." Every person who truly looks to God receives His light, and no one who truly looks is ever disappointed! In Psalm 123:12, we find these tremendous words, "Unto Thee lift I up mine eyes, O Thou that dwellest in the heavens. Behold, as the eyes of servants look unto the hand of their masters, and as the eyes of a maiden unto the hand of her mistress, so our eyes wait upon the Lord our God, until that He have mercy upon us."

"The servant's eye is not on his task, But on his master's face,
He does not gaze on his toil, But on the Lord of grace."

Faith is beholding Christ!

In the New Testament, we find these words in Hebrews 2:8-9, "Now we see not yet all things put under Him. But (and the word "but" means that what we do see is an overcompensation for what we do not yet see) we see Jesus, who was made a little lower than the angels for the suffering of death, crowned with glory and honor: that He by the grace of God should taste death for every man." There are many, many things that we are not yet permitted to see, but we do see Jesus in faith, and what we do see overwhelms the deficiency of what we don't see. Faith is beholding Jesus! In Hebrews 12:1-2, we read, "Wherefore seeing we also are compassed about with so great a cloud of witnesses, let us lay aside every weight, and the sin which doth so easily beset us, and let us run with patience the race that is set before us, Looking unto Jesus the author and finisher of our faith: who for the joy that was set before Him endured the cross, despising the shame, and is set down at the right hand of the throne of God." The verb translated "looking" has this additional idea in it: "Looking away from all else and unto Jesus." We are to look away from ourselves. Transformation of character does not begin with subjective introspection, but with an objective vision of the Lord of glory and of the glory of the Lord. F. B. Meyer often said, "For every look at self, take ten looks at Jesus."

Studies in the Person and Work of the Holy Spirit

Alexander the Great once asked Diogenes if he could do him any favor. Diogenes replied, "The only favor I ask of you is that you do not stand between me and the sun." The Christian must make this "requirement" of every other factor in life: "Do not stand between me and my Lord, the Sun of Righteousness. I simply must behold Him in His glory on a regular basis." All distractions must be firmly rejected and the gaze of faith carefully maintained. Faith is beholding the Lord Jesus in His glory.

The word translated "beholding" in II Corinthians 3:18 is a present tense, continuous action, verb. It means that we are to "go on beholding" Jesus with an unbroken continuity. This beholding is to become a consistent habit of life.

The genius of this formula is not hard to see. It is an unwritten law of life that *whatever gets your attention gets you. You become what you behold. What you look at longingly, lovingly, and lastingly, you become like.* You see, the eye has an incredibly powerful influence on an individual's inner life, and whether that influence be for good or for evil depends entirely on what is beheld and how it is understood.

Note that this verse is not referring to an occasional casual glance at Christ, but to an occupying constant gaze at Christ. This "beholding" is a steadfast gaze that absorbs and appreciates every detail of that which we are beholding. It involves the total personality, mind, heart, and will, being fixed on Christ in an attitude of worship, faith, and willing obedience. This "beholding" becomes a spiritual reflex, like driving a car. When you first learn to drive, you must think through every move you make, every motion of the car, and every factor in your surroundings. The process is very tight and tedious. But after awhile, you get in the car and operate it with no tightness or tedium at all. It is now a reflex activity in which you have become conditioned to act automatically. So it is with faith. It becomes a conditioned reflex of constantly "looking" to Jesus.

It must also be added that "beholding" is not merely looking, but it is also seeing. And what a difference there is between the two! We "look" at many things every day which we don't really "see." One is a matter of physical vision; the other is at least a

Faith's Finest Formula

matter of mental perception. This is a kind of "beholding" that a blind man can do.

Two illustrations will allow us to grasp this great truth better. The first is a Bible story told in Numbers 21 and echoed in John 3:14. The Israelites in the wilderness had sinned their way right into the judgment of God. They murmured and complained of God's gracious provisions for them until God's patience wore thin. Finally, God loosed a plague of fiery serpents among them, and anyone bitten by the deadly snakes died. The people finally appealed to Moses, and Moses interceded for them before God. God graciously gave to Moses some strange instructions for their cure. Moses was to make a serpent of brass, erect it on a pole, place it in the center of the camp of Israel, and whoever looked upon it would live! Jesus looked through the actual historical occurrence into the very heart of the Gospel. He saw the fiery serpents as a symbol of sin in the human race. Just as the bite of the serpent loosed a fatal venom in the body of the victim, so the bite of "that old Serpent, the Devil," has fatally inflicted every member of the human race. When an Israelite was bitten by one of those serpents in the wilderness, he was as good as dead. The poison attacked the entire system of the victim. So it is with sin. The poison of sin present in every sinner affects his physical, psychological, and spiritual life. It blinds his eyes, distorts his emotions, and renders him incapable of making ultimate right choices without Divine help. Sin has done a deadly "number" on the entire human race. When sin is present, a fatal poison is loose in the bloodstream of the human race, and death will result. "All have sinned," and "the soul that sinneth, it shall surely die." But God has made a perfect provision for sinners just as He did for the stricken Israelites. God told Moses to make a serpent of brass and raise it upon a pole in the center of the camp. Note that this serpent was to be the exact likeness of the fatal enemy. Even so, "God sent His Son in the likeness of sinful flesh, and as an offering for sin" (Romans 5:8). In Scripture, brass represents sin brought under judgment, so this serpent of brass pictures sin brought under the judgment of God. What a perfect picture of the Cross of Christ, where our sins were brought under the terrible judgment of God in the Person of Jesus, who became the exact likeness of sinful flesh, and offered Himself for sin and sinners. In the Old Testament account, the formula for cure was simply to "look and live," but when Jesus used the story as an illustration in John 3:14, He said, "As Moses lifted up the serpent in the wilderness, even so must the Son of Man be lifted up, that whosoever believeth in Him should not perish but have eternal life." In the one case, the cure is by looking; in the other, by believing. And yet, these are parallel cases! So looking and believing are synonymous exercises in Scripture. Believing is simply looking to Jesus.

    The other illustration is much more modern. The day was Sunday, January 6, 1850. The place was the village of Colchester in northern England. The main figure was a 15 year old boy who started out alone to go to a Baptist church across town on that Sunday morning. This teenager was a most unusual boy. By the time he was six years of age, he had read Bunyan's classic allegory, <u>Pilgrim's Progress</u>, no less than five times. By the time he was a middle teenager, he had read the voluminous works of the great Puritan theologians, and obviously had a mind that showed an early inclination toward God. But he still was not converted. On that cold first Sunday of the New Year in 1850, he never reached his intended destination. Although the snow was already many inches deep when he set out, another blinding blizzard struck him full in the face as he trudged through the town. So severe was the cold, wind, and snow that he turned aside to escape the fury of the storm. Still determined to attend church, he remembered a little chapel on a side street of the village. He found the sign in front identifying the chapel as "The Artillery Street Primitive Methodist Chapel." He went in and quickly sat down in the semidarkness under the balcony in a back corner of the auditorium. Only about a dozen people braved the storm to attend the service, and even the minister did not come. The few leaders present consulted among themselves, and finally, "a poor, thin-looking man, a shoemaker, a tailor, or something of that sort," consented to "bring the message" that morning. After a few moments of thumbing his Bible, he nervously

Faith's Finest Formula

mounted the pulpit steps and faced the tiny congregation. He faced nearly three hundred empty seats, but the world was never to get over the impact of that small service that morning. The speaker "took as his text" Isaiah 45:22, which says, "Look unto Me, and be ye saved, all the ends of the earth, for I am God, and there is none else beside Me." The young boy later said, "The man was really stupid, as you would say. He was obliged to stick to his text for the simple reason that he had nothing else to say." Research allows us to piece together the Divinely ordered "parts" of this great drama. The old speaker apparently read his text, interpreted with a few sentences of his own, ran out of ideas, and read his text again. This procedure was repeated (out of necessity) probably more than a dozen times in his brief presentation. The boy said, "I listened as though my life depended upon what I heard." Indeed, in the providence of God, it did!

In about ten minutes, the "preacher" had run out of ideas. Then, as he squinted toward the corner where the young man was seated, he suddenly lifted a hand, clenched it into a fist, and with a protruding bony index finger, he tremblingly pointed to the dim figure under the balcony and called out, "Young man, you look very miserable. You're in trouble, and you're likely to stay there unless you look to Jesus. Look, young man, look, look, look! Look to Jesus!" The young lad later said, "Who wouldn't look with that kind of encouragement! I began to look to Jesus, and I looked, and I looked, and I looked, until I fairly looked my eyes away. And suddenly, in an instant, as I looked, I was gloriously born of God, born again, born from above!" That boy shortly afterward became one of the greatest English speaking preachers of the Gospel the world has ever seen, and his printed sermons have been circulated around the world and read by millions.

Today, the building of the Artillery Street Primitive Methodist Chapel still stands at the same spot in Colchester, England. Back in one corner, under the balcony, there is a tablet which bears this inscription: "Near this spot, C. H. Spurgeon looked and lived." Spurgeon's name is a monumental reminder of one of the most mighty preaching and publishing ministries ever known on earth.

And it began with an eternity-packed moment of "beholding Jesus in His glory." This is the method of true faith; it always involves a "beholding of the glory of the Lord Jesus."

Then, this phrase also points out the *means* of faith. Isolate the little phrase, "as in a mirror," and you will see the invariable means by which faith operates. But what does that phrase mean? What is the "mirror?" The best procedure is always to let Scripture interpret Scripture. This principle of Biblical interpretation is historically known as "the analogy of Scripture." The Bible is very plain at this point. In James 1: 22-25, we read, "Be ye doers of the Word, and not hearers only, deceiving your own selves. For if any man be a hearer of the Word, and not a doer, he is like unto a man who beholds his natural face in a glass. For he beholdeth himself, and goeth his way, and straightway forgetteth what manner of man he was. But whosoever looketh into the perfect law of liberty and continueth therein, the same being not a forgetful hearer, but a doer of the work, he shall be blessed in his deed." So the mirror is the Bible, the Word of God. You see, the Bible is absolutely indispensable for faith. Romans 10:17 says, "Faith comes by hearing, and hearing by the Word (the utterance) of God." Faith starts with the Word of God, stands on the Word of God, steps out on the Word of God, states the Word of God, and stops with the Word of God! It is not possible to exercise faith without God speaking to you. And His address is never independent of Biblical truth.

But note that the Bible is called a "mirror." When you look into its pages, it reflects both you and Jesus. In our verse, we are to "behold the glory of the Lord Jesus." Desiderius Erasmus, the great German scholar of the Reformation, gave to the world one of its greatest literary achievements -- the first Greek New Testament ever published. It was called the Textus Receptus, and became the foundation for the translation of the King James Version of the New Testament. In the preface of this work, Erasmus wrote these tremendous words: "On these pages you will see the face of Jesus. You will see the Lord Himself, the whole Christ, more fully and more completely than if He stood in the flesh before you." These words echo Paul's thought in II Corinthians 3:18, that we are to "go on beholding as in a mirror the glory of the Lord Jesus." You see, the Bible is not primarily a book for religious practice (though it certainly is that), or even a book of religious principles; it is primarily a territory of encounter, a place of meeting between the reader and the Lord Jesus Christ.

In the early 1970's, I spent a week preaching in a special crusade in mid-state New York. The meetings were held in two buildings — in the mornings, we met in a small church building; at nights, in a high school gymnasium. One morning, I had gone early to the service and was "exploring" the building. I went to examine a picture near the rear of the auditorium oh one side. I was greatly and happily surprised by what I found. The picture was a facial portrait of Jesus, but it was created and comprised of the words of the entire Gospel of Matthew. The tiny words of Matthew 1:1 formed a part of His hair line, then Matthew 1:2 followed, etc., etc. When the picture was completed, a close-up observer could read the tiny printed words of Matthew's Gospel. I suppose it could be called, "Jesus According to Matthew!" I looked around and noticed that there were three other different pictures of Jesus on the walls of the building. Sure enough, I discovered that the second picture was comprised of the Gospel of Mark, the third of the words of Luke's Gospel, and the fourth, of the words of John's Gospel. What an insight! My only regret was that there were not 66 pictures, for the entire Bible is an "album" of the image of Jesus. The entire Bible is a portrait of the Son of God. The Old Testament provides the background of the Portrait, full of many shades and shadows, but always pointing toward the Central Figure. The four Gospels present His "Face," and Acts-Revelation reveal the "garments of glory" which He wears. When we read the Bible, our primary motivation should not be to learn, or even to live, but to see Jesus through its pages.

One of the great Bible teachers of American history was a Presbyterian pastor named Donald Gray Barnhouse. Dr. Barnhouse was pastor of a great church in Philadelphia. For many years, he preached on a weekly radio broadcast, and edited an evangelical periodical magazine named "Eternity." Each summer, he would

Studies in the Person and Work of the Holy Spirit

conduct a travel tour through some part of the United States or Canada or Mexico. On one such tour, the group was traveling by bus in the western part of the United States. They had come to the Monterey, San Jose area of California, which boasted at that time one of the largest amusement parks in the world. The group took a half-day to tour the park and enjoy the rides and games as they wished. A large number stayed with Dr. Barnhouse as they moved through the park. There was one particular "ride" which fascinated the great teacher. It was a large barrel, some 30 feet long and 8 feet in diameter, turned down on its side, and connected to an engine so that the barrel rotated at different speeds. The object was for the participant to walk through the barrel without falling down as it moved at one of its three speeds. Dr. Barnhouse determined to try it, and his group stood nearby, cheering him on. He gave his ticked to an attendant seated on a stool and told him to turn the barrel on to the slowest speed. He carefully calculated his walk and the rotation of the barrel, then he finally entered the mouth of the rolling barrel. However, he had taken very few steps when his feet got above his center of gravity and he fell down. As he tried to rise, he found that he could only roll and tumble in the bottom of the barrel. Finally, the operator kindly stopped the barrel, and the embarrassed preacher stood up and unsteadily stumbled out of the barrel as his people playfully jeered and taunted him outside. Dr. Barnhouse said, "Turn that thing back on; I know I can do it!" The operator started the barrel turning again, but Dr. Barnhouse's performance was only a repeat of his first failure. As he stumbled out this time, he said indignantly, "Has anyone ever walked through that barrel?" "Why, yes," the operator replied, "many people have." "Then turn it back on; I know I can do it, too!" But this time, the operator quietly said, "Sir, before you try it again, would you like me to show you the secret?" "Oh, there's a secret, is there?" Barnhouse asked. "Yes, there is. Stand at the mouth of the barrel, look at the far end, and tell me what you see." "I see a mirror," Barnhouse said. "And what do you see in that mirror, sir?" "I see myself." "Forget that; completely put it out of your mind, and don't allow yourself to think of it again. What else do you see in the

Faith's Finest Formula

mirror?" "I see you, seated on a stool." "Sir, that's the secret," said the operator. "You need a fixed vertical object to look at as you walk. Deliberately put the rolling of the barrel and the image of yourself out of your mind, and walk through the barrel, looking only at the reflection of me in the mirror. When you get to the far end, quickly touch the mirror and turn rapidly back toward me. Get your eyes fixed on me and walk quickly out of the barrel. Barnhouse carefully calculated this procedure as the barrel rolled, then he entered it and began to walk, with his eyes fixed on the reflection of the man on the stool. Finally, he reached the other end of the barrel, touched the mirror, and quickly turned to face the operator, walking rapidly out of the barrel. As he emerged, his people were now shouting and clapping in appreciation.

A short time later, the Holy Spirit of God spoke to the great preacher's heart. He seemed to say, "Did you get the message, my son? You — the motivated person — represent the committed Christian. He is determined to complete his assignment and finish his course. The barrel represents the Christian life with all of its potential and possibility for success and failure, and with all of its "roll and tumble." The operator represents the Lord Jesus Christ, the one upright point of reference and the One who determines the "speed" of the life. And finally, the mirror represents the Word of God, and its primary purpose is to afford us a clear, captivating reflection of Jesus. We are to spend our days "beholding as in a mirror the glory of the Lord Jesus," and then one day, we will touch the mirror for the last time, and turn and see Him face to face! The one secret of balance and victory for time and eternity is to behold the Lord Jesus in His glory.

So we must understand and implement day by day this peculiar description of faith, "beholding as in a mirror the glory of the Lord Jesus."

II. THE POWERFUL DYNAMIC

As we practice "beholding as in a mirror the glory of the Lord," a most marvelous transformation begins to slowly occur in our lives. As we "go on beholding as in a mirror the glory of the

Lord," we are changed into the same image from glory to glory." I call this "the powerful dynamic of faith."

Observe the *grace* of this transformation. The verb, "are changed," is a present tense, passive voice verb. The present tense describes an ongoing process. As we "go on beholding," we "go on being changed." In the beholding, we are active, but in the becoming, we are passive; but the becoming depends upon the beholding. The word "becoming" is a passive voice verb. This means that the change wrought is something that is done to us, not something that is done by us. The "beholding" is ordained of God as the means by which He transforms us. And the transformation is totally and exclusively His work. The verb, "changed," is the massive Greek word, "metamorphoumetha." You can hear a familiar English word, the word "metamorphosis," in this Greek word. Metamorphosis is the means by which a tadpole becomes a frog, or a long, fuzzy, crawling caterpillar becomes a beautiful, flying butterfly. The word describes an inward change of nature that emerges on the outside of the life.

This is the word that is used in the New Testament in Matthew 17:2, when Jesus took Peter, James, and John and went up into a high mountain. There, as He was praying, He was "transfigured (metamorphosed) before them, His face became white like the lightning, and His garments were white and glistening." What happened? The "spiritual incandescence" of His inward Divine nature came bursting through the "house of mortal clay" in which He lived, and it lit up His body like a light bulb with the light turned on! Also, this is the same word used in Romans 12:2, which says, "And be not conformed to this world, but be ye transformed by the renewing of your mind, that ye may prove what is that good and acceptable and perfect will of God." There is a fascinating comparison in the words of this verse. The word "conformed" is a form of the Greek word "schema," which means an outward shape or form. It is the word that would be used if I shaped a lump of clay or if I carved a countenance on the exterior of a block of wood with a knife. The "world" as an outward shape it is always trying to "conform" us to. The Phillips paraphrase says, "Don't let the world around you squeeze you into its own mold." But the other word, "transformed," is the word of our text; "but be ye transformed inside out." This inward transformation must be produced by God, but He does it as we "go on beholding as in a mirror the glory of the Lord Jesus."

Then consider the *growth* of this transformation. This is a present tense verb, describing a process that is to occur in a continual, constant way in the believer's life. Also, it is "from glory to glory." This is a good place to explore that mammoth word, "glory." We often use the word "glory" to refer only to Heaven, but it is more often used in an even greater way in the New Testament. "Glory" is the word for the manifested or demonstrated nature of God, the word for the character of God on display. So the phrase "from glory to glory" means that we are to progress from one stage to another of the development of the character likeness of Jesus Christ within our lives. And this growth, this progress, this development should be evident to others around us. Remember that "metamorphosis" is an inward change of nature that reveals itself through an outward, visible change. It is God's design that a Christian develop consistently from one level of the development of Christ's character in us to a new and higher level of that development.

We must be reminded, and especially in this time of "quick fixes" and "instant" products, that there are no shortcuts to maturity in the Christian life. And there are no "mature Christians," only maturing ones! I saw a "Dennis the Menace" cartoon in which Dennis was standing on tiptoe beside a card table where his Dad and Mom were playing cards. He was pulling himself up to the side of the table to be able to see over it. And he was saying, "I'm tired of being this little! Can't we move to a house that's got higher floors?" Sooner or later, every Christian going through the painful, pressurized growth process of advancing "from glory to glory" wishes for instant transformation, a quick "move to a house that's got higher floors." But this simply isn't possible! It simply isn't possible! Growth is necessarily slow, usually involves starts and stops, steps and stages, stretching and straining, and much pain.

Studies in the Person and Work of the Holy Spirit

Peter closed his two letters in the New Testament with this command, "Grow in grace (grace is "letting God do things for you") and in the knowledge (the word for heart-knowledge or relational knowledge) of our Lord and Savior Jesus Christ." This is the greatest possibility in the Christian life — the only way to become the best you can be is to grow in the manner prescribed here. But here is also the greatest tragedy in the Christian life to remain at the same "dead level," never growing, actually degenerating, and vulnerable to all the diseases of the weak. The only way to prevent this tragedy is to "go on being changed.... from glory to glory."

Think, too, of the *goal* of this process. The goal is identified in the phrase, "into the same image." What is that image? It is the image of the Person whom we are beholding. In the great eighth chapter of Romans, the Holy Spirit tells us what God's great purpose is in our lives. In Romans 8:29, we are told that we are saved "to be conformed to the image of His Son, or to be made like Jesus in His inner character. Toward this end, God "foreknew and predestinated" us. So we were included in God's purpose before the foundation of the world. When you visit a local airport in any city, you can tell the size of the planes that land there by the length of the runway. A short runway means that only small planes may land there. A long runway means that the largest planes may land there. Do you want to know how "big" God's purpose is for you? Then measure the length of the runway down which He has "taxied" in order to get His program underway. The word "predestinated" indicates a long runway and a gigantic project! That gigantic project is to change each believer into the inward character likeness of Jesus Christ. Certainly no small project! A task worthy of the Savior that Jesus is! John said, "Behold, now are we the sons of God, and it doth not yet appear what we shall be; but when he shall appear, we shall be like him, for we shall see Him as He is."

In recent years, there has been a great deal of discussion and controversy over the renowned "Shroud of Turin," a piece of cloth which many believe to have been the burial cloth of Jesus when He was laid in Joseph's tomb near Golgotha after His death. Recently, the cloth was tested by a scientific dating process and it was determined that it came from a period centuries after the time of Christ. However, any real student of the New Testament knows that the cloth in question could not have been Christ's burial cloth. The "Shroud of Turin" is an elongated piece of cloth on which the body image runs with the length of the cloth. But, according to John's Gospel, no such cloth was used in the burial of Jesus. The body was wrapped or wound with long but narrow strips of cloth such as would be used in wrapping a mummy. And the head cloth was "twirled" or "wound" separately about the head (John 20:7). So, logistically, it is not possible that the "Shroud" could have contained the body of Jesus. *But what difference would it make if it had?* Neither the piece of cloth nor the death and burial of Christ would have had any greater or lesser value! You see, it was never (ever) God's intention to place the image of His Son on material cloth, but on man's character! And what is this image? It is the character of Jesus, described as "the fruit of the Spirit" in Galatians 5:22-23. The truth is that God loves His Son so much, and values us so much, that He purposes to fill Heaven forever with a population of people modeled after His likeness! And God implicates us and our faith in this purpose. This is the powerful dynamic of faith: as we go on beholding as in a mirror the glory of the Lord Jesus, we go on being transformed into the same image from glory to glory. To summarize: As the child of God sees the Son of God in the Word of God, the Spirit of God changes the child of God into the character likeness of the Son of God to the glory of God!

III. THE PERSONAL DISCIPLINES

We have seen the peculiar description of faith given here, and the powerful dynamic of faith revealed here. Now, we must examine the Personal Disciplines of faith that are suggested in our verse. The Christian life is a wonderful cooperative venture between Jesus Christ and each born-again believer. God challenges us to "look to Jesus," and then He changes us into Christ"s likeness, but in between, we must CHOOSE to look. What disciplines are involved on our part? Surely the text suggests at least two disciplines which we must practice.

First, we must cooperate with God in the *removal of all veils* from our faces. The story should be read very carefully at this point, especially verses 12-18. Note the recurrence of the word "veil" again and again. Then, when we reach our "formula," we read that "we all, having had our faces unveiled, and going on beholding the glory of the Lord Jesus, are being changed." The verb translated, "with unveiled face," or literally, "having had our faces unveiled," is a perfect tense verb. The perfect tense describes action which occurred at one decisive point in time, with continuing and lasting results. The unveiling of the face in the first part of our verse took place once and for all in one great act of God in grace and power when He removed the impediments from our spiritual eyes and gave us the "Beatific Vision of Jesus" which converts the soul and saves the sinner forever. He opened the eyes of our understanding and unveiled Jesus to our hearts, and His image is forever stamped on our inner lives. This occurred when we were saved, when we were born again, when we were regenerated.

However, any serious Christian who has sought to keep His eyes on Jesus and walk with God knows that he certainly does not always have an unclouded view of the Son of God. His vision is not always clear. Indeed, it easily becomes dim or altogether distracted from the face of Christ. To follow the analogy of the text, veils tend to accumulate again on his face. He may stay away from the "mirror," or he may be transfixed with other things. If you look at evil, you become evil; if you behold trivia, you become trivial; if you behold good, you become good; if you behold Christ, you become Christ-like. These rules hold in a believer's life as well as an unbelievers's life. If you are not progressively becoming more like Christ "from glory to glory," it is because you have allowed veils to fall again over your face. How many Christians go through all the outward motions of the Christian life-church attendance, saying of prayers, formal Christian functions but never become more like Jesus simply because they are ignorantly wearing thick veils over their faces. Let me identify just a few of the veils.

The veil of pride often dims our vision of Christ. Verse 14 says, "Their (the Jews') minds were blinded." It was pride that

Faith's Finest Formula

blinded them to the glory of Christ (their Messiah). And pride will always preclude the possibility of seeing Jesus in His glory. Pride is the anti-God state of mind, and will always blind our eyes. This veil must be regularly removed and prevented in the believer's life.

Another veil is professionalism. This is the veil worn by the "veteran" Christian who gauges his success in terms of institutional growth. He is regularly attacked by the "Killer B's" – budgets, bodies, Bibles, bulletins, and buildings. The church instead of Christ is the focus of his attention.

Another veil is prejudice. Prejudice means an individual judges before the judgment! He plays God's role and does it before all the returns are in!

Another veil is made of daily problems. We sometimes become so conscious of our problems that we lose all sight of Jesus. I read somewhere of a man who lived along the Via Dolorosa, the path Jesus followed to His death. On the day of the crucifixion, he heard the commotion of the crowds in the street. He saw Jesus carrying His Cross and heard some of the discussion about Him in the crowd. But because the man had a slight toothache, he went back into his home and missed the greatest Event in world history.

Another veil is preoccupation. We often give primary attention to many secondary things, and there is simply neither time nor interest to see Christ.

Another veil is pretense. II Corinthians 4:2 says, "We have renounced the hidden things of dishonesty, not walking in craftiness," but how many believers play "pretend" games continually.

It is possible for us to wear thick layers of subtle veils over our faces so that it is impossible for us to see Jesus. So the discipline is obvious. Hebrews 12:2 says, "Looking unto Jesus, the Author and the Finisher of faith." The word "looking" is a unique word in the New Testament; it only occurs in Hebrews 12:2. It is the word, "aphorao," which literally means "looking away unto Jesus." It is the vocation and discipline of the Christian life to devotedly and deliberately look away from all distractions and obstructions, to look away from our experience, to look away from the difficulties, to look away from the past with its sins and failures, to look away from our personal triumphs and successes, and to look away from the future with its uncertainties and fears. We must never allow anything — anything — to replace our beholding of Christ. Charles Spurgeon once said, "I looked at Jesus, and the dove of peace flew into my heart. But then, I looked at the dove of peace, and it flew away."

A little girl traveled with her mother to visit her grandmother in a distant city. While they were there, they slept in the guest room in the same bed. The first morning, the girl awakened and began to examine the unfamiliar room. She looked down at the foot of the bed where a large mirror was hanging on the wall. When she looked at it, she saw the reflection of a picture of Jesus that was hanging over the head of the bed. She sat up to get a better look, but when she did, her body blocked the reflection of the picture and she saw herself instead. She laid down again to see the picture of Jesus, but when she got up, she again obscured the reflection of the picture of Jesus. Soon she awakened her mother and told her of this exercise. Then she said, "Do you see, Mommy? When I can see myself, I can't see Jesus! But when I can see Jesus, I can't see myself!" Exactly! We must consciously remove all "veils" in our daily lives.

Then, we must continually *redirect our vision* to Jesus. "Turn your eyes upon Jesus, Look full in His wonderful Face, And the things of earth will grow strangely dim, In the light of His glory and grace." F. B. Meyer seemed to have the right ratio when he said, "For every look you take at yourself, take ten looks at Jesus."

A Christian poet named William Cowper wrote these sad words:

"Where is the blessedness I knew, When first I saw the Lord?
Where is that soul refreshing view, Of Jesus and His Word?"

Is this your testimony today? If so, you must cooperate with the Holy Spirit by choosing to remove all obstructing and distracting veils from your face and redirect your vision toward "the light of the knowledge of the glory of God in the face of Jesus Christ" (II Cor. 4:6).

Faith's Finest Formula

IV. THE PERPETUAL DELIGHT

There is one last feature of this captivating text which invites our attention. It is typical of the Bible, God's glorious Word, that it often has subtleties and riches that are hidden like "a rich mother lode of ore" beneath the surface. There are several such treasures in this verse. Strangely, the word translated "beholding" has another marvelous possibility of translation. It may be translated "reflecting" as well as "beholding." When I was first researching the verse, I consulted twenty familiar translations of the New Testament. Ten (half) of them translated the word "beholding," and ten (half) of them translated it "reflecting." And they both were right! The Greek word contains both meanings. So we see in this verse, also, the perpetual delight of faith. What we see determines what we show; what we perceive determines what we project. Our motto might be like that of the moon: "What I get, I give; what I receive, I reflect."

W. E. Sangster, the late great Methodist pastor of London, wrote this wise paragraph about this verse: "Gazing on his Lord, the believer becomes a mirror in which the likeness of Jesus is more and more clearly seen. Yet it is more than reflection. Under the necessity of truth, Paul mixes his metaphors and says that it is a transformation, as though the mirror were changed by the reflection that falls on it. The saint is transformed into the same image. He has held himself steadily where his Lord's reflection could fall. That has been his one concern. All his mind has been given to Jesus. He has practiced His presence, studied and copied His deeds and kept His living image before His eyes. And the reflection has become a transformation, and the transformation in turn produces a greater reflection." Peculiar, but surely true!

Dr. A. T. Pierson, a great Christian teacher, once described a Christian as "God's Photography." When a person goes into a photographer's studio to have a picture made, Pierson said, four things occur. First, the sitter must be in focus. In the Christian life, the "sitter," the subject, is Jesus. Second, the veils must be removed from the camera. In the Christian life, the "camera" is the individual believer, and the "veils" are those factors in life that keep us from seeing Jesus. They must be removed. Third, the shutter is opened and the "image" of the "sitter" is etched upon the sensitive film. In the Christian life, our eyes are opened by a miracle of the grace of God, we see Jesus, and His character likeness is fixed upon our inner heart. Fourth, the film is taken into the darkroom for the development of the picture. In the Christian life, God takes His child into the darkroom of daily experience, and by means of the acids of life, He develops the latent image of Jesus so that it becomes patent for any observer to see.

A man returning from an overseas journey brought his wife a matchbox that supposedly would glow in the dark. When she received it, she expectantly turned out the light, but the matchbox could not be seen. Both thought they had been cheated. Then the wife noticed some French words on the box and called a friend to translate. And this is what the inscription said, "If you want me to shine in the night, you must keep me near the light." They left it near the light for awhile, then it glowed brightly in the dark. So it is with us! We must expose ourselves to Jesus, revel in His Word, and look upon His Face. As we keep near the Light, we will shine in the night.

In her book, <u>Rivers of Living Water,</u> Ruth Paxson illustrates this truth in this manner: "On one occasion I was traveling upon the Yangtze River in Central China. A heavy rainstorm had just cleared away and the sun had come out brightly from behind the banked-up clouds. I felt an inward impelling to go out upon the deck and the Lord had a precious message awaiting me. The water of the Yangtze River is very muddy. But as I stepped to the railing and looked over, I did not see the dirty, yellow water that day but, instead, the heavenly blue and fleecy white of the heavens above and all so perfectly reflected that I actually could not believe that I was looking down instead of up. Instantly the Holy Spirit flashed II Corinthians 3:18 into my mind and said, `In yourself you are as unattractive as the water of the Yangtze River, but when your whole being is turned God-ward and your life lies all open to Him so that His glory shines upon it and into it, then you will be so transformed into His image that others looking at you will not see you but Christ in you.' Oh, friends, are you and I 'reflecting as in a mirror the glory of the Lord'?"

Suppose that you had a large mirror placed out in the open air under the sky. Its motto might be, "What I receive, I reflect; what I get, I give." Suppose you tilt it toward the earth; it will reflect only the earth. This is like the natural man (I Cor. 2:14), whose whole perspective is "earthy" and earthbound. He is himself totally oblivious of the vast universe of reality he is missing, and he reflects only what he receives. Or suppose that the mirror is tilted toward the horizon. It will reflect a mixture of earth and sky. This is like the "double-minded man" of James 1:8, or the "carnal" man of I Corinthians 3:3. He tries to divide his attention between spiritual and material things as the objects of devotion in his life. But suppose the mirror is tilted only toward the sky. It reflects cloud, sky, and sunshine. This corresponds to the man who is "of the heavens, and heavenly." He lives "in the heavenlies" (Eph. 1:3), and he reflects "the Lord from heaven." What a vocation in a world largely filled with disturbed, dissatisfied natural and carnal people!

Remember that you are God's mirror. When you look into a mirror, you are not looking for the mirror; you are looking for a reflection of yourself. In Malachi 3:3, there is a fascinating picture of God. "He shall sit as a refiner and purifier of silver." The illustration is that of a silversmith seated beside a crucible filled with silver ore. His task is to remove any corruption from the ore and refine the silver that remains. This is God's purpose in our lives. He wants to remove any corruption that is in our lives, and refine our character so that His purpose may be perfected in us. How does the old time silversmith know when the process is completed? He ladles off the corruption and looks for the pure silver. He leans over the crucible as he works, and when he sees a clear image of himself, he turns the fire down, because he knows the process is completed. Even so, God observes our lives with equal care, looking for the image of His Son. When He is satisfied with what He sees, He may then turn down the fires of discipline, suffering and chastisement, gratified by the display of the Lord Jesus through us.

My favorite American author is Nathaniel Hawthorne. His writings have intrigued me, moved me, frightened me, and inspired me. My favorite story by Hawthorne is the short story entitled "The Great Stone Face." Like all of Hawthorne's writings, the story is Gospel-haunted. It is the story of a boy named Ernest, who lived in a village at the mouth of a valley. One of the nearby mountains had fixed upon it by Nature the giant image of a man's face. It was a strong, kind, noble, honorable face, and it could be viewed at different times of the day in its great variety of appearances, according to the sunlight and shadows which exposed the various features. The brow itself was over a hundred feet high. In the nearby village, a legend had developed among the inhabitants. The legend said that someday a man would arrive in the village who would bear an exact resemblance to the great stone face. From earliest boyhood, the face on the mountain and the legend in the village thrilled the boy Ernest. Each day, he would look several times and at length at the great stone face. Then, he would examine the faces of newcomers in the village, always looking for the matching counterpart. Ernest grew to manhood and maturity. Four times in his life, rumors circulated that the matching man had arrived. Each time, Ernest went eagerly to see for himself, and each time he was sadly disappointed. As the years passed, Ernest himself developed into a wise and respected citizen of his community. The people often requested that he speak on certain subjects of interest, and he would conduct open air lectures. One day late in his life, he was speaking before a large group when suddenly, one of his listeners threw his hands into the air and shouted, "Look! Ernest himself bears the likeness of the great stone face!" And all the crowd admitted that it was so. You see, he had looked lovingly, longingly, and lastingly at the great stone face, and over a long period of time, his own countenance had been transformed into the likeness of that face. Dear friends, this is faith's finest formula: "We all, with unveiled face, beholding as in a mirror the glory of the

Faith's Finest Formula

Lord Jesus, are being transformed into the same image from glory to glory, even as by the Spirit of the Lord."

We have observed a peculiar description of faith from the Word of God. When the Lord Jesus was here, He spoke of varying degrees of faith. He spoke of "faith," of "more faith," and of "great faith." How do you measure faith? Interestingly, you measure faith in exactly the same way that an optometrist checks your eyesight. If you go into an optometrist's office and he says, "Now, I will remove your eyeball so that I can check your eyesight," you had better quickly make yourself scarce from his office! But that is precisely the way most Christians try to check, or measure, their faith. They seek to examine and analyze and criticize their faith in order to measure it. No! When you go to an optometrist for a check of your eyesight, he puts a chart on the wall in front of you and he measures your eyesight by your perception of the object he has placed before you. Even so, God measures your faith (totally and exclusively) by your perception of the OBJECT, the Lord Jesus, He has placed before you. May we ever be beholding Him!

Insights into Beholding

2 Corinthians 3:18;

But we all, with open face beholding as in a glass the glory of the Lord, are changed into the same image from glory to glory, even as by the Spirit of the Lord.

Beholding

Novelist Harold Wright said he always kept before him a picture of Christ. "I write the best chapters in my books while looking into the face of the Son of God." We who know Him always write the best chapters of our lives while looking into His face.

Leonardo Da Vinci asked a friend to evaluate his painting, "The Last Supper." The artist companion exclaimed, "The chalice is absolutely beautiful." Da Vinci immediately took a brush and painted out the chalice. He explained, "It is Christ alone who should be preeminently seen as the center." Every believer should hold this as the rule of his life – no other feature of life should receive as much attention as Jesus.

During World War II, the Nazis treated the Belgians in Breendonk prison like animals. "How did they stand it?" a tourist asked. A guide took him to a dark cell, where the face of Christ was carved in stone on the wall. The guide explained, "We are told that they would come in here and look on the face of Jesus and remind themselves that they were not alone."

The pure in heart will know God because they have narrowed their focus to Jesus Christ. They are not distracted by their own spirituality, or their ideas about what God ought to be like, or anything else.

Studies in the Person and Work of the Holy Spirit

Donald McCullough shares this experience in his book, Finding Happiness in the Most Unlikely Places. "The last time I visited the National Gallery in London, I planned to do something different from the usual high-speed tourist sweep. I determined to look very carefully at just a few paintings. So I placed myself in front of Rembrandt's re-creation of a famous biblical scene – the woman caught in adultery. I had seen it before, but this time I wanted to see deeper into it, let it do something to me. Staying in one place was harder than I expected. My compulsive, achievement-oriented personality wanted to visit all the rooms and see all the paintings. But I forced myself to keep looking at Rembrandt's masterpiece. Other visitors came and went; I tried not to notice them. The painting was what I wanted to see, simply the painting. And indeed I began to see things I had never seen before; like the gospel itself, it had layers and layers of meaning waiting to be discovered. One woman helped me keep watch. As others passed by, she stayed. We did not move, two embedded rocks in a swift stream of humanity. I thought I saw, out of the corner of my eye, a tear step down her cheeks. Was she identifying with the woman in the painting? Or the arrogant Pharisees? One thing for sure: the Lord was touching her, too. And together we stood there, aware of each other but focused on the painting, a community of faith, silent as Quakers before the mystery of grace. What it did for her, I can't say; we never spoke. But I was changed. I saw things I hadn't seen before, in the painting, in the Gospel, in me. The pure in heart look to God revealed in Jesus Christ, and keep on looking. When shall they see God? Today and tomorrow – as they keep looking."

A scientist who is also a Christian said, "At one time, I kept my telescope pointed toward Saturn for several evenings. The view was sometimes obscured by clouds and haze in the atmosphere, and at other times the view was breathtakingly clear, but I kept the telescope pointed toward the planet no matter what the view. The view may not always be perfectly clear, but a Christian keeps the telescope of faith pointed at Jesus Christ and keeps looking at him."

Insights Into Beholding

Andrew Bonar once prayed, "When anything intercepts our view of Christ, may we feel what loneliness is."

In Collodi's renowned children's book, <u>Pinocchio</u>, the puppet brought many miseries upon himself by irresponsibility, low ambition and terrible choices. Slowly, however, he was brought by the processes of life and by wiser people to realize a better way. The climax of the book is reached when Pinocchio looked one day into a mirror. Collodi writes, "He thought he was someone else." He was! He didn't see in the mirror the image he had become accustomed to. He had seen other possibilities for himself, and was greeted in the mirror by the image of a bright, intelligent boy. A similar transformation occurs in a believer's life when Jesus shows him Himself and *himself as He sees him*.

In John Steinbeck's <u>Grapes of Wrath</u>, there is a memorable moment as a dust storm approaches in the Oklahoma "dust bowl." A family has gathered in front of their farmhouse to watch. The children hang onto their parents' legs, watching the horizon. But the women watch only the men's faces. All that matters to the women, they can find there. So it is with a spiritual Christian. Storms come and go, the Family gathers to watch, the immature family members anxiously watch the horizon, but the spiritual Christian looks to Jesus. All that matters to him he will find in the Person of Christ.

A new Christian had a strange dream in which he was trapped down in a very deep well at night. He looked up and saw a single star shining far above him, and it seemed to let down lines of silver that took hold upon him and lifted him up. Then he looked down, and he began to go down. He looked up, and began to go up; he looked down, and began to go down. He found that by simply keeping his eye on that star, he rose out of the well until his foot stood on the firm ground. Hudson Taylor said, "Get your eyes off yourself and on your Savior, get them off your disease and on your physician. Satan the hinderer may build a barrier about us, but he can never roof us in so that we cannot look up."

Bobby Jones as a boy lived near the East Lake golf course in Atlanta. Every afternoon he followed the club pro around the course, watching him play. His golf swing became a perfect imitation of that of the pro.

In Mark Twain's The Prince and the Pauper, Tom Canty (the pauper) became so preoccupied with the life of the prince that (according to the author) "he began to act the prince, unconsciously." When Christians become that preoccupied with Christ, they will be transformed – unconsciously.

Horace Bushnell said, "No one can look very long upon Immanuel's face and remain the same."

Reflecting

In a book entitled Open Windows, Christian author Philip Yancey wrote, "Previously, my main motivation in life was to do a painting of myself, filled with bright colors and profound insights, so that all who looked upon it would be impressed. Now, however, I find that my role is to be a mirror, to brightly reflect the image of God through me."

In 1873 a humble woodcarver in the little village of Oberammergau, Bavaria, posed for his picture. Nothing noteworthy was observed in the picture. In 1902 the same man posed for his picture again, but this time observers declared that the picture bore a startling resemblance to the portrait of Christ. What made the difference? In the 29 years between the two pictures, Anton Lang had played the role of Christ in the famous Passion Play which is staged in Oberammergau. Nearly 30 years of studying the life of Jesus, memorizing His teachings, exploring His characteristics, absorbing His concerns had so completely changed the simple woodcarver that his neighbors saw his Master living in him.

"Glory" in the text refers to the character of God on exhibit. Glory is a demonstration of what is within – both with God and with the growing Christian.

We are being changed here and now into a real reflected likeness of Christ's glory. However, the likeness is not the same as the original and constantly needs to be exposed to it afresh, and the process of transformation, though real, is partial and incomplete, so that the life of the church continually needs to be renewed in order to be brought into nearer conformity with the life of the Lord.

Note that the formula of II Corinthians 3:18 begins with "we all," not "I." It is the individual "I" that is being changed into the likeness of Christ, but that is occurring in the corporate community of Christians. What the Holy Spirit does personally in each has its full significance only in relation to what he is doing corporately.

John Redhead tells of an episode that occurred at the showing of "Snow White and the Seven Dwarfs." The witch was portrayed in such a frightening way that several parents had to take their children out of the movie. One little boy stayed. Someone asked him later, "Weren't you afraid?" He answered, "No, I kept my eyes on my father, and I never even saw the witch." Keep your eyes on Jesus, and many of the frightening realities of life will be unknown to you.

Some translations say that "we ... reflect like mirrors the glory of the Lord." Toyohiko Kagawa, the great Japanese Christian, said that "the manifold sufferings of life simply serve as polishing powder in the process of further burnishing the mirror."

Chapter Fourteen

THE SADDEST OF ALL SINS

Ephesians 4:30;

"And grieve not the Holy Spirit of God, whereby ye are sealed unto the day of redemption."

A pastor friend of mine preaches a simple three-point sermon about sin. The points are: Sin is *selfish*, sin is *stupid*, and sin is *sad*. All three points are tragically, tragically true! But what is the saddest of all sins? Measured by its inner effects and its outer results, I would say that the saddest sin of all is the Christian's sin of grieving the Holy Spirit of God.

There are four major sins which people may commit against the Holy Spirit. Two of them are committed by lost people, and two of them are committed by saved people. In an outlined arrangement, they look like this:

I. The Sins of Lost People Against the Holy Spirit
    A. *Resisting the Holy Spirit (Acts 7:51) — a sin against Salvation*
    B. *Blaspheming the Holy Spirit (Matthew 12:31-32) — a sin against Spiritual Sensitivity*

II. The Sins of Saved People Against the Holy Spirit

A. Grieving the Holy Spirit (Matthew 12: 31-32) — a sin against Sanctification

B. Quenching the Holy Spirit (I Thessalonians 5:19) — a sin against Service

There is a close relationship between each pair of sins listed above. When a lost person commits the sin of *resisting* the Holy Spirit, and persists a long time in that sin, it is very likely that he will finally *blaspheme* the Holy Spirit, or commit "the unpardonable sin." This means that he will have so sinned against the Holy Spirit that he has lost all sense of accurate moral evaluation. *His good is evil and his evil is good.* There is a fatal confusion of all moral reality. This is seen in the Pharisees in Matthew 12 when they dogmatically declared that the devil was behind all the miracle-works of Jesus! Their values system had gone completely upside down. Their moral sense was topsy-turvy. They were guilty of the unpardonable sin.

Note the connection in the other pair of sins. When a Christian *grieves* the Holy Spirit, he is also necessarily *quenching* the Holy Spirit. Grieving the Spirit is an inner sin committed against the indwelling, sanctifying Holy Spirit, while quenching the Spirit is a sin which prevents the Holy Spirit from working around the Christian. The word "quench" has the idea of putting out a fire by smothering it. In fact, the Living Bible paraphrases I Thessalonians 5:19 in these words: "Do not smother the Holy Spirit." The New International Version says, "Do not put out the Spirit's fire."

We are examining today the Christian's sin of grieving the Holy Spirit of God. Who is the most important person living on earth today? After a little thought, the answer is obvious. The most important person living on earth today is the Holy Spirit of God. This is "the age of the Holy Spirit." The Old Testament time could be called the age of God the Father. The time of the Gospels could be called the age of Jesus the Son. And since the Day of Pentecost, we have been in the age of the Holy Spirit. The Holy Spirit is man's

The Saddest of all Sins

last chance to know God! So any sin committed against the Holy Spirit is serious indeed!

Let me spend the remainder of this study presenting a simple profile of the Holy Spirit.

I. INDIVIDUAL

First, the Holy Spirit is an *individual* Person. This is indicated by the use of the word "grieve" in the text. An impersonal object simply cannot be grieved. It may be abused, mistreated, damaged, or destroyed, but it cannot be grieved. The fact that the Holy Spirit may be grieved indicates that He is a Person.

The Holy Spirit is often perceived as a mighty influence, or a vague essence, or an ecstatic energy, or an impersonal force. Thus, even Christians tend to refer to the Holy Spirit by the impersonal pronoun, "it," instead of by the personal pronoun, "he." It is easy to think that this is an incidental matter, while it is actually very serious.

Suppose I walked up to you and said, "I'm glad to see *it*. How is *it* getting along? Is *it* having a good day? Has *it* had a good week? I hope *it* has a good evening. Well, I'll see *it* later." What would *"IT"* think of me? You would probably think I had a little room for rent upstairs — unfurnished! You see, it is an extreme insult to personality to refer to a person as an "it." And this is certainly true of the Holy Spirit of God. He is a Person, and must be acknowledged and honored as such.

II. INDWELLS

Then, the Holy Spirit *indwells* every child of God. Grieving the Holy Spirit is a sin that is committed within a Christian. It is an inside job.

In I Corinthians 6:19-20, Paul concludes a passage about the Christian use of the human body with these words: "What! Know ye not that your body is the temple of the Holy Spirit which is in you, which ye have of God, and ye are not your own? For ye are bought with a price: therefore glorify God in your body, and in your spirit, which are God's." Look at these words carefully, and then glance in your Bible at the entire chapter, I Corinthians 6. You will see that Paul uses the words "know ye not" to introduce six different rebukes which he delivers to the carnal Corinthian believers (verses 2, 3, 9, 15, 16, and 19). In two of these rebukes, he adds the exclamatory word, "What!", to intensify the seriousness of the rebuke. In effect, he says, "I can't believe that you are acting as if you do not know these basic truths. These truths should be automatic, first-nature, and dominant in your thoughts and your lives, but instead, I am constantly having to remind you of the obvious. What is going on here?" Thus, he severely rebukes them for their intolerable ignorance. I wonder what the Apostle Paul would say if he witnessed the appalling ignorance that often prevails among Christians today?

In his rebuke, Paul states the basic truth that "your body is the temple of the Holy Spirit Who is in you." In the Greek language, there are two different words that translate into our English word "temple." One is the word, *hieron*, which is the word for the total temple property, or the total temple precincts. If your church owned seven acres of land, this property would be called the *hieron*. The other word, *naos*, is the word for the small specialized compartment of the temple called "the Holy of Holies." This was the place where God dwelt among His people. Dear Christian, this word, *naos*, the Holy of Holies, is the word that is used in I Corinthians 6:19 for *your body! Your body is God's Holy of Holies!* So your body is absolutely the holiest place on the face of the earth! It is the place where God has chosen to live among men by the indwelling Presence of His Holy Spirit. Your body is the Holy Spirit's temple. What is a temple? A temple is the dwelling place of a god. For what purpose? To reveal and publicize the indwelling God to the entire community around the temple. Christian, this is your assignment. Your life is to be a demonstration point for the God Who dwells in you in the Presence of His Holy Spirit. You are to "glorify God in your body, which is God's."

Several years ago, Dr. James M. Gray was preaching in The Church of the Open Door in Los Angeles, California, one Sunday morning, in the absence of Pastor Louis Talbot. Dr. Gray was expounding Romans 12:1 in his message: "I beseech you, therefore,

The Saddest of all Sins

brethren, by the mercies of God, that you present your bodies a living sacrifice, holy, acceptable to God, which is your reasonable service." It was later reported that Dr. Gray removed his glasses at one point, leaned on one elbow on the pulpit, lowered his voice and said, "Have you noticed that we are not told in this text *to whom* we are to present our bodies? However, I think there is only one possibility. We are surely not meant to present our bodies to God the Father, because He is pure Spirit, and furthermore, He remains in Heaven and doesn't *need* a body. Nor are we to present our bodies to Jesus the Son of God, because He is in Heaven right now *in His own body*. But there is one Member of the Godhead Who has come to the earth *without a body* — the Holy Spirit — and He wants to dwell in your body." What a beautiful statement of a "true truth" (C. S. Lewis' term)! If you have been "born from above," then the Spirit of God literally dwells inside of you.

One of the early church fathers, Ignatius, changed his name to "Christophorus," which means "Christ-carrier." He was finally put on trial and martyred for his faith in Christ. At his trial, he was questioned about the changing of his name. "Why did you choose to be called, 'Christoporus,'" they asked. He answered, "From the moment I was born again, I have carried about in my body the Presence of God the Holy Spirit, so I chose a name that would constantly remind me of the glory and responsibility of that stewardship." You, too, Christian, are a Christ-carrier, a Spirit-container. You are like a germ-carrier, carrying the infection of a serious epidemic. If your Christianity is not contagious, it is necessarily contaminated! The Holy Spirit dwells within every child of God.

III. INTIMATE

The third great truth about the Holy Spirit is that He is deeply and gloriously *intimate* with every child of God. Since He indwells the Christian, He is continuously with him — without interruption. He knows everything that the Christian feels, thinks, says, or does. No thought, word, or deed escapes Him. This is an obvious outcome from His indwelling Presence. However, it is richer even than that. The fact that the Holy Spirit is intimate with the Christian means that it is impossible to detect where the Holy Spirit "stops" and the Christian "starts" within. It is impossible to sever the two persons, I and the Holy Spirit, once He comes to live in me. Unless I sin, our thoughts and feelings are common. Furthermore, the Holy Spirit and I are so intimate that, when I sin, He is implicated in my sin — as though He were guilty of it, though He is not!

We dare not get preoccupied with the negative aspects of the Holy Spirit's intimacy with us. Instead, we must capitalize the positive side and the benefits and responsibility of it. Two close friends were described in this picturesque way: "They are as close as the fingernail and the quick of the nail." The Holy Spirit and the believer are closer even than that! The believer and the Holy Spirit are in inner spiritual union in the believer's spirit. So close are the two, as an old poet wrote, that

"Every virtue we possess, And every victory won,
Every thought of holiness, Are His and His alone."

Samuel Rutherford, the great Scottish Christian and writer, recognizing the importance of the Holy Spirit in a believer's life and His intimacy with us, wrote, "I am resolved that not so much as a thread shall ever be allowed to pass between me and the Holy Spirit." The secret of the Christian life can be simplified into one sentence: I must learn to live with an ungrieved Holy Spirit within me. How polite are you to the Holy Spirit all day long each day? Are you courteous to Him? Do you honor Him? Do you cultivate a consistent relationship with Him? Do you hold polite running conversation with Him all day long?

IV. IMPLEMENTS

The fourth great truth about the Holy Spirit is that He *implements* all the great works and purposes of God in each believer. Conviction of sin, without which no sinner would ever be saved, is the work of the Holy Spirit. Jesus said, "When he (the Holy Spirit) has come, He will reprove the world of sin" (John 16:8). The word translated "reprove" contains the ideas of contradicting, convincing, and confuting — the entire meaning of the conviction

The Saddest of all Sins

of sin. The conversion of the sinner is the work of the Holy Spirit. In regeneration, or the new birth, the sinner is "born of the Spirit" (John 3:5). So the sinner's salvation is the work of the Holy Spirit. The sanctification of Christians is the work of the Holy Spirit (see II Corinthians 3:18). If you are saved, then you were awakened by the Spirit, quickened by the Spirit, born of the Spirit, baptized by the Spirit into the Body of Christ, indwelt by the Spirit, filled with the Spirit, and anointed by the Spirit. And these are only a few of the many works and purposes of God which the Holy Spirit performs in the life of a Christian. You see, the Holy Spirit is very, very important to a Christian, and a right relationship with Him is vital to everything that being a Christian means.

The entire Christian economy could be pictured as a giant law firm with two branches in it, one in Heaven and one on earth. Each branch is operated by a very capable "paraclete," or Counselor, or Lawyer. The "Lawyer" in the Heavenly branch is Jesus, who pleads, wins and secures *our case in Heaven*. The "Lawyer" in the earthly branch is the Holy Spirit, who pleads, wins and secures *Christ's case on earth*. So Jesus is *our* Lawyer in Heaven, while the Holy Spirit is *Christ's* lawyer on earth! Thus, all of Christ's work that is conducted on earth today is the work of the Holy Spirit.

A little boy was sitting at the window inside his house watching the heavy rain pouring down the window pane on the outside. Obviously deep in thought, he asked his mother, "Mama, how does God make it rain?" Before she could speak, he said, "Oh, don't answer. I already know. He gets the Holy Spirit to do it. The Holy Spirit does all the work!" *The Holy Spirit does all the work!* He was so right. All the work that God does on earth today is done by the Holy Spirit. He is the Executor of the Godhead, and the Educator of all of God's people. We must do everything possible to prevent grieving Him.

V. INSULTED

The final great truth about the Holy Spirit for our study is that the Holy Spirit may be deeply *insulted*. He may be "grieved," the text tells us. "Grieve not the Holy Spirit of God." It is very important to understand the grammar of this sentence. The word "grieve" is grammatically a negative present imperative verb, which means that it literally says, "*Stop* grieving the Holy Spirit of God." To whom was Paul writing these words? He was writing to the intensely spiritual and mature Ephesian Christians, perhaps as spiritual as any Christians who have ever lived. And yet, he tells them to stop grieving the Holy Spirit. This means that even the mature Ephesian Christians were grieving the Holy Spirit when Paul wrote to them. What does this mean? It means that *this is a very common sin*, and that *it is a sin that is very easy to commit.* The Holy Spirit of God is very, very sensitive, and is easily grieved.

I do not personally believe that the Holy Spirit is ever angry with a child of God, but the text reveals that *He may be deeply hurt.* The word "grieve" means to "disturb, distress, offend, hurt, wound, put to pain, or make sorrowful." It is the very word Jesus used of Himself in the Garden of Gethsemane when He said, "My soul is exceeding *sorrowful*, even unto death."

The word "grieve" is a love word. You cannot grieve an indifferent person, or an enemy. You may amuse such a person, or arouse him, or vex him, or infuriate him, but you cannot grieve him. You can only grieve someone who loves you. Thus, you may grieve your mother, father, husband, or a friend, and you may grieve the Holy Spirit. Christian, the Holy Spirit of God is deeply and passionately in love with you. I have heard many preachers and teachers speak about the love of God the Father and the love of God the Son, but I have never heard a single sermon on "The Love of the Holy Spirit." Yet, in spite of our poor perception, the Holy Spirit of God loves us just as God the Father and God the Son love us.

Christian, at this very moment, is the indwelling, loving Holy Spirit being grieved or gratified by you? Is He perturbed or pleased with you? Is He hurt by you or happy with you? Be very, very careful, because everything of importance depends on your relationship with Him. If you are aware that you are living with a grieved Holy Spirit within, confess directly to Him the sin that is grieving Him and ask Him to cleanse you of its pollution and

The Saddest of all Sins

deliver you from its power. God the Father prescribed the solution in the diagnostic laboratory of Heaven, God the Son provided the solution in the Calvary clinic on earth, and the Holy Spirit is like a registered nurse who is quite willing to apply the solution to the heart of the convicted sinner or saint. The very One whom you have grieved will apply the cure when you agree with Him about the sin that grieves Him. Once you are cleansed of the grievous sin, and He is able to be free in your again, begin immediately to cultivate a continuous relationship with Him that allows Him to use you as the agent of His work where you are.

Louis Evans, Sr., the founder of the Fellowship of Christian Athletes, told a story that occurred in his ministry as a west coast pastor. The story illustrates our message. Pastor Evans said that he was asked to marry a man and woman who were very much in love. After extended counseling sessions, the day of the wedding came, the vows and rings were exchanged, they were officially pronounced husband and wife, and they departed for their honeymoon. Several days later, they returned to the home where the man had lived for some time before they were married. When they arrived there, he picked up his bride and carried her across the threshold of the home as was customary in those days. He placed her down in front of the sofa in the living room and then soberly asked her to be seated. "There is something I must tell you," he said to her. When she was seated, he said, "Honey, you have always thought that I previously lived here all alone. But during the several visits you have made to this house during our courtship, someone else has been living here, also. My aged mother has lived upstairs during all this time, but her personality is so distasteful to me that I have kept her hidden from my friends, and even from you. But, since you are now going to live here with us, it is necessary that you meet her." And he left the room and climbed the stairs to an upstairs room, while his new bride sat in shock on the sofa. A few minutes later, he returned, holding the hand of an old, bent, white-haired woman. When they reached the sofa, the bride stood up abruptly and said firmly, "Am I to understand that this woman is actually your mother?" "Yes," he replied, "this is my mother." "Are you telling me that it was through the birth canal of her body that you entered this world?" "Yes." "She is the one who nursed you as an infant?" "Yes." "And she is the one who undoubtedly built into you many of the character traits that I have found attractive?" "Yes, I suppose you could say that." "I can't believe that you have treated your own mother is such a manner! I want to make a proposal. I propose that we bring her from the obscurity of that upstairs room and give her the very best room in the house to live in. I propose that we place her at the head of the table when we eat our meals. I propose that we give her the first voice in every decision that we make in this household. I propose that hereafter we give her the place of honor which she deserves in this house."

Friends, it is tragically easy to treat the dear Holy Spirit of God worse than that man had treated his own mother. Remember, it is He who brought us to birth in the Family of God. It is He who nursed us as infant Christians. It is He who has nurtured into us all the characteristics that God the Father finds attractive in us. Is it not time for us to bring Him out of anonymity and obscurity and give him the lead role in our lives? May the Holy Spirit find in us a disposition and a faith that will please Him all the days of our lives.

Chapter Fifteen

THE HOLY SPIRIT — GRIEVED OR GRATIFIED?

Ephesians 4:30;

"And grieve not the Holy Spirit of God, whereby ye are sealed unto the day of redemption."

Having profiled the Person of the Holy Spirit in the first message of this series, we will now examine the peril of grieving the Holy Spirit of God. Remember that the Holy Spirit is the most important Person living on earth today. The celebrity of greatest attention among men is, in comparison, totally unimportant when considered alongside the Holy Spirit. Also, I remind you that there are two major sins against the Holy Spirit which lost people may commit — the sins of resisting the Holy Spirit and blaspheming the Holy Spirit. The latter sin is also known as the unpardonable sin. Resisting the Holy Spirit is a sin against salvation, and blaspheming the Holy Spirit is a sin against spiritual sensitivity.

Then there are two major sins which *saved* people may commit against the Holy Spirit — the sins of *grieving* the Holy Spirit and *quenching* the Holy Spirit. When a lost person resists the Holy Spirit, he is progressing toward the unpardonable sin. When a saved person grieves the Holy Spirit, he is also necessarily quenching the Holy Spirit. Grieving the Holy Spirit is a sin against *sancti-*

fication, a sin against the indwelling Presence of the Holy Spirit within the believer. Quenching the Holy Spirit is a sin against *service,* a sin against the Spirit's work through and beyond the believer. A Christian cannot grieve the Holy Spirit without also quenching Him. In other words, any sin against the indwelling Holy Spirit is also automatically a sin against the outworking Holy Spirit. That is, any sin a Christian commits against his own sanctification is also necessarily a sin against the service he might have rendered.

In this study, we are considering again the sin of grieving the Holy Spirit. Let me summarize the several truths which were presented in the first message.

WHO IS THE HOLY SPIRIT?

First, the Holy Spirit is a Divine *Person*. The Holy Spirit has the *traits* of personality, such as intelligence (He "knows"), emotion (He "grieves"), and will (He "gives gifts as He will"). The Holy Spirit performs such *tasks* as only a person can perform. He reminds, testifies, reproves, guides, speaks, hears, shows, glorifies, receives, strives, searches, sanctifies, etc. Each of these tasks are performed by persons. The Holy Spirit receives such *treatment* as only a person may received. For example, He is grieved and lied to, and only persons can receive such treatment. It is impossible to grieve an impersonal object. And the Holy Spirit *talks* like a person. He refers to Himself as "I." Only persons talk, and only persons have a center of self-consciousness which they refer to as "I." So the Holy Spirit is a Person, and He is clearly presented in the Bible as God Himself.

Second, the Holy Spirit is a Person of *passion and purpose*. The Holy Spirit is passionately involved in all the purposes He initiates and approves. He is not morally neutral. Indeed, the Holy Spirit is the most morally committed Person in the world. There are some things He is decidedly for, and there are some things He is decidedly against, and we don't have to guess about His moral stand. He is also a Person with very sensitive, tender, and delicate feelings. He is present in every child of God to turn a seemingly hopeless sinner into a transformed and productive saint.

Third, because the Holy Spirit is such a Person, He is *subject to potential pain.* C. S. Lewis, the Oxford/Cambridge British scholar, wrote in his <u>Four Loves</u> that "when a person decides to love, he opens himself to the possibility of extreme pain." The Holy Spirit has chosen to love, and to love sinners, and to love them unconditionally, so He has exposed Himself to the possibility of extreme pain. Because He loves you as God, you may hurt Him even as we hurt Jesus on the Cross.

Fourth, it is the Holy Spirit's *Person, performances and purposes* which indicate the nature and seriousness of the sin of grieving Him. The determination of what grieves a person totally depends on the character and feelings of the person grieved. *You* cannot *determine* or *dictate* what grieves *me* — only *I* can do that. Remember, the Person we are commanded not to grieve is the Holy Spirit of God, who is the Executor of all of God's purposes, and the Educator of all of God's people.

The Holy Spirit is the *best* and *kindest* person you have ever known, He is your warmest well-wisher and well-doer. In our text, the Holy Spirit is the seal of the Divine inheritance in us. This is just one of many, many reasons for not grieving Him. It is *our own eternal and highest good* that the Holy Spirit is desiring to work out, and *we are actually being commanded not to obstruct Him in working out that good!* This is incredible and infinite grace! Martin Luther said, "It would not do for me to be God. I would have kicked this world all to pieces a long time ago." But the Holy Spirit, who *is* God, offers us infinite and eternal good, watches as we sin against it, and begs us to stop such sinning!

HOW DO WE GRIEVE THE HOLY SPIRIT?

When we recognize the work which the Holy Spirit is assigned to perform in a Christian, we may better see how we grieve Him.

First, the Holy Spirit is present in every believer to effect the purposes of God and to perfect holiness. Thus, we grieve Him when we *disregard His Presence.* Suppose an important dignitary were residing in your home. How should he feel if you flagrantly ignore his presence and impolitely go about your own business as if he were not even there?

Second, the Holy Spirit has authored a Book for us to teach us about God and eternal realities. Thus, we grieve Him when we *distrust His promises.* The Bible is an incredible Book. It appears so "regular" to an unbeliever that he honestly believes he is warranted to reject it as "merely a human book, written by men." But the treasures hidden in this seemingly "human" book are so vast and intriguing that they leave the Bible student breathless in wonder.

I was traveling by plane on a trip some years ago. As the plane was departing a certain city, the young woman seated two seats away from me stiffened conspicuously in her seat. I watched her, and her apparent fear intensified as the plane slowly moved toward the runway for takeoff. I leaned over toward her and said, "Ma'am, do I detect that you are nervous because you are on this plane?" She confessed that she was very nervous. She said, "I am the world's worst 'white-knuckle' flier. An airplane is the biggest thing I ever tried to hold up — from the inside!" I said, "Believe me, I understand. I used to have that same problem myself." "You *used* to?" she asked. "What did you do about it?" "I got help," I replied. "I read a book that showed me how to solve the problem. And guess what? The Author of that Book is on this plane with us right now?" She asked suspiciously, "What was the book?" I pulled my hand-sized New Testament out of my hip pocket. "Ohhh," she said, "the *Bible!*" "Yes, and when you meet the Author of this Book, He will become your Peace and will show you how to overcome those fears. You see, as a Christian, I have an incredible advantage over a non-Christian. If this plane falls nose-first from the sky, I bounce higher than the plane started down from! In fact, my last neighbors are going to be angels!" What I told her about the Bible is gloriously true. Whenever or wherever you read it, you always have the Author with you. Who would you rather have to teach you any book than the person who wrote it? The Christian has the Bible's Author, the Holy Spirit, living inside of him, always

The Holy Spirit -- Grieved or Gratified?

willing to teach him the things of God. When a Christian ignores or neglects the Book the Holy Spirit has provided, He is grieved.

Third, the Holy Spirit desires to lead us continually. In fact, the Bible says, "As many as are led by the Spirit of God, they are the sons of God" (Romans 8:14). Thus, we grieve Him when we *disobey His promptings*. Frank Laubach, the great champion of international literacy, the founder of the "one-teach-one" campaign, said, "God is always speaking, always speaking, always speaking" — and he was absolutely right. Frances Schaeffer said, "God is there, and He is not silent." All day long every day, the Holy Spirit is like a prompter off-stage giving cues to the actors on stage. He is always championing the right and opposing the wrong (from God's point of view, not man's). Whether man is in a classroom, in a living room, in a workroom, in a bedroom, in a drawing room, in an automobile — wherever he is — the Holy Spirit is speaking to him all day long every day, anywhere and at all times. This is only altered by man's mishandling of the Holy Spirit. The unpardonable sin silences him altogether for a lost man, and grieving the Holy Spirit may produce His silence in the life of a Christian, though *never His absence.* When the Christian disobeys His promptings which may come in a million messages and methods, the Holy Spirit is grieved.

Fourth, the Holy Spirit seeks to condition and transform our lives moment by moment. Not only does He *speak* non-stop; He also *works* continually through circumstances, conscience, Divine arrangements, etc. Thus, we grieve Him when we *disrespect His processings*. Every circumstance of life is a kind of appeal, a kind of overture, from the Holy Spirit. In short, everything that happens in life has a Divine frame of reference. All of human life is lived "in reference to God," whether the individual knows or acknowledges it. To be human is to live in reference to a Creator-God at all times, and He has clearly revealed expectations, claims, and demands with regard to all human beings. The Holy Spirit is always working in a "hands-on" manner to advance God's purposes. To disrespect these attempts grieves the Holy Spirit.

Fifth, the Holy Spirit inwardly mediates the Presence of Christ in the inner spirit of every Christian. It is the business of the Holy Spirit to make Christ real to us, and yet He does not dishonor our choices, our desires, and our ongoing lives. Jesus said, "He (the Holy Spirit) will take the things of mine, and show them unto you." The Holy Spirit is not on earth to engage in a self-adulating, self-publicizing mission. Any experience of the Holy Spirit that constantly calls attention to itself is to be regarded with extreme suspicion among Christians. The more a believer talks about Jesus, celebrates Jesus, serves Jesus, senses the near Presence of Jesus, the more His experience of the Holy Spirit is truly and Biblically Christian. Thus, we grieve the Holy Spirit when we *dishonor His Presentation* of Christ — within us, among us, and through us.

We may sum up the nature of the sin of grieving the Holy Spirit with this statement: Anything that *neutralized His Divine Presence* or *Negates His Divine Performance* deeply grieves Him. No wonder the Apostle Paul used a negative continuous present-tense verb, which means, "*Stop* grieving the Holy Spirit of God."

WHAT HAPPENS WHEN WE GRIEVE THE HOLY SPIRIT OF GOD?

Since the Holy Spirit is the Executor of all of God's works and purposes on earth today, it is an extremely serious matter when any human being fails to properly adjust to His Person or ministry. It is a very, very serious sin to grieve the Holy Spirit of God. A great number of things happen when He is grieved. In summary and synopsis, let me mention four crucial things that happen in the life of a believer when he lives with a grieved Holy Spirit within him.

First, the *Person* of the Holy Spirit is *saddened* within the believer when He is grieved. This, of course, is the meaning of the word, "grieve." As we have earlier mentioned, the word means "to put to pain, to hurt, to wound, to offend." Jesus used the word in the Garden of Gethsemane when He said that His soul was "exceeding sorrowful." Christian, think carefully of this. You may be living at this moment in union with a Person who is deeply hurt

The Holy Spirit -- Grieved or Gratified?

within you. All of His actions and communications within you are determined by His pain and offence. You may be forfeiting all the positive benefits of His Presence by grieving Him. He simply will not favorably adjust Himself to anything that displeases Him in order to accommodate you. Remember, He is the *Holy* Spirit of God!

Second, the *Peace* of the Holy Spirit is *stifled* in a Christian's life when the Holy Spirit is grieved. When a sinner is saved, he is brought by the Holy Spirit into peace with God (Roman 5:1). He also receives the peace *of* God in his inner spirit. His status of peace with God is permanent and eternal, but his experience of the peace of God will be determined by His walk with God. This walk with God is monitored by the Holy Spirit, Who maintains the peace of God within him as he walks in the Spirit (Galatians 5:16, 25).

Every Christian should study and master Colossians 3:15 as a touchstone for his daily Christian life. It says, "And let the peace of God rule in your hearts." Here is a giant truth: the word translated "rule" gives us our sports-word, "umpire." The peace of God is the umpire of the Christian's heart! And he is to "let" the peace of God fulfill this role. What does an umpire do at a baseball game. He states the "ground rules" of the game. The Holy Spirit is the One who *states the ground rules of the Game of Life, and the peace of God lets us know if we are properly adjusted to those rules!* The game is not played by the whims, wishes, or preferences of the fans in the stands or the participants on the field (!). Then the umpire enforces the rules by which the game is played. The Holy Spirit *enforces the moral and spiritual rules by which God governs the Game of Life, and the peace of God is His inner witness within us!* Indeed, the Holy Spirit wrote the "Rule Book" for this Game, the Bible! So He always knows how every rule is to be understood and applied. The umpire at a baseball game calls every close play, and his judgment is final. The Holy Spirit calls all close plays within the Christian, the "questionable calls," and *the peace of God assures us of our agreement with the Holy Spirit* (or abandons us, thus allowing us to know that we are making wrong decisions and wrong moves).

Years ago, I coached a Little League baseball team while I served as pastor of a church in a small Arkansas town. I later facetiously said that I always thought that the wire fence between the playing field and the stands was to prevent baseballs from going into the stands, but I discovered that the fence was actually there to keep the parents from coming onto the field! Question: Have you every heard a home team crowd scream *in favor* of an umpire's call *against* the home team? No, and you never will! Everybody has a self-favoring bias in him, and it is very difficult for him to "deny himself." In fact, I have heard numerous sports crowds erupt with the cry, "Kill the ump!" and they were somewhere between frivolity and murder in their cry! How many Christians have lived out the cry with regard to the peace of God, "Kill the ump!" Christians need to be very, very careful in their relationship to the Holy Spirit. When He is grieved, His peace is stifled in the Christian, and prolonged grieving of the Holy Spirit may lead to undesirable disciplines.

    Third, the *plan* of God is *stalemated* in a believer's life when the Holy Spirit is grieved. Romans 12:1 provides a valuable descriptive commentary on the will of God for a Christian. It says that the will of God is "good, well-pleasing and complete." What a study of the will of God! The will of God is always *good*, even when it may appear otherwise. Now, the will of anyone else for your life is not good. Your own will for your life is not good; the will of others for your life is not good; and the will of Satan for your life is not good. Indeed, the outcome will always be undesirable when you pursue any other will than the will of God for your life. Then, the will of God is *well-pleasing*. This simply means that it will always lead to final gratification. A person who pursues the will of God with a submissive heart and an obedient walk will finally find the greatest pleasure in the universe. And the will of God is "complete," which means that it lacks nothing that will produce a total and fulfilling life. However, when the Holy Spirit is grieved, the will of God is thrown out of sync in the believer's life.

    Finally, the *power* of God is *suspended* in a Christian's life when the Holy Spirit is grieved. He simply will not give His power to the person who is selfishly motivated or following his own agenda. A good case in point may be seen in the Biblical story of

The Holy Spirit -- Grieved or Gratified?

Samson, the strong man of the Bible. Samson had demonstrated the power and prowess of his life in one encounter after another with the Philistines, the perennial enemies of the people of God. Samson had won battle after battle against impossible odds. However, he "laid his head in the lap of wicked Delilah," and the power of God was suspended in his life. The Bible says that he arose to oppose a group of Philistine warriors, but "he knew not that the Spirit of God had departed from him." He had grieved the Holy Spirit by his sin and immorality, and he further grieved Him by depreciating His importance in the accomplishments of his daily life. Even so, when we live with a grieved Holy Spirit, the power of God, which is absolutely indispensable for Christian service and victory, is suspended in our lives. Many Christians never know the difference, because they live so regularly at a mediocre level of defeat and powerlessness that they have adjusted to it. Thus the problem is compounded, and there is no anointing of the Spirit upon them and among the people of God. How tragic!

These, then, are some of the many things that happen when Christians grieve the Holy Spirit. Do we not need to give much greater attention to the work of the Holy Spirit and the possibility of committing this sin? Do we not need to repent and readjust our lives to the precious Holy Spirit of God?

Many years ago, Mahmoud, the famous conquer of India, arrived at the fabulously wealthy city of Gujarat in the Gujarat district of India. He had discovered that it was vital to destroy a people's gods if he was to subjugate the people. So he brought all the local idols into a public place in Gujarat (and remember that Hinduism has approximately 330 million gods!). He assigned his military commanders the task of manually destroying these icons in sight of the local people and their leaders. As the ceremonious destruction was nearing its conclusion, one giant idol of gleaming white marble was reserved until the last. As the military commanders came closer and closer to it, the local magistrates begged Mahmoud with intensifying appeals to please spare this one "god." He wavered under the force of their appeal, but finally, he took the battle-ax himself and struck the great idol a smashing blow. When he did, his army saw the reason for the local appeals. The idol broke with his blow, and it proved to be a hollow shell. Inside the compartment was a vast fortune of gold, silver, and precious gems. When the idol broke under a mighty blow, this fortune came pouring out into the dazzling sunlight.

May I spiritualize a lesson from this story for each of us today? If we ignore it, it will still enforce its truth in our lives for eternity. The lesson? *He who spares the idol forfeits the treasure!* Dear Christian, you have an inestimable, incalculable treasure in the Presence and performance of the Holy Spirit in your life. If you retain any idol that grieves Him, you will be forfeiting all the practical benefits of His Permanent Presence within you. "Grieve not the Holy Spirit of God."